MEXICAN AMERICANS WITH MOXIE

MEXICAN AMERICANS WITH MOXIE

A TRANSGENERATIONAL HISTORY OF
EL MOVIMIENTO CHICANO IN VENTURA
COUNTY, CALIFORNIA, 1945–1975

Frank P. Barajas

UNIVERSITY OF NEBRASKA PRESS   LINCOLN

© 2021 by the Board of Regents of the University of Nebraska

An earlier version of chapter 2 appeared as "Community and Measured Militancy: The Ventura County Community Service Organization, 1958–1968" in *Southern California Quarterly* 96, no. 3 (Fall 2014): 313–49. Parts of the conclusion originally appeared as "An Invading Army: A Civil Gang Injunction in a Southern California Chicana/o Community" in *Latino Studies* 5, no. 4 (2007): 393–417.

All rights reserved

Publication of this volume was assisted by the Offices of the President, Provost, and the Dean of the School of the Arts and Sciences, as well as the Departments of Chicana/o Studies and History at California State University Channel Islands.

Library of Congress Cataloging-in-Publication Data
Names: Barajas, Frank P., 1964– author.
Title: Mexican Americans with moxie: a transgenerational history of el Movimiento Chicano in Ventura County, California, 1945–1975 / Frank P. Barajas.
Description: Lincoln: University of Nebraska Press, [2021] | Includes bibliographical references and index. |
Identifiers: LCCN 2020038861
ISBN 9781496207630 (hardback)
ISBN 9781496227348 (epub)
ISBN 9781496227355 (mobi)
ISBN 9781496227362 (pdf)
Subjects: LCSH: Chicano movement—California—Ventura County. | Mexican Americans—California—Ventura County—Politics and government—20th century. | Mexican Americans—California—Ventura County—Social conditions. | Mexican Americans—California—Ventura County—Ethnic identity. | Ventura County (Calif.)—Ethnic relations.
Classification: LCC F870.M5 B36 2021 | DDC 305.868/72079492—dc23
LC record available at https://lccn.loc.gov/2020038861

Set in Garamond Premier by Laura Buis.
Designed by N. Putens.

There is that great proverb—that until the lions have their own historians, the history of the hunt will always glorify the hunter. That did not come to me until much later. Once I realized that, I had to be a writer. I had to be that historian. It's not one man's job. It's not one person's job. But it is something we have to do, so that the story of the hunt will also reflect the agony, the travail—the bravery, even, of the lions.

—CHINUA ACHEBE

CONTENTS

	List of Illustrations	ix
	Introduction	1
1.	What's Their Provenance?	13
2.	Mexican American Role Models, 1958–1968	37
3.	The Young and the Restive	55
4.	Racially Segregated Schools, 1968–1971	81
5.	No Way, José! School Busing	99
6.	Laying the Groundwork	121
7.	*¡Que vivan las huelgas!*	139
8.	Chicana-Chicano Agonists	161
	Conclusion	185
	Notes	193
	Bibliography	233
	Index	241

ILLUSTRATIONS

Following page 80

1. Map of Southern California
2. Yvonne De Los Santos, Marcha de la Reconquista
3. CSO Quonset hut with Tony Del Buono and César Chávez
4. John Soria at Ventura County CSO office
5. Javier Santana KOXR La Mexicana
6. Diana Borrego Martínez under LAPD arrest
7. César Chávez speaking at a rally in Colonia Park
8. Ray Reyes Ventura College faculty and MEChA advisor
9. La Raza Peace Moratorium flyer
10. Bert Hammond and the NAACP
11. Rachel Murguia Wong, 1972 edition of the *Oxnard Press-Courier*
12. Rachel Murguia Wong, Oxnard Elementary School District Board trustee
13. Roberto Flores, 2020
14. Moorpark College Movimiento Estudiantil Chicano de Aztlán (MEChA) flyer, ca. 1973
15. La Colonia "cauldron of racism" cartoon

MEXICAN AMERICANS WITH MOXIE

Introduction

From the United Farm Workers (UFW) Boycott Office in Delano, California, Jessica Govea, twenty-four, examined a clipping of a full-page advertisement in the *Ventura County Star-Free Press* sent to her by Ray Ortiz, the union's organizer in the city of Oxnard. Published on January 30, 1971, after the "In Support of Cesar Chavez" title, it declared, "WE ARE MEXICAN-AMERICANS, non-farmworkers who support Cesar Chavez and the work he is doing in [sic] behalf of the farmworkers." The 240 signatories denounced the attacks of the agricultural industry that branded their champion a deceitful Marxist revolutionary. They also consisted largely, but not exclusively, of Spanish-surnamed residents—many born before World War II, others afterward. The j'accuse intrigued Govea. In her reply letter, she thanked Ortiz and closed with "Looks like you guys are doing some good boycott work. Viva la Causa!"[1]

Three years later, after months of underground organizing on the part of gritty UFW *apio-fresa* (celery-strawberry) harvesters from Salinas with local compeers, a strawberry strike erupted in Ventura County on May 26, 1974. As part of a migrant syndicate, ethnic Mexican farmworkers on the Oxnard Plain demanded the improved work conditions won by brethren at the sister Salinas Valley operations of the Dave Walsh Company—one dollar for a tray of strawberries, a twenty-cent increase.² At one field in the eastern part of Oxnard, on Sturgis Road and Rice Avenue, 150 strikers formed a picket line. On the fourth day of the walkout, Wednesday, May 29, a Ventura County Sheriff's Department helicopter pilot zeroed in on UFW strikers at a dirt parking lot as they prepared to protest a Vujovich strawberry farm near Gonzales Road and Rice Avenue in Oxnard. To break up the muster, the pilot conducted an aerial attack. When not mowing back and forth in a tilted assault position, the helicopter hovered directly on top of them; the violent storm generated by its propellers, coupled with kicked-up gravel, forced the picketers into a scramble—especially Isecelia Quiroz, who stumbled and fell to the ground. Terrified, she thought she was going be killed as the aircraft descended over her.³ To distract the pilot away from Quiroz, Roberto Flores, twenty-six, a former Brown Beret and UFW leader in Oxnard, hurled rocks at the aircraft. For this, sheriff's deputies arrested him on charges of felony assault. No to be outdone, the Oxnard Police Department (OPD) detained seven other picketers.⁴

Three days later UFW president Chávez, forty-seven, traveled from Delano to lead a protest march of two thousand people through the streets of the La Colonia barrio of Oxnard. Then, after a Mass at La Virgin de Guadalupe Church, Chávez, followed by his fans, strutted to nearby Colonia Park to deliver a speech. Once there he indicted Ventura County law enforcement—judges, the district attorney, sheriff, and OPD—with collusion in the service of the agricultural industry. He exclaimed that of all the places where the UFW had fought for the rights of farmworkers, Ventura County was the most vicious—perhaps worse than Texas, with its Rangers' terrorism.⁵

Within these abridged narratives exist a composite of historical subjects. In the first, the sponsors of the newspaper ad instantly proclaimed their discrete status as "MEXICAN-AMERICANS, non-farmworkers," even though most of the listed people were the progeny of agricultural workers, if not long-time Mexican migrant residents themselves. Within this cohort also existed two generational groups: one born before World War II that came of age prior to the 1960s, and the other subsequently. Historically, ethnic Mexicans born before 1945 have been labeled the "Mexican American generation." I label activist youth born afterward the "Chicana-Chicano generation." The former primarily approached their adulthood during the decades of the Great Depression, World War II, and conflict in Korea. The latter, in their youth, witnessed in one form or another the nation's escalated intervention in the civil war of Vietnam, the assassinations of iconic political and civil rights leaders, as well as momentous marches and demonstrations. Another demographic dimension of the people recognized was that, before settling in Ventura County, many lived as migrants, not only from Mexico—with and without authorized residency—but also places outside of Southern California, such as the valleys of Salinas and San Joaquin, and South Texas.[6]

Moreover, the same year that self-proclaimed Mexican American residents took out their newspaper ad, conga player Andre Baeza of the band El Chicano opened a live performance of its Brown Sound hit "Viva Tirado" with the proclamation "By the way, we're all Chicanos!" Hence I argue that a collection of people from the Mexican American and Chicana-Chicano generations defined El Movimiento (the Chicano movement) in Ventura County. Certainly, not all ethnic Mexicans identified themselves as Chicanas-Chicanos,[7] from the start or ever (such as Chávez), but many, whether they did or not, expressed an emblematic moxie in relation to an emotive spirit of righteous indignation (i.e., anger) that instigated valiant fights against systems of racism to realize the nation's ethos of equality and the pursuit of happiness for all.[8]

I also aver that social-political currents of California, in particular, rallied persons from all walks of life in Ventura County to communally challenge local injustices. Yet, in the case of the Salinas Valley, as deftly narrated by Lori Flores in *Grounds for Dreaming: Mexican Americans, Mexican Immigrants, and the California Farmworker Movement* (2016), Chávez did not kindle El Movimiento in Ventura County. A transgenerational tradition of collective resistance existed here that dated back to at least the 1903 Japanese-Mexican Sugar Beet Strike. In this regard both a transgenerational network of local support coupled with the UFW fight from afar fanned embers of righteous indignation among incipient Chicanas-Chicanos of all ages. And, whereas Flores portrays the Salinas Valley as an agricultural staging ground, I contend that Ventura County was home to a diversified economy of farming and the industries of defense and technology.[9] Geographically, Ventura County was also situated between the public higher education institutions of San Fernando Valley State College (SFVSC) and the University of California, Los Angeles (UCLA), to the southeast and the University of California, Santa Barbara (UCSB), to the north. It was at these campuses, as well as at the local community colleges of Moorpark and Ventura, that first-generation ethnic Mexican college students conveyed their experiences and recently learned perspectives to and from their hometowns.

To prove my theoretical framework, both explicitly and inherently, I interlace transgenerational perspectives with translocal and transnational features. Therefore, the people highlighted in this book consist of the U.S.-born, native to Southern California as well as migrants from other parts of the state, the nation, and North America. If not Mexican nationals themselves, they were often the sons and daughters of at least one migrant parent. This is to say that families and communities consisted of a hybrid of U.S. citizens (by birth or naturalization) and migrant Mexican nationals, some with authorized residency and others not, at least at first.

But, no matter their citizenship and age, many ethnic Mexicans adopted a Chicana-Chicano mentalité, if not the label itself, as a continuity of racist exploitation, subordination, and violence persisted in and out of the environs of an agricultural economy. Concurrently, a tradition of resistance united the Mexican American and Chicana-Chicano generations. In fact, many in both cohorts accompanied their parents to ethnic Mexican mutual aid and service center organizational meetings. In the process they heeded a spectrum of grievances in their community: economic, educational, and political. Consequently—as was the case with Govea's parents, who were founding members of the Community Service Organization (CSO) in Bakersfield—comparable organizations and unions integrated three cohorts of the ethnic Mexican community: migrants, Mexican Americans, and those born after World War II. In this context Mexican American generation adults in particular imparted lessons of organized resistance as younger Chicanas-Chicanos provided fresh doses of moral outrage to fight for the rights of the disenfranchised in and out of the fields of agriculture.[10]

Incipient Chicanas-Chicanos of all ages in Ventura County also resided in neighborhoods that corresponded with their family's occupation. Migrant farmworkers largely lived in barrios, and "non-farmworkers" more likely resided outside of migrant dominant enclaves as post–World War II residential developments flourished with Veterans Administration and Federal Housing Administration financing. The developments where distinct working-class people lived were not so discrete, but patterns existed that highlighted a diversity among ethnic Mexicans in terms of their residency, English- or Spanish-language dominance, and income. But, as Tomas R. Jiménez cogently contends, exchanges between the recent Mexican migrant with the long-term resident and U.S.-born replenished and redefined the transgenerational character of many ethnic Mexican families during El Movimiento—however, not in the distinct sense of eras both before and after the Mexican Revolution, the Great Depression, and World War II.[11] I argue that the dynamics of migration, citizenship, and the length of residency restyled the identities of Chicana-Chicano youth and their elders during the 1960s and 1970s. So, Chicanas-Chicanos did not just consist of the U.S.-born, as often suggested by scholars.[12] In fact, Mexican migrants—as family members, *vecinos* (neighbors), friends, and classmates—played a vital role in the identity of Chicanas-Chicanos during El Movimiento. This was especially true given that the U.S.-Mexican border was only four hours away from Ventura County. Mexican migrants also became Chicana-Chicano as they witnessed, participated in, and adapted to the cultural crosscurrents of the time.

Historians have examined the acculturation of ethnic Mexicans largely from a biological generational lens. In 1989 Mario T. García opened this conversation with *Mexican Americans: Leadership, Ideology, and Identity, 1930–1960*. Then, in 1993, Emilio Zamora and George J. Sánchez published *The World of the Mexican Worker in Texas* and *Becoming Mexican American: Ethnicity, Culture, and Identity in Chicano Los Angeles, 1900–1945*, respectively. The former detailed the existence of a fundamental Mexicanist identity; the latter narrated how the migrant and U.S.-born "became" Mexican American via adaptations when confronted with momentous forces of political and cultural disruption such as the Great Depression of the 1930s. Prior to 1989 and subsequent to the works of García, Zamora, and Sánchez, Vicki Ruiz analyzed the identity formation of ethnic Mexican women in relation to Los Angeles unionism and the cultural coalescence of the traditions of Mexico and the United States in her germinal

Cannery Women and Cannery Lives: Mexican Women, Unionization, and the California Food Process Industry, 1930–1950 (1987) and *From Out of the Shadows: Mexican Women in Twentieth-Century America* (1998). In fact, Ruiz, in her characteristically poetic prose, states that "immigrants and their children pick, borrow, retain, and create distinctive cultural forms. There is not a single hermetic Mexican or Mexican-American culture, but rather permeable *cultures* rooted in generation, gender, and region, class, and personal experience."[13]

Next, Douglas Monroy's 1999 *Rebirth: Mexican Los Angeles from the Great Migration to the Great Depression* examined the congress that "rebirthed" a Mexicanist identity—so much so that a *México de afuera* (an outer Mexico) community formed in Los Angeles. These books demonstrated, in sum, how identity formation by way of mass culture, consumerism, and labor-political activism was not a linearly advancing one-way street. Along the way to "becoming" distinctive from their origin past, ethnic Mexicans revised their identities with the recession and surges of migrant streams from and back to Mexico throughout the mid-twentieth century. I also claim that by the 1960s and 1970s select Mexican Americans (i.e., activists), born before and after World War II, as well as long-term and recent Mexican national migrants, whether they realized it or not, became Chicana-Chicano as they were equally influenced by, and adapted to, the spirit of the time.[14]

And, whereas David G. Gutiérrez's *Walls and Mirrors: Mexican Americans, Mexican Immigrants, and the Politics of Ethnicity* (1995) traced intragroup ramparts and reflections among ethnic Mexicans, more recently academics have examined the asymmetries of identity in places previously underexamined, if at all, such as Chicago, Illinois; Garden City, Kansas; San Diego and Santa Maria, California; St. Paul, Minnesota; and Milwaukee, Wisconsin, prior to and leading up to El Movimiento. A shared theme among these books, and others, is how both authorized and unauthorized coethnic Mexican migrants, from South Texas as well as the rest of the nation, to a significant extent invigorated both tensions and affinities with their U.S.-born and -raised counterparts in accordance with geographic and temporal circumstances.[15]

More recently, Mario T. García has published a series of books that center on the Chicana-Chicano generation in Los Angeles.[16] But, rather than focus on the context that transformed identities, the argument of *Mexican Americans with Moxie* demonstrates the transgenerational condition of El Movimiento Chicano in Ventura County. In this manner this narrative will detail how young men and women in their teens to late twenties, such as Roberto Flores and Jessica Govea, and adults in their early thirties to late forties, like César Chávez (in particular, but not so tidily), became Chicanas-Chicanos as they heeded militant protests in other parts of the nation that involved long marches, boycotts, sit-ins, and the seizure of college buildings. The emotive effrontery of the Black Panther Party for Self-Defense, the Black Student Union (BSU), and the Students for a Democratic Society (SDS), moreover, indirectly provoked ethnic Mexican students to develop an unapologetic, politicized identity of their own—a moxie, if you will—as many Chicana-Chicano youth and the more maturated made their bones in defiance of state injunctions to force change. In the process they risked the collusive wrath of reactionaries and law enforcement infamous for inflicting violence without hesitation upon protestors, such as in the helicopter attack and by the Texas Rangers.

The primary motivation to write *Mexican Americans with Moxie* comes from the 2012 publication of my book *Curious Unions: Mexican American Workers and Resistance in Oxnard, California, 1898–1961*. Upon its completion sources pointed to a continued and geographically wider story of ethnic Mexican agency as Chávez's 1958–59 CSO assignment concluded in Ventura County. As a result this book similarly demonstrates the curious unions for social justice among men and women from diverse classes, ethnicities, and races that provided oxygen to the verve of ethnic Mexicans becoming Chicana-Chicano in their mentalité and deeds. Simultaneously, more moderate activists of the Mexican American generation fretted over the security of youth as well as recently arrived migrants that entered the labor market at its lowest and most exploited tier: agriculture. In the process, many of the Mexican American generation embraced *la causa* (the farmworker cause) side of El Movimiento, if not the Chicana-Chicano label itself.[17]

Print, television, and radio media synchronously covered spectacular events of the larger civil rights movement, farmworkers, and President Lyndon Baines Johnson's wars on poverty and in Vietnam. In the process local affairs complemented those of the national and foreign. Thus, archival material informs this project. Primary sources consist largely but not solely of newspaper accounts from local publications such as the *Oxnard Press-Courier*, *Los Angeles Times*, and *Ventura County Star-Free Press*. The first daily provides a perspective from the largest community in the county, the second a more regional angle, and the last a county-wide outlook. To understand the nature of movements on the campuses of Moorpark College and Ventura College, I studied their student newspapers: the *Raider Reporter* and the *Pirate Press*. For more individualized and personal perspectives, the book relies on oral history interviews.

To situate this narrative within the larger context of El Movimiento, I point to touchstone events and personalities that surfaced within the previously mentioned sources in relation to the East Los Angeles student blowouts (i.e., boycotts) in high schools; the Chicano Moratorium; and the struggle of farmworkers in Chávez's UFW in the food-basket valleys of Coachella, Salinas, and San Joaquin. Collectively and over time these actions of mass rage contributed to the alchemy of the Mexican American becoming Chicana-Chicano in Ventura County.

To provide a sense of the distinct sociogeographical terrain from which El Movimiento emerged in Ventura County, chapter 1 examines the Cold War era in Southern California in relation to the rise of industry and its concomitant population growth, which drove residential as well as commercial development projects. As a great number of families moved into the middle class, with more men and women obtaining private- and public-sector employment subsidized in one way or another by the military-industrial complex, a demographic shift occurred in the five counties of Los Angeles, Orange, Riverside, San Bernardino, and Ventura, as white flight accelerated with the Watts riots of 1965. In this respect Ventura County was home to both rural and emergent urban environs. Carey McWilliams, the ever-prescient doyenne of California's history, named such liminal communities as the city of Oxnard "rurban."[18]

Meanwhile, youth of the baby boom generation raised in Ventura County's barrio enclaves came of age not only collectively but also sociopolitically, with the civil rights movement, youth culture, and Vietnam War. In the overview of this milieu, chapter 1 highlights the breakdown of Ventura County's provincialism, especially, as a significant number of young men and women ventured off to not-so-faraway places such as UCLA and UCSB, on one hand, and local community colleges and SFVSC, on the other. This not only provoked a gestalt of thought and action among first-generation college students, but also spread infectiously to friends and family in their home communities.

Chapter 2 contends that the CSO of Ventura County, founded by Chávez in partnership with ethnic Mexican members of the Oxnard Civic Improvement Association (OCIA) in 1958, embarked upon measured strategies of militancy while working behind the scenes with civic and elected leaders to effect change. In the mobilization of the community, CSO men and women of the Mexican American generation—who retained a Mexicanist identity as they served migrant families—mentored and modeled a politicized agency for youth of the incipient Chicana-Chicano generation. As a result, collective resistance did not dissipate with Chávez's departure. In fact, an overlap of militant stratagems existed among activists of the Mexican American and Chicana-Chicano generations.

Chapter 3 details how Chicana-Chicano youth advanced the campaigns of the Mexican American generation by way of independent direct actions. This consisted of, but was not limited to, the establishment of a tutorial program in the Oxnard Elementary School District (OESD) and college recruitment prior to the widespread institutionalization of Educational Opportunity Programs (EOP). This chapter also demonstrates how Ventura County Chicanas-Chicanos linked their activism with counterparts and groups both in the region of Southern California and across the nation. This culminated in La Marcha de la Reconquista in 1971, which protested, for the most part, incessant police violence and the Vietnam War.

Sixteen years after the Supreme Court's *Brown v. Board of Education* decision in 1954, another system of abuse continued in the OESD with the maintenance of racial segregation that restricted the life chances of ethnic Mexican and Black students. In this regard, chapter 4 details how the CSO and National Association for the Advancement of Colored People (NAACP) in Ventura County petitioned district officials in the 1960s to remedy the segregation of students. As the board of trustees and administrators dismissed their grievances and proposed solutions, John Soria of the Mexican American generation championed a federal lawsuit against the OESD that garnered the summary judgment of Judge Harry Pregerson in May 1971 that mandated school busing as a means to achieve integration. In the course of this discussion, I reveal nuanced and ironic outcomes. For example, many in the barrios of Oxnard did not support busing to desegregate as they valued, first and foremost, an equal education in their neighborhood schools. But the more the OESD resisted reforms, Blacks and Chicanas-Chicanos accepted busing. The issue of school desegregation, moreover, galvanized a larger ethnic politics in the county.

Chapter 5 details how the OESD unsuccessfully filed appeals all the way to the U.S. Supreme Court to derail Judge Pregerson's order. In the process, however, the Ninth Circuit ordered a trial that ultimately decided that de jure—by policy—segregation had existed in the district since the 1930s. Emblematic of extant dual systems of education in the region, this chapter examines the nuanced nature of opposition to busing as well as how Rachel Murguia Wong, as a Mexican American board member with a Chicana flair, collaborated with the Chicano Studies Department at San Fernando Valley State College to implement Operation Chicano Teacher (OCT) as part of the racial integration of the teaching faculty in the OESD.

From the discussion of school segregation and the fight for its dismantlement, chapter 6 further advances the book's thesis by detailing how the Mexican American generation modeled militant resistance for Chicana-Chicano youth. Such direct actions also benefited from the support of a cross-cultural spectrum of people who collectively advocated on behalf of the farmworker—both local and migrant—after Chávez's departure in 1959, with the establishment of federally funded war-on-poverty programs. By way of paid job training and education, these initiatives developed local leaders. Indeed, veteran organizers and civic activists coached Chicana-Chicano youth to carry on a tradition of resistance with a moxie all their own.

Chapter 7 then reveals how Chávez's National Farm Workers Association (NFWA), later renamed the UFW, inspired and supported labor protests in

Ventura County.[19] And, as Chávez's union garnered domestic and international recognition for its grape boycott, organized labor disputes arose in Ventura County citrus orchards and strawberry fields, as well as in a poultry plant. This in turn attracted popular and political attention. Although the stimulus for these insurgencies resulted to a significant degree from the UFW's fight in the grape orchards of the San Joaquin Valley, the work of the CSO and the war-on-poverty initiatives of Operation Buenaventura and the Farm Worker Opportunity Project provided the grounds for grassroots leadership by individuals such as Al Rojas and Armando López (the latter one of the founders of the Oxnard Brown Berets). The agricultural strikes of this time in Ventura County benefited from the wisdom of veteran activists of the Mexican American generation and the exuberance of Chicana-Chicano youth. This led to direct actions not only against the satraps of the agricultural industry but also complicit law enforcement agencies (i.e., the courts, police departments, sheriff's offices, and immigration agencies). These battles resulted in media coverage that encouraged picket lines at government agencies and grocery stores as well as community protest marches.

The final chapter narrates the activism of students in Ventura County's high schools and two community colleges. Raised in a tradition of collective resistance dating back to the early twentieth century, for many Chicana-Chicano students their politicization flowered in and out of the classrooms and quads of academe. Whether at high schools, community colleges, or universities, they heeded the dissent of groups such as the BSU and SDS. This compelled Chicana-Chicano students from both rural and urban settings to ponder, "What are we doing?" In this spirit chapter 8 examines how Chicana-Chicano youth exerted their collective sovereignty on campuses and in their communities to recruit peers (many Vietnam War veterans) into academe. Once on college campuses, they mobilized campaigns of self-determination in the form of El Movimiento Estundiantil Chicano de Aztlán (MEChA) student organizations, aesthetics of cultural affirmation, to win campus space, as well as elected positions on Associated Students boards. In the midst of this fervor, Chicana-Chicano youth took bold stances in local dailies on issues as they proclaimed their new identity.

Finally, I hope that *Mexican Americans with Moxie* will inform the leadership of adult mentors and youth alike for the present and into future. In this regard educators, community volunteers, and activists cannot assume that youth and young adults can recognize or successfully resist systemic forces that oppress them on their own. Although previous works on El Movimiento Chicano included the central involvement of people like Sal Castro in East Los Angeles and organizations of the Mexican American generation, the role of elder leaders has been represented to a large extent as following the lead of activist youth when in reality they were directly behind them, if not shoulder to shoulder, at their side. The wisdom obtained via experience, often painful, must be shared with the upcoming generation of leaders so they can recognize the landmines and traps inherent to social systems and institutions. The elder generation, moreover, must come to the defense of youth when threatened by the authorities of agencies, often ethnic Mexican themselves.

And, for upcoming generations, I hope this book encourages incipient activists to seek out and consider the advice of people who have already gone through the phases of life in which they find themselves. Concurrently, youth need to hold older folks in positions of power accountable, to address their needs in order to realize their own aspirations. From this, both cohorts will be encouraged to make the communities in which they live better places.

1

What's Their Provenance?

How did ethnic Mexicans of distinct generational cohorts and citizenship in Ventura County move to becoming Chicana-Chicano? This chapter answers this question with the claim that a historical block of economic expansion, exploitation, and racism bound people of different age groups: primarily Mexican Americans and Chicanas-Chicanos. These forces spanned the first sixty years of the twentieth century. From these shared experiences and remembrances, I argue two points. First, that a foundation of advocacy on behalf of the farmworker predated César Chávez's return to the county with his gutsy union. Second, that ethnic Mexicans—youth to middle-aged adults, U.S. citizens as well as Mexican nationals—internalized an identity of resistance, or an incipient Chicanismo, based on a cacophony of transgenerational and translocal discourses in their public and private lives.

Adios, César

The Ventura County city of Oxnard lies sixty miles northwest of Los Angeles. Named after sucrose tycoons, the Oxnard brothers established in this seaside community the American Beet Sugar Company (ABSC) factory in 1898. At one point it was the largest refinery of its kind in the nation. As sugar beet production expanded, so did the ethnic Mexican population. The men, women, and children who toiled in the cultivation and harvest of sugar beets labeled themselves *betabeleros*. In 1903 Japanese and Mexican betabeleros—in an exceptional interracial partnership that included labor contractors—formed the Japanese Mexican Labor Association (JMLA) to protest a 50 percent wage reduction. The bitter strike ended in a short-lived JMLA victory. Thirty years later another betabelero strike erupted. This time the satraps of agriculture interlocked their rule with law enforcement and the local press to defeat this job action. The Great Depression also undermined the overall struggle of the union of the betabeleros—the Cannery and Agricultural Workers Industrial Union. Eight years later, in 1941, a strike exploded in Ventura County's citrus orchards and packinghouses. Dead set not to yield to the demands of organized labor, elites from the private sector and public agencies again colluded to quash this insurgency.[1] Landowners, and the agricultural associations to which they belonged, made stingy concessions in wages to placate workers as they repudiated the recognition of the Agricultural and Citrus Workers Union as their collective bargaining agent.

Before and after these labor revolts, the ethnic Mexican community of Ventura County organized mutual aid organizations. Civic groups like La Unión Patriótica Benéfica Mexicana Independiente, La Alianza Hispano Americana, Las Guardianes de Colonia, and the Oxnard Civic Improvement Association (OCIA) sponsored events that integrated the cultural vigor of the ethnic Mexican community into the fabric of the mainstream as they lobbied elected officials for equitable municipal services. In his recognition of the social capital of the ethnic Mexican community in Oxnard, Ralph Helstein, president of the United Packinghouse Workers of America (UPWA), paid the Community Service Organization (CSO) $20,000—adjusted for inflation, approximately $180,000—in the summer of 1958 to establish a Ventura County chapter to complement his union's foothold in the region's citrus packinghouses and orchards. But on one condition: that the CSO's crackerjack organizer, César Chávez, personally lead the campaign.[2]

Within a year of his arrival in 1958, Chávez, with the support of the OCIA, founded a CSO chapter in Ventura County. In the process of building its membership to a healthy five hundred residents of largely second-generation Mexican American lineage and long-term-resident Mexican nationals, it serviced the migrant community via citizenship classes, voter registration drives, the navigation of public bureaucracies, and get-out-the-vote campaigns. The CSO and the UPWA then tapped into the organization's leadership capital to combat the agricultural industry's corruption of the Bracero Program, which imported male contracted workers from Mexico to systematically depress the wage rate. Due to white supremacist fears of race suicide, lawmakers engineered this exclusively male program that barred the inclusion of women to preclude the replication of ethnic Mexican families in the United States with all the rights—especially voting—and immunities that came with both birthright and naturalized citizenship. As braceros became the workers of choice, the program displaced domestic laborers (or locals, as they were also known). The Chávez-led CSO politicized the ethnic Mexican community as it exposed the agricultural industry's fraud for the exploitation of tractable labor. For a fleeting moment, the CSO compelled state and federal agencies to hold employers accountable to the dictates of Public Law 78, which, for one, mandated an employment preference for domestic workers, as braceros were supposed to supplement a labor shortage at the extant wage rate. So, whereas the Bracero Program in the Salinas Valley "slowed the evolution of a postwar Latino civil rights movement," as historian Lori A. Flores argues, in the more mixed economy of Ventura County, adjacent to urban Los Angeles, it jump-started a movement that would continue into the mid-1970s.[3]

With his mission completed, in May 1959 Chávez left Ventura County to serve as the CSO's national director in Los Angeles. Soon after his departure, José Rivera of the Ventura County chapter informed Chávez of the dissipation of gains that had been achieved in privileging the employment of domestic farmworkers. As before the California Farm Placement Service (CFPS) required domestic workers to first register at its offices each day to obtain referral cards to present to the grower-controlled labor associations. After domestic workers jumped through this hoop, each morning they found that the labor associations dispatched braceros to worksites prior to their arrival. Furthermore, if a local had been fired three times, the growers marked the person ineligible for reemployment. The CFPS also disqualified applicants from obtaining a referral card if a person registered for work more than twice. These provisions did not apply to braceros. Consequently, domestic workers largely found themselves systematically barred from agricultural employment.[4]

In Defense of the Farmworker

Despite the addiction of growers to bracero labor, the Ventura County CSO continued to champion the cause of domestic workers. In January 1961 chapter president Ygnacio Coronado angrily pointed out in a letter to the *Oxnard Press-Courier* that taxpayers subsidized the importation of braceros to the detriment of "our citizens" (i.e., domestic farmworkers, longtime migrant residents, and U.S. citizens). Coronado thought that Edmund G. Brown pandered to the growers, and he characterized like politicians as craven for their refusal to stand up to "farm bosses." Coronado also sardonically likened Governor Brown's expressed opposition to minimum wage legislation for farmworkers as a press release from the agricultural industry.[5]

Later in the year, William Tolbert, manager of the Ventura County Citrus Growers' Committee, defended the Bracero Program in a speech to the Rotary Club of Ventura County. Criticism of the program was a public relations ploy on the part of unions, he held. The federal Department of Labor did not pay workers; it funded $1,400,000 only to supervise the program. Tolbert then cited the average pay of a bracero as one dollar an hour and claimed that the inability of unions to organize farmworkers was due to the "individualistic and independent" thinking of its employees.[6]

The perspective of commercial agriculture did not go uncontested as CSO vice president José Rivera penned a point-by-point rebuttal to Tolbert's Rotary Club address. In a letter to the *Oxnard Press-Courier*'s letters section, Voice of the People, Rivera emphasized CSO's opposition to the Bracero Program, not the contracted guest worker, due to it being "nothing short of 'Legalized Slavery.'" To counter the myth of rugged individualism that was closely linked to a white and male nationalist ideal, he highlighted stratagems of the grower class to advance their moneyed interests. The fact that the federal government facilitated the agricultural industry's access to braceros was itself a subsidy. Rivera went on to contextualize Tolbert's own statistics to evidence the economic inequities that farm labor faced. These realities underscored the aggregate subordinate status of ethnic Mexicans in the United States.[7]

The CSO critique of the Bracero Program stemmed from its short-lived victory two years before. Its national office also collaborated with Ernesto Galarza. A Stanford- and Columbia-trained academic and labor organizer who entered the United States as a migrant child during the Mexican Revolution, Galarza published writings in syndicated newspapers that exposed the agricultural industry's exploitation of this federally sponsored system. Meanwhile, CSO men and women conducted "educationals" on the Bracero Program's endemic problems. And, to advance a wider consciousness, CSO chapters publicly debated questions that affected the interests of ethnic Mexican communities.[8]

As in the case of the civil rights movement, during this era television sensitized the general public to the plight of migrant farmworkers with the 1960 broadcast of Edward R. Murrow's *Harvest of Shame* the day after Thanksgiving. In this exposé U.S. secretary of labor James P. Mitchell identified migrant farmworker families as "excluded Americans." Like Rivera, the documentary compared the condition of migrant farmworkers to that of slaves. *Harvest of Shame* so moved comedian and talk show host Steve Allen that he contacted William Becker, secretary of the California Committee for Fair Practices, to express his alarm and volunteered to chair the organization's Committee on Farm Labor Problems. Becker took advantage of Allen's offer to build a statewide network to address this twentieth-century version of bondage.[9]

Old Age Pensions for Farmworkers

Prior to *Harvest of Shame*'s airing, the national CSO worked for the passage of old age pension legislation for noncitizens. Chapters from around California lobbied state legislators as Dolores Huerta, the organization's cunning legislative chair, met with politicians in the state capital. Mexican American generation CSO men and women of migrant parentage, if not Mexican nationals themselves, demanded that the seniors in their community be treated with dignity. When the old age pension campaign started in 1953, only four CSO chapters existed. By July 1961, with the enactment of Assembly Bill 5 (AB 5), titled the

Old Age Security Adjustment, that number rose to forty-two statewide. The progression of an ethnic Mexican voting bloc via a sequence of English-language instruction, naturalization classes, voter registration, and get-out-the-vote campaigns produced dividends. But the victory would not have been possible without the help of unions, clergy, and the cross-cultural political capital of Black, Jewish, and Asian American organizations, as the California legislature did not include one member of Mexican ancestry.

The day Governor Brown signed AB 5 into law, two hundred CSO representatives from around the state traveled to Sacramento to witness the ceremony. The *Oxnard Press-Courier* reported Rivera—at the time second vice president of the Ventura County CSO—to be in attendance. But, as historian Kenneth C. Burt points out, "the old age bill was only a part of CSO's aggressive legislative agenda that included new efforts to curtail police abuse of minorities and the negative impact of urban redevelopment.... Nor was the pension bill the only legislative victory."[10]

The CSO's AB 5 campaign impressed Governor Brown and Assemblyman Philip Burton. At the bill's signing, they declared a farmworker minimum wage law their next goal. Excited by this, Chávez urged the CSO to assert itself as the undisputed organization of agricultural workers; hence, CSO momentum should have been channeled "right away." But, to achieve this, the CSO needed a labor committee, money, and, most important, *ganas* (the will). When the organization refused to venture into this arena, Chávez resigned at the 1962 organization's annual national convention.[11]

After his departure from the CSO, in April 1962 Chávez and his family moved to Delano, where his wife, Helen, had family. As he worked the crops to "cleanse" himself, Chávez imagined a strategy to create a union of his dreams. To start he tapped into his CSO network, both in and out of the San Joaquin Valley, to recruit true believers to his cause. Meanwhile, Ventura County CSOers continued to condemn the agricultural industry's continued employment of braceros over domestic workers. In May 1962 local CSO leaders John Soria, Val Lucero, Joe Pérez, Joe Reta, and Rivera traveled to Delano to persuade Chávez to return to Ventura County to join their own outfit, the Oxnard Farm Labor Service Center (FLSC), which organized farmworkers with the external support of Max Mont of the California Committee on Fair Practices and Katie Peake, an affluent Santa Barbara ranch owner and member of the Emergency Committee to Aid Farm Workers. Soria offered Chávez the opportunity to form a second labor service center in Delano, so that he would not need to abandon his own unionization efforts. Chávez refused the proposition; he wanted no part of an operation dependent on external funds. In comparison to Oxnard, he also preferred to organize grape workers in the San Joaquin Valley because they were relatively younger denizens as opposed to itinerant farmhands.[12]

The determination of Soria, Rivera, and the others to organize farmworkers created a schism within the CSO, as the organization refused funds from Peake; although sympathetic to farmworkers' plight, the Ventura County chapter decided that this project belied the policy of its national headquarters to stay clear of this realm of organizing. To publicly clarify its position, the Ventura County CSO issued a press release that declared the organization's autonomy from the FLSC.[13] In February 1963 Soria addressed the city council of Oxnard regarding the importation of Mexican and Japanese braceros that displaced domestic workers. And, to distance his work from CSO, Soria stated that he represented the FLSC, an unattached local union.[14]

¡Que viva César Chávez!

Two years later, in the community of Delano, some 130 miles north of Ventura County, Chávez's National Farm Workers Association (NFWA) demonstrated the boycott during its grape strike. The significance of this labor walkout connected the urban experience of incipient Chicanas-Chicanos with those who lived not only in the agricultural communities of the San Joaquin Valley, but also the Ventura County farm towns of Piru, Fillmore, Santa Paula, and Saticoy, as well as the more "rurban" cities of Camarillo, Oxnard, and Ventura that enjoyed mixed economies of agriculture, commerce, and industry, which provided employment opportunities in municipal, state, and federal agencies. Moreover, Chávez, a diminutive, swarthy man with raven hair, carried himself with a Mexican Americanist savoir faire that inspired incipient Chicanas-Chicanos—farmworkers and nonfarmworkers alike, of all ages—to collectively fight the economic oppression of their employers as betabeleros and citrus workers had done hitherto.[15]

This was huge. Rarely, if ever, did young ethnic Mexicans witness people from their communities in positions of authority, much less taking on the man (the white man) with such moxie in the articulation of the trials and dreams of the farmworker. At worksites the parents of many Chicanas-Chicanos with restricted employment options took orders; unless they were *mayordomos* (supervisors) themselves, they rarely gave direction. So, as Chávez voiced the demands of his union to growers with the accompaniment of his partner, NFWA vice president Dolores Huerta, and younger acolytes such as Jessica Govea, he animated both authorized and unauthorized immigrant residents with Mexicanist identities, and incipient Chicanas-Chicanos. In the process, not only did they honor the secondary boycotts of *la unión* (the NFWA) in front of mom-and-pop grocery stores and supermarket chains such as Safeway that carried nonunion grapes, they also formulated demands of their own in and out of the environs of agriculture.

From the fight in the fields to the north, complemented by a tradition of resistance, labor insurgencies in Ventura County erupted in the communities of Fillmore, Santa Paula, and Moorpark. While Chávez commanded union strikes in the valleys of San Joaquin and, later, Salinas, he visited Ventura County at the request of friends and workers with similar grievances to raise funds as well as to demonstrate his moral support for local struggles.

The audacity of putatively obedient farmworkers to demand that the NFWA be their bargaining agent motivated Chicana-Chicano youth to exercise their own self-determination. Yvonne De Los Santos, as the daughter and granddaughter of migrant workers raised in the unincorporated community of Saticoy, was one such person, whose family struggled to subsist on the measly wages set by grower cartels. As a latchkey child, she often returned from school to a home with barren cupboards as her parents toiled in fields and orchards. While in school, teachers and peers emotionally punished her for speaking the *idioma* (language) of her family—Spanish. This devastated her sense of self. In recalling this experience in a familial collective sense, De Los Santos stated, "I felt good except when we went to school when we were forced to speak English. . . . I remember at one point I became ashamed of my mother and father. I felt embarrassed when mother and father went to the school." This shame grew as De Los Santos was bussed to a school in the city of Ventura. Here she became conscious of the economic divide along a white-brown color line. Fifty percent or more of demoralized Chicana-Chicano students dropped out of high school by the ninth grade, when they were able to. Psychologically, the process commenced much earlier. Pushed out by the educational system, so fell their life chances compared to others with high school diplomas. In fact, De Los Santos stated, "all the kids were passed by in all respects. I could see that there were different classes. Whites were usually in the higher groups. . . . I was one of the very few that continued but I did poorly."[16]

The Lay of the Land

The Chicana-Chicano youth of Ventura County lived contiguously to, and at the center of, the sister counties of Kern to the northeast, Santa Barbara County to the northwest, and Los Angeles to the southeast. The labels of the latter two spoke to the successive settler-colonial regimes of Spain and Mexico. Subsumed but not entirely erased from public memory, the history and survival of the Yokut of Kern, Yang-Na of Los Angeles, and the Chumash of Ventura and Santa Barbara counties remained standing. Whites and others often misidentified the first people of the state for Mexicans, due to their brown skin and Spanish surnames, although they were the true founders of California. As an indigenous people under occupation, they also often resided within the colonias and barrios of Southern California. This further obscured their existence.

Ethnic Mexicans lived in a Cold War–era economy in Southern California that entailed the five counties: Los Angeles, Orange, Riverside, San Bernardino, and Ventura. In 1963 the Los Angeles Chamber of Commerce viewed the region as economically consolidated.[17] Consequently, even though a large proportion of ethnic Mexicans in Ventura County lived and worked in communities centered in agriculture, they were not completely marginalized economically. Military and commercial bases and ports, as well as suburban developments, opened new vistas of employment that prompted Chicanas-Chicanos approaching their early adult years to incrementally transcend the economic status of their parents. Freeways, in particular, facilitated the creation of networks among young men and women who explored the campus life of colleges and universities in the region. Many of their family members commuted to work in the region's military-industrial complex.[18]

Civic managers and developers transformed the pasturelands, orchards, and fields of the valleys of Conejo and Simi into suburban tract homes and shopping centers. But, as this shift occurred, Ventura County continued to be the number-one producer of lemons in the nation. In 1958 the total gross value of lemons stood at $29,446,851. Despite this citrus bonanza, the county's uneven topography of orchard acreage—consisting of valencia and navel oranges, lemons, and grapefruit—gave way to real estate development. Oil production also drove the county's economy. As people entered from the Los Angeles region and beyond, residential tracts metastasized, as did road construction. Concurrently, the Cold War economy compelled companies such as Packard Bell Electronics, Technology Instrument Corporation, the Northrop Institute of Technology, and California Lutheran College to open shop there in 1961.[19]

The Cold War economy afforded a significant proportion of ethnic Mexicans a working-middle class competence. No longer did this segment have to be preoccupied with food and residential insecurity as their incomes rose with employment prospects beyond agriculture. But, since many ethnic Mexicans, especially incipient Chicanas-Chicanos, were the sons and daughters of agricultural migrants, they did not disremember the deprivations of their family. As the children of parents who worked in orchards and packinghouses, they either attended or knew of union rallies, picket lines, and the designated leaders at camps and halls. Many first- and second-generation ethnic Mexicans worked in the citrus industry and appreciated the high stakes involved in the struggle for a living wage and the right to bargain collectively—in other words, the demand to be treated with dignity.

Jim and Juan Crow

Black and brown families in particular ventured to Ventura County after World War II to pursue new lives. Lily Watkins, an African American recruited in the

1960s by officials of the Oxnard Elementary School District (OESD), recalled how advertised rental homes she inquired about over the phone were suddenly no longer available when she arrived with her husband. Racist tenants also vacated apartment complexes as Black families became neighbors. Indeed, a survey conducted by the California Fair Employment Commission in 1971 found that 20 percent of the civilian rental housing units were not available to Black military personnel at the Point Mugu Pacific Missile Range southeast of Oxnard and the city's air force base.[20] Black Seabee servicemen also experienced discrimination at Port Hueneme during this era, as white southern migrants did not abandon their Jim Crow racism. This similarly impacted residents of the Mexican American generation as a National Association for the Advancement of Colored People (NAACP) report of April 4, 1946, declared, "Longtime residents here point out that such occurrences were uncommon until recently. In varying degrees, this racial animosity also has backfired against Mexicans here the same as against Negroes."[21] In response to local NAACP protests, the Oxnard City Council passed a resolution of housing nondiscrimination; the council, however, did not pass an ordinance, as it contended that the problem was a federal matter.[22]

In 1968 Ureal B. Brown, chapter president of the Oxnard and Ventura Branch of the NAACP, along with other members of the organization, met with the city of Oxnard's Human Relations Commission and private interests to discuss racist residential practices. The NAACP also met with the commanders of local military installations, Ventura County's Real Estate Board, the Human Relations Commission, and faith and civic groups to address the problem of chauvinist landlords.[23]

Bigots, however, did not limit their racism against the Black community to housing. In 1946 four Black women sat in a section of the Oxnard Theater designated for white patrons; management called the police to eject them from their seats. Similarly, an usher directed Fred Tolston, also of Oxnard, to sit in the section designated for Black and Mexican patrons. As he was being escorted from the designated white seating area, he witnessed the removal of Irene Turner, a Black woman, from the theater after she objected to the segregated seating.[24] In addition, Black families of Ventura County discovered burning crosses and Ku Klux Klan (KKK) signs staked in front of their homes. And in the city of Ventura businesses brazenly discriminated against Black customers as a bus terminal café posted a white trade only sign.[25]

The year before, in 1945, Richard (Dick) Abrams, described as a "prominent" resident of Oxnard and president of the Oxnard branch of the NAACP stated that "the influx of southern whites here, who bring with them their provincial and distorted racial views, in my opinion, is directly the cause of this new friction. Secondly, southern Negroes, who have moved here in large numbers, haven't helped the situation any. Generally speaking, they have gone from one extreme, that of being almost completely suppressed in the south [sic], to the other extreme, that of taking advantage of comparative freedom by unnecessary bulldozing tactics in the relationship with other groups."[26] In other words, the Black community now lived in a social environment that allowed them to more freely contest white supremacy. No longer did Black migrants now living in Southern California need to fear KKK-led lynchings and other forms of white terrorism. Some in the Black community, according to Abrams, now took full advantage of their new freedoms by the confrontation of racists.

Twenty years later, in June 1963, San Fernando Valley State College professor and Simi Valley resident Jack D. Forbes, as a trustee of the Ventura Junior College District, declared at a Democratic Club meeting, "We in Ventura County do not need to look at Mississippi or Alabama for examples of segregation of Jim Crowism. We have it right here—and we should do something about it." Forbes pointed to systemic racism "in housing, private employment, public employment, appointments to civic committees, and in education as well as in private clubs and organizations which make use of public facilities."[27] The next month the *Oxnard Press-Courier* interviewed people about race relations in the city. Most expressed support for equal rights as movement activists demonstrated and marched in the nation's southern states; many, however, opposed tactics of direct action. Others denied the existence of racism locally. But a Mrs. J. N. Poss, a city of Port Hueneme resident and recent migrant from Anniston, Alabama, affirmed Forbes's testimony as a white woman. She confessed that many southern white migrants imported

Jim Crow traditions, and that Blacks did not enjoy the same rights as ethnic Mexicans or Italians. Poss then divorced herself from the Black community when she stated that the "Lord loves them as much as He loves the white, but I believe that if He'd wanted us to live together He would have made us all the same color."[28]

Consequently, the NAACP, American Civil Liberties Union, CSO, Ventura County Jewish Council, Human Relations Council, and United Church Women worked to eliminate racism in residential housing. In 1967 the NAACP, with a membership of 180, convened five meetings with the leadership in the city of Oxnard, Ventura County Human Relations Commission, and Real Estate Board to abolish racist practices.[29]

As residential developments boomed after 1945, the city's council, school boards, and private developers worked in unison in the de facto segregation of largely Black and ethnic Mexican schoolchildren within the barrio of La Colonia. A 1963 OESD plan, for example, to construct a junior high school in this quarter would prove this, prompting cross-cultural opposition.[30] The segregation of nonwhite teachers to these schools followed. Lily Watkins recalled that, in fact, all four Black teachers in the district taught at Juanita Elementary, in the heart of the La Colonia barrio. The district also systematically barred the transfer of Black teachers to white neighborhood schools.[31] Other forms of racism consisted of blackface theater. The Camarillo Players' production of *You Can't Take It with You* provides an example. The Oxnard and Ventura County chapter of the NAACP met with the Camarillo Players and successfully persuaded the group to cancel the production.[32] On the north side of Oxnard, I recall a home off of C Street that displayed a Black lawn-jockey statue in its front yard. Another racial trope of the era consisted of a middle-aged Black man paid by the proprietor of the Colonial House Restaurant to wear a white chef's uniform and wave to customers. Then there was the Elks Lodge, which barred Blacks from membership. All of this evidenced a milieu of white supremacy in Ventura County—not of the variety of Southern Redemption after the nation's era of Reconstruction, characterized by lethal KKK terrorism and Huck Finn–like language, but that underpinned privileges of power and discretion in nearly all aspects of life and society.

Somos jodidos (We're Screwed)

Consciously and unconsciously, people of the Mexican American and Chicana-Chicano generations understood their condition as a disadvantaged community. In a two-part *Los Angeles Times* series in 1966, José Antonio Villareal, author of the germinal 1959 novel *Pocho*, articulated this vexation as he identified a tension between Chicana-Chicano youth on the one hand, and more experienced elders on the other. Villareal contended that "youth seems to be carrying the day in the leadership battle among Californians of Mexican descent." A transgenerational intersection, however, existed, as members of the Mexican American generation mentored incipient Chicana-Chicano adolescents and young adults. The emblematic hand-off of the scepter of leadership of the Mexican American Political Association (MAPA) at this time from sixty-three-year-old Eduardo Quevedo to forty-eight-year-old Bert Corona, a civil and labor rights activist whose crusades dated back to the 1940s, exemplified this shift as Corona straddled the generations born before and after World War II.[33]

This inchoate cohort demanded equal protections under the law while emphasizing to a greater degree a mestizo, if not an indigenous, identity. Opposed to the emphasis of earlier scholars, this Chicana-Chicano politics, again and moreover, was not limited to those born in the United States. Rather, anyone who had experienced racist acts of subordination and disparate treatment in public facilities and institutions often embraced the once pejorative Chicana-Chicano label. Not uncommon verbal assaults of "dirty Mexican," "wetback," "taco," and "beaner," to name a few, galvanized their righteous indignation. Additionally, a political economy of tokenism and exploitation buttressed this sensibility. Indeed, the fluid migration of Mexican nationals both young and old, authorized and the unauthorized, "replenished"—to use the definition of sociologist Tomás R. Jiménez—the ethnic Mexican identity of people who came to call themselves Chicana-Chicano.[34] In this context, Villareal stated, "the first and greatest of these is the fact that the Mexican community in California is in a state of flux. There are more immigrants coming into the United States from Mexico than from another country. Add to this the number of illegal entries who will remain, especially in rural areas and who will eventually marry and have children who will be American citizens."[35]

So, in 1966, Villareal, as a person of the Mexican American generation, recognized how migrant Mexican nationals refashioned the identity of many ethnic Mexicans as a whole. As intraethnic divisions and tensions existed, Chicana-Chicano youth and their activist mentors, such as Corona, understood that all ethnic Mexicans, regardless of citizenship, in the eyes of the general public formed a racialized suspect class vulnerable to systemic violence. In this regard MAPA, via electoral politics, committed itself to the redress of grievances of poverty, exploitation, and all forms of racism without the abnegation of any segment of the ethnic Mexican community. Furthermore, as will be detailed later, MAPA's rise represents an organizational shift in the mentalité of many Mexican Americans to becoming Chicana-Chicano. This mindset entailed working with and within institutions as well as the deployment of external direct actions. Moreover, a preoccupation with the life chances of children, no matter their resident status, bound together ethnic Mexican activists of the Mexican American and Chicana-Chicano generations.

As an example of this intergenerational bridge, Rachel Murguia Wong's ethnic Mexican parents met and ultimately started their family at Rancho Sespe, a citrus labor camp between the communities of Santa Paula and Fillmore. The Murguia family worked in the citrus industry during the 1930s until the countywide Citrus Strike of 1941, after which her parents briefly relocated the family to the city of Port Hueneme, before settling in John Steinbeck's Cannery Row in Monterey. As a young woman of the Mexican American generation, Murguia attended the University of California, Los Angeles (UCLA), where she met her husband, Alan Wong, and from which she graduated. In 1966, after a one-year stay in Hong Kong, Murguia Wong and her young family moved to Oxnard, where they lived in the northern, predominantly white and white-collar middle-class area of the city.[36]

In this sense Wong's early adulthood linked the Mexican American and Chicana-Chicano generations. As an analyst for the La Colonia Youth Services program in Oxnard, Murguia Wong abhorred the self-annihilation of alienated youth. One of the most horrific entailed kids who inhaled paint and gasoline fumes, coupled with the illicit use of drugs and alcohol, as anodynes to barrio life. To address this problem, the La Colonia Youth Services program worked with the police department, businesses, and city agencies.[37] Oxnard social services created employment summer programs to keep adolescents of all backgrounds constructively occupied. Concerned Chicanas-Chicanos of the county such as Murguia Wong also worked with the Neighborhood Youth Corps (NYC) of Oxnard in cooperation with the Ventura County Community Action Commission. To finance such initiatives, Ventura County communities pursued war-on-poverty funds for the Youth Employment Services program (YES) started in 1965. One of YES's initiatives provided on-the-job training for low-income youth. By the summer of 1968, public and private agencies in Ventura, Camarillo, Newbury Park, Thousand Oaks, and Santa Paula sought YES workers. The following year the YES program in Oxnard (OYES) attracted 3,060 applicants ranging from the ages of fourteen to twenty-one. Ethnic Mexican youth made up the largest percentage, at 45 percent.[38]

The OYES program not only provided youth with jobs, but also trained them in soft skills to work in professional environs. In a June 1970 report, Ann Ward, OYES's executive director, listed the reasons why youth desired such employment. The first tier consisted of poverty caused by the unemployment of one or both parents; such economic stress meant food and clothing insecurity. Second, OYES youth indicated the basic human need to feel loved. This encompassed support for their development and treatment for the emotional, physical, or substance abuse that often intersected.[39]

Other youth of the Chicana-Chicano generation experienced their fair share of toil in the fields, nurseries, orchards, vineyards, and packinghouses of Ventura County. In the process they witnessed the top-down indignities, violence, and outright wage theft endured by family members at the hands of unscrupulous employers and *mayordomos*, many of the latter ethnic Mexicans themselves. This included verbal abuse, physical and sexual violence, and the ripping off of workers in their piece-rate production and hours of labor. Chicana-Chicano youth committed to memory folktales of labor insurgencies and evictions that spanned the first half of the twentieth century. Many were also the children of riveters named Rosa that worked in the industries of World War II; others were the offspring of bracero fathers and women-led households.[40] Then there were those who witnessed firsthand the violent campaigns of the Immigration and Naturalization Service (or *la migra*, as this agency was known), one in 1954 crassly labeled "Operation Wetback." As *migra* officers raided worksites, they indiscriminately detained or chased and decked any suspect ethnic Mexican. There was also the regular harassment, surveillance, and brutality suffered by the working poor at the hands of racist law enforcement officers. Combined, all of this created a milieu of occupation in communities such as La Colonia in Oxnard, Santa Paula, and Ventura.[41]

To survive a system of wage slavery fixed by a cartel of agribusiness associations and bureaus that prohibited food, clothing, shelter, and medical security to maximize profits, many Chicana-Chicano youth embarked upon the harvest circuit with their parents (and, often, extended family) up and down the state to places such as King City, Madera, Salinas, San Jose, Watsonville, and Healdsburg. Few gender and age restrictions existed in the labor ranks of the agricultural industry. All workers physically able to fill or carry a sack or tray did. Growers boarded migrant families in barns, tents, shanties, and barracks, at times adjacent to braceros. At one site, Kika Friend, my *tía*, suffered the indignity of having to sound a whistle with fellow strawberry pickers so that the mayordomo would know that the workers were not consuming the fruit. This was in addition to pesticide exposure by aerial crop dusters. All the while men, women, and children racked their spines as they utilized the infamous short-handled hoe (*el cortito*, outlawed in California in 1975) to cultivate row crops.[42]

For most "a Mexican was a Mexican." Even Chicanas-Chicanos, before their politicization by El Movimiento, largely identified themselves as Mexican, even though the majority in Ventura County were U.S.-born citizens or longtime residents. As eloquently detailed by Ana Rosas, many children entered the United States with their mothers after their bracero fathers economically solidified themselves.[43] Incipient Chicana-Chicano youth also understood and spoke Spanish with divergent degrees of fluency. Young migrants or the offspring of migrant parents who entered the United States as adolescents were often fully bilingual in English and Spanish. As they matured some preternaturally code-switched back and forth in both languages; others, not so much.

Within ethnic Mexican communities there existed also households with mixed parentage in relation to residency, citizenship, and generation. Thus, a melodious bilingualism defined and united Chicanas-Chicanos of El Movimiento, no matter how extensive or limited their fluency or comprehension in either language. Of course, at times there was tension around and derision of both language speakers. Nevertheless, a ubiquitous Spanish language sounded in the *barrios*, *campos* (fields), *colonias*, and *huertas* (orchards) of Ventura County, especially by Mexican nationals, who often performed the most physically taxing and least remunerative labor.

The Private and Public

As with English-Spanish communication, the semiotics of petit entrepreneurs, public and private conversations, and the propaganda of El Movimiento itself reinforced an alloyed, collective Chicana-Chicano identity. Prior to the advent and widespread proliferation of television, especially in poorer households, radio synthesized news as parents tuned into Spanish-language stations during the predawn hours and after dinner. Spanish-language talk programs, such as Javier Santana's KOXR radio show *El Pueblo Opina* (The people opines), mediated debates on issues that impacted the community in relation to education, and politics (local, state, national, and transborder). After their politicization in the late 1960s, Chicana-Chicano youth embraced their bilingualism, no matter the level of their facility, as a central aspect of their collective self-confidence, unity, and action.[44]

When not on the migrant route, Chicana-Chicano youth often lived in the barrios and colonias of Ventura County, segregated from more affluent white neighborhoods by custom and policy. Two of these communities were La Colonia in Oxnard and the Avenue barrio in the city of Ventura. It was in quarters such as these that Chicana-Chicano youth comingled with an ethnic and racial cross-section of disenfranchised households of ethnic Asians, Blacks, and whites. Raised in the enclave of the Avenue, Moses Mora poignantly declared in an interview that "poor people are poor people, no matter what color they are."[45] It was in these cross-culturally integrated yet economically segregated spaces that Chicanas-Chicanos not only befriended peers of different races and ethnicities but also adopted a melange of styles of cuisine, dress, and music. Motown sounds and rhythm and blues in particular boomed throughout the courtyards and alleyways of congested public housing projects. At city parks working-class Black, white, and ethnic Mexican men and women coached and supervised their kids and other Chicana-Chicano youth in extracurricular activities, especially Little League baseball and drill teams such as the Colonades of La Colonia.

As they reached adolescence, Chicana-Chicano youth carpooled to adjacent cities such as Oxnard and Ventura with larger populations to enjoy the sounds of Cannibal and the Headhunters, Thee Midniters, Ike and Tina Turner, and Sam and Dave with Dick Clark's Caravan, who performed at Ventura's National Guard Armory, the Green Mill Ballroom, or Carousel. In Oxnard the Roller Gardens at Wagon Wheel Junction booked similar shows. As on Los Angeles's Whittier Boulevard, Chicana-Chicano youth cruised the avenues, boulevards, and main streets of Oxnard, Santa Paula, and Ventura. To the vexation of elder residents, lowriders blasted the music of the Impressions and the Salas Brothers (later known as Tierra). Cruisers fostered an esprit de corps as they listened to artists who embedded in their lyrics a politics that conveyed notions of ethnic pride. While they socialized in parks or the parking lots and the courtyards of their high-density public housing projects, to escape crowded households, youth gossiped and bantered as they listened to and identified with the messages of James Brown's "Say It Loud, I'm Black and I'm Proud" and the Impressions's "This Is My Country."[46]

The Folklore of Labor

Tales of organized resistance passed on by people born before World War II, complemented by firsthand experiences with racism, further defined the worldview of the Chicana-Chicano generation. The Ventura County Citrus Strike of 1941 was one touchstone event. This cohort also witnessed intraethnic schisms. In fact, many of the families of the countywide citrus labor battle of 1941 did not agree with the strike leadership and left the region for places such as San Jose, California, to return later in their lives, if at all.[47]

The ideal circumstance for many families was for one or both breadwinners to obtain unionized employment. Collective bargaining agents and written contracts afforded these households a living wage with the benefits of health insurance, vacation, and retirement. De Los Santos recalled the indigence her family suffered as migrant agricultural workers. But when her father obtained unionized employment in construction, the family relished new clothes and a more salubrious home environment. Even when work ran out in construction, De Los Santos's mother encouraged her husband to remain current with his union dues in order to maintain certain benefits, particularly his seniority, which better positioned him to be reemployed.[48] Households headed by unionized wage earners, furthermore, modeled for their children not only the importance of collective action but an empathy for all workers, especially the destitute. Mora of the Chicana-Chicano generation recalled his construction-worker father honking the car horn in solidarity when they drove by a picket line. Ethnic Mexican adults also inculcated in their children the centrality of collective action by their active membership in mutual aid lodges and service centers such as La Alianza Hispano Americana, La Unión Patriótica Benéfica Mexicana Independiente (UPBMI), the CSO, the Mexican American Opportunity Foundation, the Latin American Veterans Club, and upshot women auxiliaries. In these outfits transgenerational and cross-citizenship ethnic Mexicans participated in social and political functions. Many came from refugee families that experienced the cataclysms of the Mexican Revolution. As such Chicana-Chicano youth heeded the conversations and folklore of elders that witnessed *la revolución* firsthand and who valorized the leadership of insurgents such as Ricardo Flores Magón (an anarchist journalist who befriended the likes of Emma Goldman in the United States) and military leaders Pancho Villa of the Mexican state of Chihuahua and Emiliano Zapata of Morelos. These revolutionary icons were mythic figures that families of Ventura County referenced as part of a tradition of resistance.[49]

In addition to a rich community history of struggle, Chicanas-Chicanos both consciously and unconsciously fathomed their own subordination as they suffered indignities: in elementary school, not having new clothes or even shoes to wear, then their peers and teachers pillorying them for being unable to speak English. Many Chicanas-Chicanos, migrant and U.S.-born, share the memory of being prohibited from speaking their mother tongue in school under the threat of corporal punishment or social stigmatization.

Then there was the entitlement exuded by some of their middle-class, white, and acculturated ethnic Mexican peers. Often monolingual Spanish-speaking students spent spans of time in school mute and alienated, if not terrified, as they fell behind in an unaided English-only curriculum. This humiliation scarred them.

Furthermore, the curriculum failed to speak to their history. Disaffected by all this, many started the psychological process of educational withdrawal at an early age, to be fully actualized by dropping out by their ninth-grade year, if not sooner. Other young men and women gravitated to neighborhood street gangs for acceptance, recognition, and expression. Then there were those who resisted their oppression through their involvement in extracurricular activities before and after the eruption of the 1968 Blowouts in East Los Angeles that boycotted the racist conditions within the Los Angeles Unified School District.[50]

The educational system's negligence that circumscribed the life chances of Chicanas-Chicanos made young men especially susceptible to the military draft or enlistment into one of the armed forces as the U.S. intervention in Vietnam's civil war escalated. Chicano recruits often left Ventura County with an identity that lacked a politicized consciousness. After they witnessed the horrors and absurdities of war, however, Chicano veterans began not only to question their government's foreign policy but also their own identity and status in society. Chicanas, on the other hand, experienced concern for the military inductions of their *hermanos* (brothers), *primos* (cousins), and *amigos* (friends). This consciousness increased with Ralph Guzman's 1968 report, which documented disproportionate Vietnam casualty rates among Chicanos from the Southwest. Chicano Vietnam veterans, such as Armando López, a resident of Oxnard and a founder of the Brown Berets, returned home to support and encourage recently discharged compeers to take full advantage of their veterans' benefits. Chicano veterans and those they recruited into academe found themselves woke by campus teach-ins and antiwar demonstrations conducted by clubs such as Students for a Democratic Society (SDS). Others acquired a political consciousness while incarcerated with political prisoners (e.g., members of the Black Panther Party for Self-Defense, or SDS) who led reading groups grounded in history and current events. No matter the institution, academic or carceral, Chicano Vietnam veterans of Ventura County experienced consiousness-raising exercises.[51]

In their participation in student organizations such the United Mexican American Students (UMAS) and El Movimiento Estudiantil Chicano de Aztlán (MEChA), women more often than not found themselves in subordinated roles, excluded from positions of visible leadership, even though Chicanas conducted much of, if not all, the required administrivia and event preparation. Young and naïve, Chicanas often found themselves victimized by predatory Chicanos who viewed them largely as sexual objects. As a result many young women found themselves emotionally fractured as some Chicano leaders took advantage of them. Other men resented women leaders and sought to destroy them by the deployment of rumors and innuendo. Occasionally this occurred with the complicity of other Chicanas. Drug and alcohol abuse compounded the vulnerability of women to false-hearted men.[52]

More positively, Chicanas teamed up with supportive allies in their rise to positions of leadership. In 1970 Manuela Aparicio-Twitchell experienced this at the start-up campus of Moorpark College. As a cross-country runner, interethnic male teammates encouraged her to enter—unsuccessfully—the election for campus queen. She then went on to be elected chair of Moorpark College MEChA. Five years later Graciela Casillas became president of Ventura College's Associated Students' board after MEChA mobilized an electoral campaign in coalition with other students. Therefore, the world of academe afforded Chicanas-Chicanos the opportunity to contrast experiences in which to (re)assess their own place in society.[53]

Professors and peers also exposed students to new perspectives. This allowed them to develop a greater social consciousness, which led to their participation in demonstrations and conferences near and far. For example, MEChA de San Fernando Valley State College elected Diana Borrego Martínez, from the citrus community of Santa Paula, and a classmate to attend the Denver Youth Conference of 1969. The next year Borrego Martínez attended antiwar protests and was arrested more than once for her activism. Others attended the moratorium marches spearheaded by the Brown Berets and Rosalio Muñoz in East Los Angeles in 1969–70. As a complement to Chávez's leadership in the fields, the valiant direct actions of the Brown Berets struck the fancy of many young Chicanas-Chicanos not accustomed to seeing the authority of "the man" challenged. This motivated youth to educate themselves and embark upon collective direct actions of their own for the uplift of *la raza* (the underdog community).[54]

Jess Gutiérrez, an immigrant and the son of a father who was a bracero, attended the September 1970 Chicano Moratorium Peace March in his community of Oxnard, the second largest after the August 29 demonstration in East Los Angeles that resulted in a riot instigated by the Los Angeles County Sheriff's and Police Departments. Wounded by a land mine in Vietnam and recently discharged from the army, the moratorium speeches of Bert Corona, UCLA instructor Blase Bonpane, Oxnard resident Richard Carmona, and Rosalio Muñoz intrigued Gutiérrez. Marchers from in and out of the county carried a black coffin representing ethnic Mexican Vietnam War casualties with the words "8,000 Chicanos." Chants sounded: "*¡Raza Sí, Guerra No!*"; "Chicano Power!"; and "Hell No, We Won't Go!" The event prompted Gutiérrez to consider his own experiences in relation to the war.[55]

As they articulated discrete yet intersectional problems of oppression, the power movements of Blacks, Native Americans, and second-wave feminists influenced the activism of Chicanas-Chicanos, and vice versa. In households that could afford the relatively new technology of television, many families witnessed movement demonstrations on the nightly news. From this a collective consciousness emerged near and far among Chicanas-Chicanos. The Black civil rights movement, moreover, with its militant actions involving sit-ins at lunch counters, bus boycotts, marches, and voter registration campaigns, often in the face of ruthless state violence, impacted Chicana-Chicano youth. Inaccurate, if not negative, media portrayals of such events compelled Chicanas-Chicanos to create their own literature and newspapers such as *Con Safos, El Chicano, El Malcriado, El Popo, La Raza*, and many others to challenge the narratives of the commercial press. As part of an informal network in and out of college campuses and correctional facilities, these grassroots publications circulated among young men and women hungry for alternative perspectives that contextualized and affirmed their experience. This storytelling advanced the creation of a cultural nationalism rooted in degrees of fact and fiction. The power of the written word politicized readers to not only adopt a ritual of study that they may or may not have held previously but also author their own narratives. This was the power of culturally relevant knowledge.[56]

Takeaway

A continuity of exploitation and subordination in agricultural work coupled with a tradition of resistance psychologically tethered the Mexican American generation to that of the Chicana-Chicano. Many in the latter accompanied their parents to lodge and service center meetings, where they listened to the spectrum of grievances in their community: economic, educational, and political. Hence, organizations such as the CSO and MAPA united three cohorts of the ethnic Mexican community: the immigrant (the Mexicanist generation), the Mexican American generation, and the baby boom generation, who were often the offspring of mixed-citizenship families. In the process Mexican American generation adults modeled an organized resistance to injustice. This was nevermore salient than in the fight in the fields. Chapter 2 will examine the work of service organizations of the Mexican American generation that catechized Chicana-Chicano youth in the art of civic—at times militant—engagement.

2

Mexican American Role Models, 1958–1968

This chapter argues that ethnic Mexicans of the Mexican American generation role-modeled tactics of resistance for incipient Chicana-Chicano youth. This occurred to a significant degree during the 1960s, with the measured militancy of the Ventura County Community Service Organization (CSO) as it contested the Bracero Program, school segregation, residential displacement via redevelopment, and ever-persistent police violence. The CSO campaigns underscore the agency and leadership development of men and women of the Mexican American generation in relation to other organizations as it continued to engage institutions after César Chávez's departure from Ventura County in the summer of 1959. Whereas extant literature focuses largely on the CSO's history in Southern California with respect to its founding chapter in Los Angeles—particularly with the election of Edward R. Roybal to the Los Angeles City Council in 1949 and Chávez's involvement prior to his resignation in 1962 to found the National Farm Workers Association—this chapter spotlights the Ventura County chapter. In the process it highlights the significance of this national organization within a geographical setting with a liminal rural and emergent urban character.[1]

Vote!

As the national CSO sacked Chávez's proposal to develop a farmworker union, the Ventura County chapter continued to engage government agencies. The organization enhanced its goodwill in the community with a progression of services for immigration, English as a second language, and naturalization followed by voter registration drives and get-out-the-vote campaigns. As a result government functionaries and elected officials paid attention to the group's work in the community. By 1960 the CSO had recruited one thousand paid members in the counties of Ventura and Santa Barbara. At one point the Ventura County chapter was the largest in the nation, which allowed the organization to pay staff and fund projects. By 1964 it had expanded its civic action programs to include job training for unskilled workers. CSO women and men attended workshops on how to support migrants, authorized and unauthorized, in relation to their residency status, social security and unemployment benefits, driver's licenses, and citizenship applications.[2]

Tony Del Buono—a founder of the Oxnard Civic Improvement Association (OCIA), from which the local CSO evolved—along with other committed leaders spearheaded a countywide door-to-door voter registration drive. To this end the CSO encouraged members to become deputy registrars, as part and parcel of a larger national initiative, while Anthony P. Rios, the organization's national president, hoped to register half a million new voters in the Spanish-speaking community. After 1947 CSO volunteers registered 217,000 citizens to vote, the goal being to motivate elected officials to address the needs of all people. From this campaign the CSO integrated ethnic Mexican communities into the civic fabric of the country to achieve equity in education, housing, and public safety.[3]

On election day CSO crusaders, in some cases, escorted voters to precincts. If a poll denied a person this right, they investigated the situation on the spot. In the November election of 1960, for example, Oxnard Precinct 22 refused Luisa Bustillo of La Colonia a ballot based on the presumption that she did not read English. The English-speaking Bustillo, a native-born citizen of La Cruces, New Mexico, had voted since 1925; hence, she fumed that the poll officials questioned her eligibility—and citizenship—based on the criterium of language facility that most likely served as a pretext to deny her suffrage because of her ethnicity. When poll workers turned Bustillo away, she made a beeline to the CSO office for help. CSO leaders Del Buono, Eddie Pérez, and John Soria contacted Jane Tolmach, chair of the county Democratic Central Committee, who took the case to Ventura County clerk Robert Hamm and the state attorney general. In the end Bustillo cast her ballot.[4]

As CSO teams canvassed neighborhoods to register eligible voters, Soria decided to run for a seat on the city council. Soria's family's history influenced his civic consciousness. As a packinghouse worker, Soria's mother capitalized on her bilingualism to organize workers during the Ventura County Citrus Strike of 1941. As a boy Soria listened to émigré narratives of the Mexican Revolution. His uncle's discussion of anarchist, socialist, and Marxist ideas further piqued his consciousness. Generationally, Soria, as a Mexican American, stood in between elders with Mexicanist identities and youth with an emergent Chicana-Chicano sensitivity.[5]

As a nonpartisan service organization, the CSO avoided the endorsement of candidates. As a result Soria resigned as president of the chapter in 1960, after declaring his candidacy for a seat on the city council. Ernie Villanueva, a fellow CSO officer, also recused himself from the organization's leadership. Nonetheless, the *Oxnard Press-Courier* expressed its concern about the CSO allying itself with the UPWA the previous year and targeted Soria as a person that helped the union organize domestic farmworkers. The newspaper patronized candidates Soria and Villanueva with the admonishment that they should appreciate the responsibility of the council to represent the whole community, not just the interests of an organization. The newspaper's snarky editorial, however, did not direct a similar reproach to the white male council candidates. Ultimately, the unsuccessful campaigns of Soria and Villanueva made the point irrelevant.[6] But electoral victory was not the sole measure of success. The fact that the candidacies of Soria and Villanueva raised the profile of the ethnic Mexican community served as an achievement.

The Ventura County CSO advanced its civic goodwill in the sponsorship of forums for municipal, county, state, and congressional races. To ensure effective communication between monolingual English-speaking candidates with audience members with limited English-language comprehension, organizers stationed translators at these events, which were held at the Juanita Elementary School in the heart of the La Colonia barrio of Oxnard. In March 1960, for example, 150 people listened to candidates as CSO president Del Buono moderated the program. At a Sunday afternoon debate two months later, 75 people attended the event at the Juanita school followed by a *tardeada* (soirée) at the adjacent Colonia Park that attracted a total of 700 people. Four years later, in 1964, the Ventura County chapter hosted the CSO national convention in Oxnard. Two hundred CSO chapter delegates arrived with their families, as well as elected officials of both parties, such as State Controller Alan Cranston, State Attorney General Stanley Mosk, Assemblyman Burt Henson, State Senator Robert Lagomarsino, and Oxnard mayor Robert Howlett. The benediction of Reverend Brendan Nagle of Oxnard's Santa Clara Church urged brisk social change as he underscored the convention's élan vital when he stated, "Guard us from the temptation to be satisfied with tokenism or gradualism. Make us see both the value of negotiation and the necessity for direct action against discrimination when negotiation has failed." In relation to nondiscrimination, the CSO declared its opposition to Proposition 14, the anti–Rumford Fair Housing Act initiative that ultimately passed that November by a 2–1 margin.[7]

Women of the CSO

In registering voters, organizing get-out-the-vote drives, conducting English-language and naturalization instruction, and serving as poll deputies, women directed the expansion of the CSO. Early CSO leaders included Oxnard residents Vera Gonzales, Nellie Gutiérrez, and Carmen Yslas, who had been involved in the 1958–59 campaign to end the Bracero Program. For the most part, however, reports in the local press and archival records neglected to recognize these central women members by name. Like their counterparts in other service organizations, women performed most, if not all, of the same duties as men—except in exceptional instances—such as functioning as executive officers or spokespersons.[8] As historian Margaret Rose points out, "Mexican American women became the backbone of the CSO."[9] At the organization's 1960 national convention in Fresno, California, Del Buono stated "I think it's the females in any organization that do the work. Men do the Bull." And Laura Flores Espinosa, the daughter of Edward Flores, one of the founders of the Ventura County chapter and a trade unionist of the Hod Carriers Building and Common Laborers Union, recalled how CSO women attended to a bevy of residents that sought the services of the organization at its La Colonia headquarters. Moreover, many wives of CSO activists indirectly supported the organization as they managed households and family businesses while their spouses attended meetings that often went late into the night or called them out of town.[10]

CSO women also tapped into a network of civic organizations, such as the Latin American Veterans Club, the Sociedad Internacional de Beneficios Mutuos, and the Cristo Rey Catholic Church, among others, to encourage electoral participation as well as to augment its own membership. To ensure that ethnic Mexican U.S. citizens could exercise their right of suffrage, women CSO members performed duties as judges and clerks at poll precincts. Since the Ventura County CSO headquarters on 435 East Hayes in Oxnard served as a polling site, and many of the poll officers there had Spanish surnames, it is conceivable that the CSO trained most of them. Women then went on to participate in other projects. For example, in 1965, Yslas worked for President Lyndon Johnson's Head Start program, which served the prekindergartners of La Colonia.[11]

Shall We Dance?

Community programs advanced the CSO's social network, which in turn increased its goodwill in the county. *Quinceañeras* (debutante balls), pageants, and holiday fetes showed the organization as a civic agent in the larger polity. The proceeds from these events infused the organization with critical funds for paying staff and sponsoring community building initiatives, like candidates' forums, followed by *tardeadas* to promote public awareness of the issues that impacted the lives of barrio residents. For example, when the city claimed that it could not afford an Easter egg hunt in 1960, the CSO donated money to purchase prizes while thirty members of the organization supervised the event activities. This volunteerism complemented the organization's more politically charged advocacy, to avoid being typecast as a gadfly outfit.[12]

In March 1961 the CSO leadership appointed Ernestine Webb, an African American, to supervise a youth group. Webb explained to an audience of women, educators, and local merchants that one of the program's goals was to remedy an internalized inferiority complex instilled in youth by a white-dominant society. This was achieved by way of an ethnic studies–styled curriculum that educated youth about their heritage, believing that love of self and one's community would assist them in the achievement of economic mobility.[13]

CSO programs, moreover, capitalized on family networks to advance a dues-paying membership. For young women the organization sponsored pageants, and the contestant that sold the most tickets was crowned CSO queen. In order to make *quinceañeras* affordable for the families of fifteen-year-old girls, the organization on at least one occasion sponsored this life-cycle celebration.[14] The coming-out gala, however, served as another initiative that solidified the chapter's relevancy with Ventura County ethnic Mexican communities, especially youth who not only enjoyed these cultural events but also observed how members served as community advocates as they mobilized residents to question policymakers.

Urban Redevelopment, No!

Beckoned by the CSO, 450 people squeezed into the auditorium of Juanita Elementary on November 30, 1961, to comment on the city of Oxnard's proposal to apply for federal funds to survey the housing needs of La Colonia. For many the study portended the creation of a redevelopment plan that threatened barrio residents with displacement. One of the CSO's specific concerns was that the redevelopment proceeds ultimately disbursed for the relocation of La Colonia residents would be insufficient. This was on top of racist residential covenants and the interlocked practices of the Federal Housing Authority, lenders, and realtors that blocked people of color from purchasing homes in white neighborhoods. With this in mind, the CSO announced its opposition to the city's prospective application for these federal funds.[15] In addition, the consequences of urban redevelopment projects in other communities piqued the skepticism of many. The May 1959 televised eviction of residents in the Los Angeles barrio of Chávez Ravine, to make way for the construction of Dodger

Stadium, perhaps served as the most dramatic of such episodes in the history of Southern California. With Los Angeles city councilman Edward Roybal being the highest-profile ethnic Mexican voice against the evictions, CSO members learned of the dynamics of urban renewal projects in workshops at their national conventions.[16]

From its national headquarters in Los Angeles, CSO director Chávez advised the Ventura County chapter. When contacted by the *Oxnard Press-Courier*, he stated that the city's deficient inventory of low-income housing and the existence of substandard residences owned by absentee landlords stood at the core of the problem. Sensitive to the circumstance of the working poor—especially the migrant farmworker, who earned the lowest of wages—and having experienced residential dislocation as a boy when his parents lost their home in Yuma, Arizona, during the Great Depression, Chávez undoubtedly feared for the housing security of ethnic Mexican families. So the CSO "primed" three hundred of its members and residents of La Colonia to attend the community meeting on November 30. With Oxnard City Urban Development Committee members Peter Flores and Walter Schlichter in attendance, the CSO Citizens Committee voted unanimously to oppose the application, proclaiming that a federally funded survey would ultimately result in a redevelopment project that displaced hundreds of La Colonia residents. One by one participants in this coordinated action denounced the city's leadership for not appointing CSO members to the Urban Development Committee and vowed to fight urban redevelopment all the way to the U.S. Supreme Court, if necessary. At the conclusion of the meeting, a friendly member of the city committee informed CSO leaders in confidence that the mobilization of Colonia residents was a "big stick" in their hands.[17]

By the end of 1961, the Urban Development Committee of Oxnard rejected the idea to submit a proposal for federal funds for the redevelopment survey. To educate residents of La Colonia on the persistent threat of redevelopment, the CSO sponsored a community cleanup in January 1962. As redevelopment conversations continued, the CSO opposed a housing tract plan in La Colonia that involved the transplantation of salvaged homes from the Los Angeles area onto four-thousand-square-foot lots. CSO held that the recycled houses and stingy-sized parcels would deteriorate the quality of life of this community.[18] In a 1962 report to the CSO National Executive Board, Cloromiro Camacho, as president of the Ventura County chapter, cited newspaper coverage along with the conduct of "house meetings and 'barrio arousements'" (i.e., actions such as that of November 30) to halt city renewal projects. Leo Alvarez, the organization's vice president, addressed the city council to voice the organization's steadfast opposition to a second attempt to conduct a federally funded redevelopment survey of La Colonia.[19]

No More Segregated Schools

Connected to the polemic of urban redevelopment was the proposed location of neighborhood school sites. In January 1962 the CSO endorsed a $3.2 million school bond for the Oxnard Elementary School District (OESD) that ultimately passed. The organization, however, qualified its imprimatur as it opposed the establishment of a junior high school in La Colonia. The Culbert site, as it was called, existed at the easternmost boundary of the city. Instead the CSO recommended that the new middle school be situated west of Oxnard Boulevard, to promote the ethnic and racial integration of schoolchildren. The Ventura County chapter of the National Association for the Advancement of Colored People (NAACP) of Ventura County agreed that the construction of a junior high school at the Culbert site would exacerbate the de facto segregation of Black students and their ethnic Mexican peers. At a meeting of twenty people at CSO headquarters, chapter president Cloromiro Camacho throatily stated, "This is complete discrimination. If a school is built here, it would be 99 percent Mexican or Negro. Therefore this is a segregated school."[20]

In response the OESD dispatched school principals James Ingersoll of Juanita Elementary and Domingo Martínez of Harrington Elementary to persuade the CSO to support the bond measure's funding of a sixty-eight-room school at the Culbert site. They were unsuccessful. OESD board president Mary Davis later conceded that school segregation existed, although due to no fault of the district; in her opinion it emerged from discriminatory residential patterns. She then defended the advantages of neighborhood schools. For example, since the proposed Culbert site would serve third to eighth graders, there would be smaller class sizes. The neighborhood school would also afford children the opportunity to participate in student government and after-school study sessions.[21]

Familiar with the racist *movidas* (machinations) of bureaucracies that portrayed its actions as neutral, the CSO remained incredulous. Indeed, the organization's executive board organized a no vote campaign that entailed an automobile caravan of protest. Members of the Ameramex Club, which originally supported the bond, joined the opposition. But not everyone in the ethnic Mexican community of La Colonia agreed. Actually, the issue divided the membership of both the Ameramex Club and CSO. Raquel Soto, CSO secretary and a Ramona-Juanita-PTA member, along with Webb, backed the bond. Armando López, a high school student who was president of the Ameramex Club and a member of Webb's Teen Toppers, also registered his support for the proposed new school.[22]

In order not to be viewed in the community as obstructionists, the NAACP and CSO respectively declared their inclination to work with the school district to find a solution. Del Buono, a mentor of López, argued as the CSO's spokesperson that interracial fights at Oxnard High stemmed from segregation. In turn the school board and district officials stated that the creation of an intermediate school in La Colonia would alleviate impaction at other elementary and middle schools in the district.[23]

The Culbert site debate took place within the context that ethnic Mexicans made up nearly 40 percent of the student population of the district, followed by Blacks at 10 percent, and ethnic Asians at about 3 percent: for a minority/majority student population, just over 50 percent. The 6,351 white students in the district made up 49 percent of the population. With this situation in mind, Althea Simmons, field secretary of the Los Angeles chapter of the NAACP, found that if the district constructed a junior high school at the Culbert site, 97 percent of enrollees in the new campus would be students of color.[24]

In March 1963 the NAACP presented an innovative plan to the district for integrating its schools. First, the proposal called for the elimination of the Culbert site plan; instead the Fremont junior high school on the west side of the city would either be expanded or a new campus would be constructed near it.

If the school district refused to abandon the Culbert site, a compromise called for it to be paired with the Fremont school: one junior high for seventh graders and the other for eighth graders. Another alternative entailed the creation of a large campus at the Culbert site to accommodate junior high students of the Fremont and La Colonia neighborhoods. To integrate the elementary schools throughout the district, Simmons similarly proposed the pairing of campuses by grades and redrawing attendance boundaries.[25]

Although the district trustees rejected the options outlined by Simmons, they disingenuously requested that she and the NAACP coordinate its plan with the CSO.[26] The *Oxnard Press-Courier* labeled Simmons an interloper who falsely likened Oxnard's de facto school segregation to a racist system the likes of the Deep South. Furthermore, the newspaper dismissed the NAACP's desegregation plans as well as the notion of busing as a remedy. In a reactionary editorial, the newspaper went so far as to assert that "there is not and never has been discrimination in Oxnard. Nor has there ever been a question raised as to educational standards. Everyone here knows that educational standards are the same and as high in Colonia as elsewhere in Oxnard."[27] As chapter 5 will illustrate, racism in the OESD indeed existed. And, as historian David G. García deftly outlines, the district engineered educational segregation over decades.[28]

Nine years removed from the *Brown v. Board of Education* Supreme Court case of 1954, which constitutionally abolished the doctrine of separate but equal, the NAACP requested that the Ventura County district attorney weigh in on the Culbert site controversy. In a mealymouthed reply, district attorney Woodruff Deem opined that the Culbert site project would "probably be valid." He went on to say that the proposal would be valid without qualification after the OESD completed an "exhaustive effort" to explore the question of race as well as alternative school construction plans.[29] Consequently, in June 1963, the OESD abandoned the junior high bid at the Culbert site. The board stated that the La Colonia neighborhood did not warrant a junior high school but would consider the establishment of an additional elementary school in its place. Trustee president Mary Davis even confessed that the board "made an error in judgment" and that she did not realize the "magnitude of the de facto segregation problem."[30]

Police Brutality

As it continued to probe the question of school segregation, CSO monitored the actions of other public agencies, especially the police. Tension between city and county law enforcement agencies on the one hand, and ethnic Mexican residents on the other, intensified during the agricultural labor strikes of the 1900s, 1930s, and 1940s, as sheriff deputies and police officers infiltrated union meetings and intimidated strikers on the behalf of grower elites.[31] Therefore, the repression of labor protests on the part of law enforcement was part and parcel of an overall violation of the rights of ethnic Mexicans in regards to racial profiling and overpolicing, of youth in particular.

For example, in December 1946 Oxnard Police Department (OPD) special officers Jack Hironymous and Bob Massie responded to an assault in progress call at the barrio quarter streets of Sixth and Meta. Upon their arrival the officers arrested seven ethnic Mexican youths on charges of public drunkenness and failure to disperse. The Mexican consul general made an inquiry as countercharges of race-based police brutality arose. After an investigation of its own, in January 1947 the state attorney general recommended the removal of the two officers from the police force.[32] Later that year the Ventura County grand jury investigated the alleged June 13 police beating of seventeen-year-old Juan Sosa of Oxnard and indicted three officers alleged to have brutalized him. Another OPD officer was also charged for an assault on an ethnic Mexican youth shortly before Christmas.[33] Subsequently, Oxnard police chief Don McFarland confessed that his captain in charge of personnel "would have hired any number of punks onto the force if he could."[34]

Due to such abuse, many residents of La Colonia, particularly youth, viewed the OPD as not their protectors but as an agency that violated their civil liberties with impunity. This made for edgy relations between the ethnic Mexican community and law enforcement. In 1958, for example, when OPD officers responded to the call of a cyclist struck by a car in La Colonia, fifteen aggrieved ethnic Mexican youths embarked upon a low-level form of what scholar-activist Armando Morales calls "curbside justice," pelting the officers with bottles and rocks.[35] Oxnard police chief Al Jewell described the event—without contextualization—as "unprovoked."[36] Perhaps the arriving police officers did nothing at the time to merit such a reception, but this does not mean that a prior history of police misconduct, if not assault, did not ultimately serve as the incident's cause. This sort of hostility characterized police relations in barrio communities throughout the Southwest, according to a 1970 report of the U.S. Commission on Civil Rights. As a result, in 1967 Chief Jewell issued his officers steel helmets.[37]

Actually, the OCIA, the precursor organization from which the Ventura County CSO evolved, charged OPD officers with the instigation of a 1956 riot. The conflict resulted after the police responded to a disturbance at a bazaar sponsored by the Cristo Rey (Christ our king) Catholic Church in La Colonia. Police fired tear gas before assaulting the attendees with their batons. For La Colonia residents this episode demonstrated yet again the use of gratuitous force by the OPD against their community. Hence, the motivation behind the OCIA's creation blended well with one of CSO's central goals: the fight against such police brutality.[38]

In Los Angeles two cases established the CSO's reputation as a vanguard against police violence. The first took place on Christmas Eve 1951, involving seven men (four ethnic Mexican and three white) from the Lincoln Heights neighborhood. After their arrest on charges of assaulting an officer, the police brutalized them at two different stations. After Anthony P. Rios, president of the Los Angeles CSO, investigated the incident, the organization voted to support the case. The next month LAPD officers arrested Rios after he attempted to stop the beating of a man by two drunken off-duty police in the parking lot of a bar. The police who arrived on the scene charged Rios and his friend, Alfred Ulloa, with obstruction. Once at the station, the cops abused the two. A jury eventually found Rios and Ulloa not guilty, and six of the seven officers in the first incident—known as "Bloody Christmas"—were convicted of disorderly conduct. Moreover, the trial instigated a grand jury investigation that led to the successful prosecution of five police officers. The department expelled from the force the other officers directly involved in the event as well as reprimanded over thirty officers implicated in it.[39]

Six years after the 1956 police rampage at the Cristo Rey Catholic Church, another controversy arose that involved the alleged excessive use of force by

OPD officers on Fred Jones, past president of the Ventura County NAACP, who accused OPD detectives Bill Lewis and Harry Papageorge of assault. Jones stated that prior to being attacked he had questioned the officers' actions in the arrest of a resident on his neighborhood street. The detectives then arrested Jones on charges of public drunkenness and interference with the conduct of their duties. At a crammed city council meeting, twelve speakers from the CSO and the NAACP addressed the counsel and called for a grand jury investigation. In a comment to the *Oxnard Press-Courier*, Chief Jewell labeled the NAACP and CSO "political pressure groups" and welcomed an investigation. He even offered to resign if the council found the charges to be true. Jewell moreover countered that the charges against his department were politically motivated, as Reverend H. H. Washington, an African American and a member of the NAACP, was a candidate in the pending council election, along with CSO members Soria and Villanueva.[40]

In the local newspaper, Camacho, as CSO president, rebutted Chief Jewell's characterization of his organization. He listed other "pressure groups" such as those of growers that kept farmworkers in "semi slave conditions." Under Jewell's definition, Camacho considered the League of California Cities another such body. Camacho also pointed out that in 1961 law enforcement organizations lobbied the state legislature for "unlimited powers" for searches and seizures.[41]

Furthermore, with an audacity that did not go unnoticed by adherents of the Mexican American generation–oriented CSO and, especially, incipient Chicana-Chicano youth, Camacho dared Chief Jewell to name an instance when the CSO acted outside the law. Camacho formulated his riposte in a context within which the voices of ethnic Mexican residents were generally dismissed, if they were heard at all. Certainly, institutions in the community such as the school board and police department, who were seldom challenged, felt threatened by the assertive advocacy on the part of ethnic Mexicans who were often stereotyped as inarticulate, passive, and apolitical. In the closing of his letter to the editor, Camacho pledged that the CSO would not "deviate from the original purpose for which we in CSO were organized, that is, for equal treatment and equal opportunity for all under our democratic system."[42]

Ultimately, a California Department of Justice investigation cleared the OPD of racial discrimination, brutality, and mistreatment in the Jones case. The forty-eight-page report supported Jewell's view, as it too characterized Jones's charges as a political maneuver. Despite the outcome of the probe, CSO defended its contention that the OPD acted with excessive force.[43] In two ways the Jones case paralleled the conclusions of Armando Morales, professor of psychiatric social work, in his foundational 1972 study on Mexican American–police conflict, *Ando sangrando / I Am Bleeding*. First, that 24 percent of arrests involving Blacks entailed intervention on behalf of people perceived to being victimized by police. For Mexican Americans, Morales contends the proportion of arrests for "interfering with police" was 58 percent. Second, as to the California Department of Justice's favorable findings on behalf of the OPD, Morales contends that the justice system has been historically "dangerously overprotective" of law enforcement.[44]

Six years later, in 1968, the CSO engaged the OPD again. At a jammed Oxnard City Council meeting, Rose Williams, as a CSO officer, pronounced the organization's support of the Brown Berets of the Chicana-Chicano generation, which presented a petition of eight hundred signatures that requested the state attorney general to investigate complaints of police brutality in La Colonia. Before hearing the representatives of the Brown Berets, the council moved its meeting to an auditorium to accommodate an overflow audience. Once reconvened in a larger venue, the Brown Berets demanded that the city grant it the authority to set employment requirements for police officers, suspend police officers, and establish a review board. As though the CSO was passing the leadership torch to the next generation, Williams declared that the organization "lent its support to the Brown Berets because we know they are the leaders of tomorrow."[45]

The Rise of MAPA of Ventura County

As the CSO continued its work and the profile of the Brown Berets of Oxnard expanded in 1968 with its protest of law enforcement's abuse of power and the Vietnam War (as will be detailed in chapter 5), the Mexican American Political Association (MAPA)—founded by several CSO members—played a prominent role in Ventura County's electoral politics. In fact, its emergence reflects the exasperation among veteran activists with the sluggish pace of reform in relation to fair housing and equity in education, as well as the organization's eventual opposition to the U.S. military involvement in Vietnam. In this regard Soria served as a critical intergenerational catalyst of both the militant spirit of the CSO and MAPA and the rise of the Brown Berets and the Chicana-Chicano generation. In fact, Armando López (mentioned in the previous paragraphs), a founder of the Brown Berets in Oxnard, served as MAPA's first vice president.[46]

In its initial year, in 1966, MAPA focused its concern on Oxnard, as its title suggested: "MAPA of Oxnard." But it soon adopted the moniker of "MAPA of Ventura County" to broaden both its membership and its influence.[47] Committed to the maximization of the electoral power of ethnic Mexican communities as part and parcel of a larger national campaign, in line with the model set by the CSO, MAPA of Ventura County engaged the political establishment with enhanced zeal. This approach signifies the vexation that many veteran activists held in their attempt to effect consequential reform in political bodies as well as achieve representation in the Democratic Party beyond tokenism. The quest for electoral power defined MAPA's temperament in a style that rejected coyness in the achievement of its goals. It refused to straitjacket itself in an organizationally oriented politics of respectability. MAPA called out elected officials whom it perceived only advanced their political careers at the expense of the ethnic Mexican community. To effectively influence the "power structure," the creation of a formidable ethnic Mexican political base was an imperative.[48]

In late January 1968, MAPA denounced the Oxnard City Council and the Oxnard Elementary School District (OESD) for their joint decisions to cement residential and educational segregation. MAPA shrewdly understood that these parallel public entities advanced a system of de facto school segregation that was de jure in character. MAPA argued that residential developments and their corollary neighborhood schools isolated largely Blacks and ethnic Mexicans in barrio enclaves such La Colonia. MAPA censured both the Oxnard City Council and OESD for their acceptance of federal subsidies to establish low-income apartment housing in La Colonia and their continued refusal to accept school desegregation plans proposed by the community, such as that presented by Simmons of the NAACP.[49]

In his comments to the city council, Soria pronounced MAPA's close watch of school desegregation in Berkeley and the organization's approval of busing. This was in the context of the combined attendance of 1,993 students in the La Colonia neighborhood schools of Ramona and Juanita. Of this total 1,562 and 340 students were, respectively, ethnic Mexican and Black. This left 91 students between the two schools that were either white or ethnic Asians. Leland Guyer, OESD director of compensatory education, responded to Soria's indictment. He stated that 500 La Colonia middle school children were bused to the Fremont school, and another 250 grade schoolers were transported to the west side of the city due to the impaction of Ramona and Juanita Elementary. Guyer also affirmed MAPA's contention that the further development of low-cost housing in La Colonia perpetuated de facto segregation. However, Paul Woven, the city manager of Oxnard, argued that the further development of low-income apartment housing in La Colonia would address the problem of substandard housing; segregation would not be maintained due to the fact that "no walls" existed to keep people there. Woven tacitly claimed that residents had expressed to the city leadership that they did not wish to "break their ethnic ties." He was not specific, however, about whether it was ethnic Mexican residents that wished not to move out of La Colonia or white residents threatened by the ethnic and racial integration of their neighborhoods.[50]

Oxnard councilperson Salvatore "Sal" Sánchez rebutted MAPA's condemnation of the city and the OESD, characterizing the organization as obstructionist. In alluding to MAPA members having ties to the CSO, Sánchez accused Soria and other critics of the city council of being longtime gadflies. He then posed the rhetorical question of what MAPA had achieved in the interest of the "so-called down trodden citizens it (MAPA) champions?" Sánchez, moreover, believed that the responsibility of segregation lay with La Colonia residents themselves, as no one compelled people to live in isolated environs. Many La Colonia residents, according to Sánchez, resided in La Colonia due to their "being in the country illegally." Unauthorized migrant residents, therefore, sought anonymity in the predominant ethnic Mexican enclave.[51] And, as founder and president of United Latin Americans Inc., Sánchez accused the ethnic Mexican electorate of being uninformed and susceptible to the political machinations of both the Democratic and Republican parties.[52]

The ideological contretemps between Sánchez and Soria continued over time; Sánchez highlighted this contrast as he publicly declared his partisan registration as a Republican. Soria, on behalf of MAPA, sardonically expressed the organization's appreciation for Sánchez's announcement and called upon other members in the ranks of the Democratic Party who were crypto-Republicans to follow Sanchez's lead in denouncing the Democratic Party and changing their affiliation to the party of Ronald Reagan.[53]

Takeaway

Emblematic of the temperament of chapters in and out of California, the Ventura County Community Service Organization leadership of the Mexican American generation tactically embarked upon direct action. To gain the attention of policymakers, it often turned to the national office for guidance on how best to "prime" the ethnic Mexican community to make its message heard. As this took place, incipient Chicana-Chicano youth connected to the CSO participated in the organization's enrichment programs and found themselves engaged in the zeitgeist of global movements for civil rights and self-determination. As a result this cohort of youth adopted the resolve of their predecessors with a flair all their own. Meanwhile, CSO leaders, and, subsequently, those of MAPA, carried on the tradition of speaking to power. By the end of the 1960s, the prominence of the CSO had faded. A new generation of activists, as Rose Williams anticipated in the Brown Berets, seized the scepter of resistance against social injustice. Meanwhile, Soria continued his activism through the 1970s, in particular as the standard bearer of the 1971 class action school desegregation case *Soria v. Oxnard School District Board of Trustees*. The federal desegregation order that resulted would be appealed by the school district to the U.S. Supreme Court, where it was denied certiorari. The notion to desegregate the Oxnard schools originally pursued by the CSO and subsequently supported by the NAACP debunked the myth that educational segregation was fundamentally a de facto manifestation of racist residential policies. In actuality, as David G. García has demonstrated, the district implemented strategies of segregation to accommodate the demands of white parents to segregate ethnic Mexican and Black students from their children.[54] As this case unfolded, Ventura County youth of the Chicana-Chicano generation made their own voices heard by way of independent direct action and community service. Furthermore, demonstrations to end the war in Vietnam, as well as La Marcha de la Reconquista, evidenced a larger network of Chicana-Chicano activism both in Southern California and across the nation.

3

The Young and the Restive

In 1968 Roberto Flores, a founder of the Brown Berets of Oxnard, charged the Oxnard Police Department (OPD) with misconduct. Flores's activism during the late 1960s to the mid-1970s in Ventura County fits the moment of the Chicana-Chicano generation. Born in 1948, as a young adult he was involved in farmworker strikes (as detailed in the introduction), anti–Vietnam War protests, and education. As with many of the Chicana-Chicano generation, mixed citizenship defined the Flores family: his mother was ethnic Mexican, born in the United States, and his father was a migrant from Jamai, Zacatecas, in Mexico. Early in their lives, his parents labored in agriculture. During World War II, his mother worked in San Diego's armament industry. After moving to Ventura County, the Flores family lived in La Colonia, where they were proprietors of a restaurant in the barrio corridor of Cooper Road. There Flores witnessed with indignation the brutality of law enforcement against the ethnic Mexican community. Dramatic—and frequently traumatic—*migra* (border patrol) raids that involved officers pursuing migrants on foot before tackling them to the ground underscored the inhumane circumstances in which the people of La Colonia lived: exploited at work, underserved in their neighborhoods, and suspected as criminal. The repressive, often violent, actions of law enforcement officers demonstrated to Flores that the people of La Colonia lived in an "occupied state." Added to this the public health symptoms of addiction and alcoholism that plagued the ethnic Mexican community concerned him. And, like many of his peers, he noticed educational inequities in the community as well. In this chapter I argue that ethnic Mexicans of the Chicana-Chicano generation resisted such institutional assaults, which defined the lives of people of color.

The Brown Berets

As a 1966 graduate of Santa Clara High School in Oxnard, Flores earned a scholarship to the University of California, Los Angeles (UCLA), some fifty miles away. While at college Flores witnessed El Movimiento from a Los Angeles perspective. On one return visit to his hometown, he listened to his mother and neighbors express their concerns about a fetid drainage ditch along their street. As a premed student, Flores acted by organizing the neighborhood and taking samples from the channel to Ventura College for testing. Analysis of the water indicated high levels of petrochemicals and bacteria. With the support of his mother—who was a citrus packinghouse union leader—and her social network, the neighborhood successfully petitioned the city council to fix the trench problem.[1] This action was one of many organized by Flores to improve the lives and future of the people in his community.

The élan of El Movimiento also motivated Flores and his hometown friends Fermín Herrera and his brother Andrés (both also UCLA students, the latter on a football scholarship), as well as Armando López, to formulate an independent Brown Beret chapter in Ventura County. As mentioned in chapter 2, López had an extensive history of activism as a member of the Ameramex Club, the Teen Toppers, and the Mexican American Political Association (MAPA) of Ventura County.

In August 1968 the *Oxnard Press-Courier* introduced the founders of the Brown Berets to its readers with an exposé titled "Who Are the Guys in the Brown Berets?" Reporter Bea Hartmann highlighted the leadership of Andrés Herrera (the organization's prime minister), his brother Fermín (administrator of discipline), López (administrator of public relations), and Flores (administrator of records). Like Flores, the Herrera brothers and López had observed in their earlier lives the inner dynamics of collective action. The Herrera brothers' migrant father, Tomás Herrera, served as the second vice president of the Ventura County Community Service Organization (CSO) during the early 1960s. Tony Del Buono, one of the founders of the Oxnard Civic Improvement Association (OCIA) that became the CSO with César Chávez's return to Ventura County in 1958, mentored López. In fact, as previously discussed, some ten years earlier community members and Del Buono founded the OCIA in response to the OPD's brutalization of church festival attendees in 1957.[2]

The Brown Berets shared office space with Uhuru, a cultural organization, at 130 Colonia Road, which was the address of the American Friends Service Committee, a branch of the Quaker Religious Society of Friends. The Berets also enjoyed the support of white liberal men and women in their midtwenties and thirties.[3] In this way the civic engagement of an older generation informed the worldview of the Brown Berets' leadership, as they discerned that their advocacy on behalf of ethnic Mexicans required a balanced combination of savoir faire and nonviolent militancy (i.e., direct action). From the civic consciousness demonstrated by groups such as the CSO, the Brown Berets understood the institutional processes in which functionaries of law enforcement, housing, and education operated. Therefore, like the CSO, the Brown Beret complemented community-based services such as tutoring, college recruitment, and lectures with nonviolent direct action that involved picket lines, marches, and spirited public addresses. In this regard reporter Bea Hartmann of *Oxnard Press-Courier* characterized them as "the proud, oft-angered, oft-pleasant-mannered young men who call themselves the Brown Berets."[4]

To this end the Brown Berets studied the history and culture of ethnic Mexicans as well as the writings of theorists to inform their demands for social justice. The sacrifices of family members in the armed forces and the mobilization in the World War II economy further ballasted their worldview. Equipped with such knowledge, the Brown Berets strategically asserted themselves in varied ways. They engaged school administrators, teachers, other professionals, and residents to assess the issues that faced the disfranchised. For example, as a fourteen-year-old freshman at Buena High School in the neighboring city of Ventura, Peggy

Larios contacted the Brown Berets about white students performing racist skits that portrayed Mexicans as both slothful peons asleep against a *nopal* (cactus) with a sombrero and as *banditos* (criminals), similar to the caricature in the Fritos corn chips commercials of the time. Based on this appeal for support, Larios would recall, Roberto Flores and Andrés Herrera of the Oxnard Brown Berets made an appointment with Buena High's principal, which resulted in an apology to the school's ethnic Mexican students. Following this experience Larios and several of her friends became members of the Oxnard Brown Berets, as the organization provided not only an outlet for resisting a multifaceted "in your face" racism but also a space for youth to develop as community leaders.[5]

To complement their dialogue with the community, the Brown Berets embarked upon direct action. For example, at an antipoverty conference at Ventura College in 1968, López castigated the moderate views of previous speakers and challenged trade unions to descend upon Ventura County to "bust up this feudal agricultural kingdom." He then urged the audience to take a more militant approach on the war on poverty.[6] López's reference to a "feudal agricultural kingdom" illustrates how the ethnic Mexican community understood the serf-like condition of the farmworker dominated by the interlocked interests of the agricultural industrial complex composed of, in part, landed elite families, petrochemical companies, financiers, insurance companies, railroads, and their associations. The agents of these interests colluded on boards and commissions—public, private, and liminal agencies—to advance their economic power to the detriment of ethnic Mexican communities as well as other disfranchised populations.[7]

Angered by the violence of OPD officers, the Brown Berets (which, at its height, grew to some fifty members, along with a ring of associates and community supporters) posted and outfitted individuals with cameras and tape recorders at the main entrances of the La Colonia barrio to shadow entering patrol cars. From this surveillance and the sworn affidavits of people who alleged being victimized by the police, in 1968 the Brown Berets—who at this point believed that the OPD could be reformed—demanded an outside investigation as well as the institutionalization of a citizen's review board and the employment of officers who would reflect the demographic makeup of the city. With the help of progressive lawyers, the Brown Berets successfully petitioned the California attorney general to investigate the OPD.[8]

Ultimately, the state attorney general's study dismissed ten cases of alleged police brutality. Special agent Richard J. Mercurio of the California Department of Justice, however, recommended that the OPD standardize its arrest procedures; apparently, officers exercised overly broad discretion in this regard.[9] Despite Mercurio's report, community confidence in law enforcement remained low. In fact, throughout California such tension characterized relations between police and residents in many barrio communities. For example, in response to the appeals of MAPA, in 1972 the California Assembly Select Committee on the Administration of Justice held a series of hearings on police brutality and misconduct, where a number of parents, activists (such as UCLA student president and anti–Vietnam War organizer Rosalio Muñoz), academics, and victims testified. Many detailed sadistic brutality meted out by law enforcement officers. In one instance a law enforcement officer bludgeoned one person so viciously that the victim's eye popped out of its socket. Others related horrific accounts of police profiling, raiding East Los Angeles homes, and shooting unarmed victims at point-blank range.[10]

A Brown Beret Tutorial Program

The Brown Berets, however, did not limit its focus to the OPD's abuse of power. It also worked with the Oxnard Elementary School District (OESD) to implement a culturally relevant tutorial program to reform an educational system whose duty was to educate all children equitably but had failed to do so. Over time approximately a dozen Brown Berets, women and men, participated in this project. In October 1968 Brown Beret member Robert Olivares contacted Norman Brekke, at the time director of special projects at the OESD, to invite La Colonia teachers to the organization's tutorial workshop. During the meeting's orientation, Flores declared that the Brown Berets would administer the tutorial and proceeded to identify the challenges that faced ethnic Mexican students. This included the recognition that the children of La Colonia required special attention, because of their singular culture. La Colonia students did not realize their academic potential due to the failure of teachers to meet their needs; hence, Brown Beret tutors sought to address the deficiencies of teachers as educators, not the students' academic aptitude. Another objective of the tutorial program entailed the elevation of the amour propre of school children.[11] Once students loved and felt confident about themselves their academic achievement would zoom.

Joe Barry, in charge of UCLA's High Potential–High Risk program and advisor to the campus organization United Mexican American Students (UMAS), along with UCLA mathematics professor David A. Sánchez, supported the tutorial program and attended the workshop. Barry situated the work of the Berets within the context of movements tied to Reis López Tejerina in New Mexico, César Chávez, and Sal Castro's leadership in the student walkouts in East Los Angeles. To effectively educate and remedy the high dropout rate among ethnic Mexican students, Barry emphasized that educators must affirm their students' culture and value system.[12]

Due to segregation in the educational system, Barry, Sánchez, and the Brown Berets further claimed that ethnic Mexican students would be best served in equitably funded neighborhood schools. Within integrated, white-dominant environs, they held, ethnic Mexican schoolchildren would lose their inimitable character and cultural sense of self. Academic achievement emanated from a paradigm of equity, not integration. In this regard, Barry stated, "integration is irrelevant, equality is the goal," and that "there's no need for rubbing shoulders just pocketbooks." The academic achievement gap resulted from substandard instruction at the schools of La Colonia based on a mediocre curriculum and the insensitivity of "second class teachers" to the cultural capital of ethnic Mexican students.[13]

Like many in his cohort, Flores had introjected his own experiences of trauma with the systemic forces of racism both in and out of school. For example, not one of his elementary school teachers had spoken Spanish. In fact, he and fellow classmates witnessed administrators, teachers, and staff berate students for speaking their first language, Spanish. This indignation intensified once he transferred to the parochial school of Guadalupe in La Colonia. Flores realized that in both systems he and his peers were not expected to achieve academically. As a result many students withdrew psychologically and exhibited signs of neurosis, if not aggression. Teachers underscored their low expectations when they skeptically interrogated students who excelled. "There was no consistency between the two realities [of school and home]," Flores held. This bifurcated experience instilled in students an acceptance of a cultural, economic, political, and social white supremacy and, conversely, a Mexican inferiority. This consciousness compelled him and his peers to attempt to reform the educational system.[14]

As a college student, however, Flores asked, "Why are we blaming the victim?" After all, perspicacious children existed in La Colonia schools just as in any population. The civil rights movement and corollary critiques of institutionalized racism inspired Flores and his cadre of some thirty Brown Berets to effect change by way of the tutorial program. Since they knew that able and talented young ethnic Mexican students wanted to learn, these audacious volunteers reproached educators of the district, not the children, as the problem.[15]

Brekke—remembered positively by interviewees for this book as a conscientious educator—and the district leadership welcomed the volunteerism of the Brown Berets, at least initially.[16] But the relationship cooled, according to Flores, when he gained access to students' IQ scores and created a report, with the help of Sánchez, that demonstrated the discriminatory character of the district's testing system. Flores also discovered that in the early grades there was virtually no difference in the scores between students from different ethnic groups. As they cycled up grade levels, however, the data revealed pronounced gaps in achievement. Flores concluded that the inherent cultural bias in the test explained the differences in scores between ethnic Mexican students and those who came from more privileged, white backgrounds. In Flores's words, "The test was for another population." As he read the literature on the issue, he discovered that his findings aligned with studies that critiqued standardized testing throughout the nation.[17] Flores's report did not sit well with the district's administration. But, after considering the findings, the IQ testing was dropped, according to Flores, as was the relationship between the district and the Brown Beret tutors. The organization contended that a culturally relevant education would instill confidence in students to achieve academically. Consequently, the Brown Berets taught their curriculum to the people.

In December 1968 the Brown Berets debuted a community workshop at Juanita Elementary. To open the event, the Berets screened the 1966 documentary *The Land Is Rich*, which revealed the plight of agricultural workers.

To hook the attention of viewers, Harvey Richards, the documentary's producer, built upon Edward R. Murrow's 1960 *Harvest of Shame* as he linked his exposé to the movement of Chávez's National Farm Workers Association (NFWA), particularly the union's 1966 Easter march from Delano in the San Joaquin Valley to the state's capital in Sacramento. The documentary contested the Jeffersonian myth of yeoman agrarianism with its emphasis on the industry's historical character of corporate monopolies. It also explained the machinations of Wall Street, the Southern Pacific Railroad, and petrochemical companies to augment their wealth off the backs of impecunious families. To connect the larger movement of farmworkers with the general public, Richards highlighted the conditions of substandard housing and unfair labor practices that denied farmworkers a minimum wage, workmen's compensation, old age pensions, and basic safeguards. The documentary featured scenes of Ventura County marchers holding picket signs that identified the communities they represented: Oxnard, El Rio, and Ventura. Based on ideas borrowed from Luis Valdez when his company, Teatro Campesino, performed at UCLA, the Brown Berets concluded the screening with a puppet show that dramatized barrio life, satirizing the culturally insensitive educational system delivered to them. To bridge the cultural chasm created by an irrelevant curriculum, Andrés Herrera recited the catechistic poem of Rodolfo "Corky" Gonzales, "I AM Joaquin." From their indigenous past in Mesoamerica to their plight under U.S. occupation after the Mexican-American War of 1846–48, the poem revealed a Chicana-Chicano imaginary with a central message: resistance.[18]

The Need for Unity

As the Brown Berets supported schoolchildren, it sought to create bridges with civic organizations. In a December 1968 forum to advance unity and alleviate intraethnic factionalism, the Brown Berets worked with others to advance shared goals specific to education, fair housing, labor rights, and equal treatment before the law. As the missions of organizations such as Los Amigos, El Círculo Social Mexicano, MAPA, and the Association of Mexican American Educators (AMAE) operated independently, they also often differed ideologically. For example, whereas El Círculo Social Mexicano was a service-oriented club,

MAPA advanced an agenda centered on electoral politics. As a professional organization, AMAE sought to advance the interests of ethnic Mexican students as well as the careers of its membership. Perhaps grounded in a divide between the Mexican American and Chicana-Chicano generations, the Brown Berets did not commit its energies to electoral objectives but rather addressed the social and cultural needs of the ethnic Mexican community. Despite these differences in goals and strategies, Raul Maynez, president of Círculo Social Mexicano and temporary chair of the Unity Council, declared the common commitment of such groups to preserve Mexican culture, advance intercultural understanding, and effect progressive change.[19]

In relation to overall community uplift, the organizations collaborated to network youth with employers as well as colleges and universities. As a UCLA student who traveled home regularly before the advent of the unity forum, Flores approached Father Joseph Arredondo at Our Lady of Guadalupe Church in La Colonia in 1967 with the idea of a college recruitment program as part of the National Work Study program. With the help of Arredondo, the program worked with residents to learn English and created tutorial programs. It also recruited educators to help students.[20] As a first step, Flores hired himself to work with Father Arredondo. He then recruited parish youth to apply to Moorpark College (which opened that year); the University of California, Riverside; the University of California, Santa Barbara; and others. After a successful first year, Flores's program placed thirty students at work-study sites throughout the county. Two factors ballasted the program's success: first, the interest of youth in pursuing a higher education while, second, being gainfully employed. This also afforded ethnic Mexican youth the opportunity to imagine careers beyond agriculture.[21]

Success enjoys many parents. Now a twenty-one-year-old senior at UCLA, Flores and the work-study program he founded attracted the support of AMAE with a membership largely of the Mexican American generation. In addition to student job placement, the program incorporated extension courses for University of California credit. AMAE became so besotted with the framework established by Flores and Arredondo that it co-opted the program and developed a nonprofit to administer night classes in La Colonia for educators and civic leaders as they mentored youth.[22]

Meanwhile, Joe Mendoza, an educator in the city of Ventura and AMAE member, brokered additional agreements with county agencies previously not disposed to cooperate due to Flores being labeled "a member of the militant Brown Berets." As a middle-aged, middle-class professional from the Mexican American generation, Mendoza assuaged the apprehensions of county functionaries with an emphasis on AMAE's history as a community "voice of reason." Mendoza stated that AMAE supported effective programs regardless of their origin, even from a member of the Brown Berets, for it was better that students use their energy in the conduct of, in his words, "research projects, rather than picket lines to identify and correct ethnic grievances." Employment, potentially for a weekly paycheck of $120 (no small amount for the time), constructively channeled the energies of thirty selected youths and encouraged their pursuit of a higher education. Considering the high dropout rate among ethnic Mexican students in comparison to their Black and white peers, the project deserved a chance—as the *Oxnard Press-Courier* titled its editorial of July 5, 1969—because it had already a proven success record.[23]

The Oxnard Union High School District (OUHSD) did not feel competently staffed, either, to serve ethnic Mexican youth. When students at Oxnard High protested racism in their attempt to access enrichment programs in the fall of 1970, district officials appealed to AMAE to mediate relations between students who demanded the establishment of an UMAS club. Initially the protest so flummoxed district officials that it appealed to the Oxnard Community Relations Commission (OCRC) for help, which recommended AMAE. The OCRC then asked AMAE, as an association of educators, if it was legal for UMAS to have an off-campus sponsor. The OCRC also petitioned AMAE to help the district in the creation of culturally relevant programs. In the spirit of self-determination, the students demanded the right to select their own sponsor. When district administrators refused the Brown Berets' assistance, tensions escalated within the district's high schools. All the while frustrations within Ventura County's ethnic Mexican community converged alongside broader dissent related to ever-persistent police brutality, the struggle for the dignity of farmworkers, and opposition to the war in Vietnam.[24]

¡Marcha sí! ¡Guerra no!
On Saturday, August 29, 1970, the largest ethnic minority antiwar protest took place in East Los Angeles. One of the central impulses behind this demonstration stemmed from the awareness that the casualty rate of ethnic Mexican servicemen exceeded their demographic proportion in the Southwest. Researcher Ralph Guzmán documented that from 1961 to 1967 Chicanos made up 19.4 percent of those who died in Vietnam, while this group consisted of 10 to 12 percent of the population. Consequently, the Brown Berets of Los Angeles formed the National Chicano Moratorium Committee (NCMC) and organized a demonstration in December 1969 that attracted the support of other antiwar activists such as Muñoz, a fellow UCLA student of Flores and the Herrera brothers. Sans the digital social media of today, the December protest attracted a yeasty two thousand marchers. A subsequent demonstration in February 1970 garnered six thousand participants.[25]

Chicana-Chicano activists networked with counterparts throughout the nation to plan and lead complementary demonstrations. In fact, after the second annual Chicano Youth Conference in Denver, Colorado, in March 1970, Chicano Moratoriums across the nation were planned, with a crowning event in East Los Angeles on August 29. This moratorium attracted some twenty to thirty thousand people from throughout the country. Students, parents, seniors, and children, many from Ventura County, took to the streets; then tragedy ensued. On the pretext of a robbery at a nearby liquor store, Los Angeles sheriff deputies and police stormed the peaceful rally at Laguna Park, wielding batons with full force and firing their guns and tear gas. In the end law enforcement killed three people, brutalized the crowd, and arrested hundreds. In the aftermath Rubén Salazar, of the Mexican American generation and a former *Los Angeles Times* reporter–turned KMEX-TV newsperson, stopped at the Silver Dollar Bar several blocks away from the melee, on Whittier Boulevard in East Los Angeles, to decompress after the assault. Here Los Angeles sheriff deputy Thomas Wilson killed him, firing a ten-inch tear gas projectile designed to pierce walls into the bar. Instantly, in killing Salazar, Wilson silenced the journalistic voice of ethnic Mexicans. Many in the community contended that the powers that be in Los Angeles orchestrated Salazar's assassination because of his refusal to temper his criticism of law enforcement. In effect Salazar had told the establishment, in the words of Gonzo journalist Hunter S. Thompson, "to fuck off."[26] Thompson also shrewdly maintained that Salazar's neutralization transformed accommodationist-oriented Mexican Americans with, perhaps, a mien of respectability, when he wrote:

> Middle-aged housewives who had never thought of themselves as anything but lame-status "Mexican Americans" just trying to get by in a mean Gringo world they never made suddenly found themselves shouting "Viva La Raza" *in public*. And their husbands—quiet Safeway clerks and lawn-care salesmen, the lowest and most expendable cadres in the Great Gabacho economic machine—were volunteering to *testify*; yes, to stand up in court, or wherever, and calling themselves Chicanos. The term "Mexican-American" fell massively out of favor with all but the old and conservative—and the rich. It suddenly came to mean "Uncle Tom." Or, in the argot of East L.A.—"Tio Taco." The difference between a Mexican-American and a Chicano was the difference between a Negro and a Black.[27]

In Ventura County, many in the Chicana-Chicano community also viewed Salazar's homicide as the system culling its leadership. Salazar's martyrdom, as well as the deaths of two others, served as an additional wake-up call. In a letter of September 3, 1970, to the *Ventura County Star-Free Press* titled "Siesta Is Over!," Arthur Gómez of Santa Paula addressed California governor Ronald Reagan, local state senator Robert Lagomarsino, and assembly member Ken MacDonald when he declared:

> Yes, the siesta is over! The siesta was broken by the murder of two innocent Mexican nationals in a Los Angeles hotel and the 10-inch projectile that shattered Ruben Salazar's head.... One day there will be a Chicano assemblyman and state senator from Ventura County.... One day we shall overcome. One day we shall not have our leaders murdered. One day we shall not have our children made ashamed of being part Mexican. One day we shall have justice and dignity.[28]

Undaunted, three weeks later, a Chicano Moratorium demonstration, billed emphatically as a peace march, took place in Oxnard on September 19, 1970. Approximately one thousand marchers from all walks of life, points of origin, and a span of generations once again took to the streets. Brown Beret Peggy Larios would recall in particular the noticeable participation of elderly ethnic Mexicans; their support at the time comforted her. For this moment, at least, no matter their generational designation (Mexicanist, Mexican American, or youth of the baby boom), they expressed their new identity as Chicanas-Chicanos with moxie. In preparing for the demonstration, the organizers declared the community's goal of liberation from, in the words of an *Oxnard Press-Courier* reporter, "Anglo-American domination." From La Virgin de Guadalupe Church, demonstrators paraded through the streets of La Colonia barrio and the downtown district with a coffin representing eight thousand ethnic Mexican servicemen killed in Vietnam. Demonstrative of countywide participation in the protest, an *Oxnard Press-Courier* report illustrated a banner that read "MEChA Moorpark." The procession concluded at the Oxnard Community Center, where national chairman for the Chicano Moratorium Committee Muñoz characterized the Vietnam War as the "systematic murder" of Chicanos. He also linked U.S. military violence abroad with domestic state violence when he stated that the "police instill more fear and harass the Chicanos more than the Viet Cong through their prejudices."[29]

Before "La Raza" (the people's) peace march, men and women of the Brown Berets leafleted neighborhoods in and out of the city of Oxnard. The group also organized the community to protect itself from catastrophe such as had occurred in East Los Angeles. To this end the Brown Berets, John Soria (as head of MAPA of Ventura County), and MEChA representatives from local colleges and high schools met with law enforcement. To ensure peace at the event, the Brown Berets formulated a code of conduct to circulate to the public, the OPD, and media. In an interview with the local newspaper, Flores informed the community that the intent of the march was to demonstrate the power of nonviolent protest; participants who did not adhere to the event's code of conduct would be removed. The organizers also established a chain of command among its monitors, who were directed to be sober and drug-free, and to not leave their assignments. The students, with Mexican American generation supporters such as Soria and others at their side, exercised their sovereignty when they convened with Oxnard police chief Robert Owens as equals. For example, when Chief

Owens, accompanied by his staff, suggested that the march's route be changed to avoid traffic gridlock, an unidentified student retorted, "It is our parade, not yours, and we don't want to change the route."[30] The larger collective, which included members of La Raza Moratorium Committee, agreed with Chief Owens. Prior to the demonstration, twenty of the moratorium leaders fasted at the Guadalupe Church in La Colonia as part of a three-day outdoor vigil with the coffin in front in honor to the sacrifices made by Chicano servicemen.[31]

The program featured the oratory of Blase Bonpane, a UCLA lecturer; Jose Ontiveros, a veteran U.S. Army lieutenant; and past president of MAPA Bert Corona, a longtime labor organizer and migrant rights advocate whose activism dated back to the late 1930s. The theme of the speeches stressed the disproportionate Chicano servicemen casualty rate. Flores contextualized the anticipated peace march of Ventura County with international events of the time when he spoke to the *Oxnard Press-Courier*:

> Because it is generally agreed that this war must stop and because the on-going peace talks in Paris now bogged down in their second year—looking for a face-saving political agreement on both sides—we are marching in protest so that our youths' lives will not be used as pawns in a political game.... While the past and present administrations in Washington approve thousands of dollars in plush accommodations to the negotiators in Paris to wine and dine, our prospective Chicano draftees live under poverty conditions under which they are victims of racial discrimination, unemployment, poor education, police brutality and the added pressures of knowing that their lives may be taken to defend these same oppressive conditions.[32]

La Raza Moratorium Committee's communication with law enforcement and the press in advance garnered goodwill in the community. Indeed, the *Oxnard Press-Courier* commended the organizers in an editorial, in which it acknowledged the disproportionate ethnic Mexican casualty rate (thirty from Oxnard alone) in the Vietnam War. It also complimented, in a backhanded manner, law enforcement in general, for its "diplomacy and restraint" leading up to and during the march. Surely this commentary was made in relation to the August 29 moratorium demonstration in East Los Angeles.

Chief Owens seconded the newspaper's praise when he extended kudos to the organizers.[33]

Voice of the People

The moratorium peace march reached hearts and minds. Jess Gutiérrez, for example, served in an army infantry unit in Vietnam. On one mission a tripped landmine exploded; miraculously, he survived the blast, but a fellow soldier died at his side. Awarded a Purple Heart medal and honorably discharged in 1968, Gutiérrez returned to his family in Oxnard. Raised in La Colonia, he knew many of the organizers of the demonstration, and although he did not actively participate in the event itself, he was sympathetic. The pronouncements of Flores, Muñoz, and other speakers resonated with him, as he held anger based on his experiences in the army. For example, Gutiérrez was disciplined for his tardy return from leave to visit family when his sister passed away. Determined absent without leave, it did not matter to his unit's leadership that his return flight had been delayed due to the Tet Offensive that year. He also took umbrage to the fact that his Purple Heart had been rudely tossed on his bed as he convalesced at a military hospital.[34]

Other peace march observers found its message an affirmation of their worth. Richard Becerra wrote the *Oxnard Press-Courier* to express his pride for the actions of Chicana-Chicano protestors in Los Angeles and Ventura County. In a contribution to the newspaper's Voice of the People section titled "Viva La Raza. Brown Is Beautiful," Becerra stated, "To those Chicanos who could, and did not [participate]: look in the mirror and see a yellow Mexican. Who needs you? Now they can pat you on the head for being a 'good Mexican' and then laugh behind your back." Becerra's rebuke underscored a sentiment that the white establishment tolerated ethnic Mexicans only as obsequious second-class citizens. In the same breath, he called out the more moderate to action. If the community's opposition to the war offended conventional sensibilities, Becerra expressed, so be it. In fact, he considered those who did not protest the general condition of the Chicana-Chicano community as duped "good Mexicans," if not traitors to the cause of social justice.[35]

Becerra's reprimand, however, did not go unanswered. A. M. García responded that he or she had looked in the mirror and did not see a "yellow Chicano." However, this person had reservations about the potential for police violence at peace marches like the one in East Los Angeles. Furthermore, García feared that if the peace march soured, the ethnic Mexican community would have been implicated as irresponsible rabble-rousers. García also viewed the goals of the protest as parochial when writing that "if you sincerely wish to help the Chicanos, find a just cause for all, not just a selfish few." Therefore, García felt that a peace moratorium that focused on the disproportionate casualty rate of ethnic Mexican servicemen blemished their cause in the eyes of the white-dominant society.[36]

Ruben N. Martínez shared this perspective. Immediately after the peace moratorium march, Martínez expressed his disdain for those who labeled themselves Chicano, as he resented the media focus on "loudmouths" and their identification as "leaders," and he spoke on behalf of the "Mexican American" that felt such dissent unwarranted, if not unpatriotic. Martínez, and the constituency he proclaimed to represent (the silent majority, perhaps), supported President Richard Nixon's policy of "disengagement and withdrawal."[37]

But Martínez's criticism of the peace march went beyond the event itself. Conceivably representative of many in the ethnic Mexican community, he held an antagonism toward "half-baked kids" that self-identified as Chicana-Chicano as opposed to Mexican American. To the older Martínez, these youth consisted of snarky elitists that demanded special privileges from the "taxpaying Anglo and those Mexican Americans." As "law-abiding Mexican-Americans," they needed to reject federal government aid, be self-reliant, and cease their political extortion of Anglo leaders.[38]

Martínez did not restrict his contempt to Chicana-Chicano activists. He also alleged an irksome "permissiveness" on the part of the city council and Chief Owens. In fact, he tacitly purported that state violence was necessary to quell the activities of the Brown Berets. Martínez held that the Brown Berets intimidated the larger community and was disloyal to the nation in their reverence for the ancestral homeland of ethnic Mexicans (i.e., Aztlán) and third world decolonization movements abroad. In his eyes El Movimiento degraded the status of the Mexican American community.[39]

Burn Baby Burn, and Burn Again

A year after the riot incited by law enforcement at the Chicano Moratorium in East Los Angeles, on the warm Sunday evening of July 11, 1971, orange-red flames from fire-bombed business buildings in La Colonia lit the sky. A glow and sounds of crackling came from the Bank of A. Levy at 629 Cooper Road. As police units and fire trucks arrived at the scene, residents pelted them with bottles and rocks, yelling "Pigs!" and other bilingual obscenities. At the east end of the street, the segregated "Mexican school" of Juanita also went up in flames. After law enforcement secured the area, a dragnet commenced. Looky-loos found themselves indiscriminately arrested. In the denial of root causes based in systemic oppression and the community's attempt to—in the words of Armando Morales, about such general insurgencies—salvage a sense of dignity in response to intolerable living conditions, Chief Owens declared that an investigation revealed that no provocation triggered the uprising.[40] Instead, he attributed the actions to "hoodlums apparently seeking only excitement" and did not foresee repeated trouble.[41]

He was wrong.

The next week a fiery insurrection ignited on Sunday, July 18. The *Oxnard Press-Courier* characterized it as a "destructive rampage" that involved one hundred youths. The estimated cost in damages was $100,000. As the week before, insurgents tossed Molotov cocktails at the Bank of A. Levy, and at both the Mexican schools of Juanita and Ramona, which neighbored each other. Leon's Pharmacy, owned by Mike Leon, at 801 Cooper Road, was also targeted; after looting it, the assailants doused the drugstore with gasoline and set it on fire. People also shattered the windows of the Legal Services Center and adjacent offices. Firefighters not only dodged bottles and rocks, as the week before, but this time also sniper fire. Thus, over one hundred youths temporarily sealed off La Colonia from additional first responders. The *Ventura County Star-Free Press* printed that the conflagration restarted after a preannounced "anti-pig" rally of about 150 Chicanos at Colonia Park. Only after an assessment of the rebellion, eighty law enforcement officers from the departments of Oxnard, Port Hueneme, and the Ventura County Sheriff's Office carried out a "massive sweep" of the barrio that resulted in thirty-eight arrests. Again, in a state of complete denial as to systemic causes tied to social injustices such as police abuse, poverty, price gouging businesses, and racist residential and school segregation, Chief Owens argued that the second revolt, like the one the week before, was not instigated by any grievances in the community. Again, it was in his estimation a "senseless attack," without purpose or cause.[42]

The *Oxnard Press-Courier*, on the other hand, in an editorial on July 20, 1971, characterized the revolts as acts perpetuated by young "hoodlums." The newspaper credited leaders of La Colonia, perhaps of the Mexican American generation, with the restoration of peace.[43] Meanwhile, the OPD imposed a 10 p.m. curfew for people under the age of eighteen not accompanied by an adult. Owens stated, "I have not been able to pinpoint any real reasons for the destructive outbursts.... But it appears the violence was just attacks by frustrated youth against the establishment and police." Euphemistically, Owens did admit, however, that in a meeting of thirty-five (two-thirds under the age of fourteen) to discuss this "anti-pig" protest, youth had informed him that the police over patrolled La Colonia and inflicted harassment that caused "confusion and anger."[44]

Newspaper coverage of the revolt in La Colonia faded quickly, and what attention remained denied the structural causes that served as the tinder for the unrest. Instead, the *Oxnard Press-Courier* deflected important questions by focusing on a minor human interest substory on the actions of Joe García in the first insurgency. As a resident of La Colonia and combat veteran who served nineteenth months in the rain forests of Cambodia and Vietnam, García watched the rebellion with his friends from Colonia Park, adjacent to the Juanita school. After he noticed the auditorium of the Juanita school in flames, he and his *camaradas* (buddies) broke into the building to save the flags of the state and nation. In his words, García felt that he had "fought too hard [in the Vietnam War]" to see the country's colors burn. Therefore, attention on García's patriotic act masked the reasons behind the social and political upheaval in La Colonia. Indeed, the Oxnard City Council, the Elks Lodge, Congressman Charles Teague, and the Ventura County Republican Central Committee issued commendations to García for his rescue of "Old Glory."[45] Although he condemned violence, García understood the anger that fueled the rebellion. In fact, he related to an *Oxnard Press-Courier* reporter his consciousness of unequal opportunities for people of La Colonia in relation to employment, education, and services.[46]

At an OCRC meeting, Commissioner William Terry made a motion to request a federal investigation of complaints against the OPD and called for the dismissal of police officers accused of harassing minorities. The motion died, as it failed to obtain a second. After three hours of public commentary that described the OPD's abuse of authority, the OCRC called for a joint session with the Oxnard City Council on the matter. In the course of this discussion, participants questioned Chief Owens about the disturbances in La Colonia and the composition of his department. At that time there were only two Black and nine ethnic Mexican officers in an eighty-member police force. Owens expressed his willingness to consider preferential points, like those afforded to military veterans, to ethnic Mexican applicants and other minorities who took entrance exams. The *Oxnard Press-Courier* quoted López: "Troubles brew from frustration and emotion . . . external social forces make them lash out." Persons from the Mexican American generation then spoke. To improve community-police relations, director of the Ventury County CSO Cloromiro Camacho proposed that youth be selected to serve as liaisons with the OPD. Robert Serros, an activist and one of the few Chicanos in the community with a doctoral degree, criticized Chief Owens for the lack of proactive measures.[47]

Soon after the OCRC colloquy, Owens petitioned the city council on July 20 to seek the assistance of the U.S. Department of Justice Community Relations Service to address the issue of police training and tactics. That same evening a bomb threat interrupted an OESD board meeting, and some three hundred people were evacuated; the controversy of busing to remedy segregation in the schools made for the high audience attendance. Finally, based on ongoing conversations with youth in La Colonia, Chief Owens acknowledged their despair. He admitted that some police officers under his command served the people of La Colonia in, he said, an "over-zealous" and "rude and discourteous" manner. The youth also asked why his department could not advocate on their behalf for the city's improvement of the quality of life in their racially segregated neighborhood, as 90 percent of the twenty thousand residents of La Colonia were ethnic Mexican and 7 percent Black. Furthermore, the average occupancy in small homes was five persons. Consequently, in addition to central squares serving as social gathering points in ethnic Mexican culture, Southern California high residential density was a reason why many youths congregated at the Colonia Park when it was prohibited after dusk—even when they knew that a police detail outfitted in riot gear would clear the grounds each night in military close order formation.[48]

Ten months late, Ventura County supervisor Frank Jewett received a report from the Social Action Committee that found that "white racism and poverty" were at the basis of the riots in La Colonia. But Jewett reproached community "attitudes" as part of the problem.[49] In other words, Jewett ignored endemic oppressions of brutality, exploitation, and indignities that residents of La Colonia suffered in the form of *migra* dragnets, police abuse and harassment, and price gouging on the part of La Colonia merchants who themselves were ethnic Mexican.[50]

From this conversation the city's political leadership learned of grievances in La Colonia toward the school district, housing authority, and other local agencies. Although Mayor R. H. Roussey referenced these issues in an equivocal manner, the implication of these agencies is not surprising in relation to the historical and systematic segregation of students, municipal neglect of housing, and other forms of institutionalized racism, as well as the city of Oxnard being a Sundown Town that—like many other communities in Southern California—prohibited the presence of people of color in white neighborhoods at the end of a workday.[51]

The Battle of Ventura County

As with the white supremacist machinations of officials in education, employment, and housing, police brutality influenced the identity of many ethnic Mexicans born before and after World War II as a historically minoritized people. Frustrations among Chicana-Chicano youth in the city of Santa Paula boiled over in the spring of 1972 with the customary hard looks (often by way of pitch-black sunglasses), verbal abuse, harassment, and gratuitous use of force on the part of the police. The youth had had it, and they fought back with fury in early April. Clashes that made the headlines of local and regional newspapers started on the night of Sunday, April 9, when Chicana-Chicano youth cruised their cars through the main streets of the city. As was the custom, Santa Paula police watched, questioned, and cited youth over the course of the night. In response, around 9 p.m., an irritated group of Chicana-Chicano youth pelted police officers with rocks and bottles. After this assault two police officers required medical attention. The conflict then escalated, with two hundred people versus the cops. With the "presence and good offices of a leader of the Mexican-American community," unnamed by the *Santa Paula Daily Chronicle*, law enforcement units from Ojai, Fillmore, and the Ventura County Sheriff's Department and Highway Patrol suppressed the uprising. Several Chicana-Chicano youth, over and under the age of eighteen, one of them from El Rio, were arrested on charges of resisting arrest and felony assault.[52]

Six days later, on Saturday, April 15, twenty Santa Paula youth picketed the city's police station for two hours with signs that charged the department with brutality and harassment. Then starting at 7:15 p.m., Sunday, April 16, fifty cars caravanned the streets side by side in protest of the actions of the police. After an hour the number of cars grew to seventy-five, with a total of two hundred participants. Law enforcement agencies from other cities in the county were once again dispatched to help disperse the demonstrators. Police chief Ray Tull claimed ignorance as to the motives behind the parade despite the picketing of his station the day before. But he did express wonder to the press, perhaps disingenuously, if the night's event could have been related to the melee of the week before.[53]

Events of the following Sunday, April 23, however, left little doubt that Santa Paula's ethnic Mexican youth loathed the city's police. As youth cruised the streets of the city, a patrol car pulled over one vehicle and discovered loaded rifles in the trunk. Then a battle broke out once again between the police and some 250 ethnic Mexican youth predominantly from Santa Paula, with others from the neighboring communities of Fillmore, Saticoy, and Oxnard. The insurrection intensified with the fire-bombing of a car and windows broken at businesses and the city's high school. The *Los Angeles Times* reported that fifteen gunshots were indiscriminately fired. At least two persons suffered minor gunshot wounds. As before, frightened by the community's resistance, the Santa Paula Police Department requested backup from the police departments of Fillmore, Ojai, Port Hueneme, and Ventura as well as the Ventura County Sheriff's Department and Highway Patrol. Some thirty people were arrested, sixteen of them juveniles, mainly on failure to disperse charges and the violation of a 10 p.m. emergency curfew. One young woman repeatedly slapped a sheriff's deputy as he arrested two of her Black male friends. Some youth who escaped arrest vowed their continued resistance the next week. Chief Tull yet again claimed obliviousness to the reason behind the latest youth rebellion. The *Santa Paula Daily Courier*, moreover, depicted local law enforcement as innocent victims of youth harassment over the past three Sundays. Coincidentally, on the same night of the April 23 uprising in Santa Paula, Oxnard Chicana-Chicano youth also resisted the OPD's military-like actions with bottles and rocks as they approached Colonia Park, perhaps in its regular sweep at dusk in full riot gear.[54]

The previous Wednesday, on April 19, adults of the Mexican American generation had accompanied one hundred youth in a meeting with the city council of Santa Paula. In this discussion Chicana-Chicano youth aired their grievances, including police harassment, the lack of a recreation center, and the closure of public parks at 11 p.m. The *Santa Paula Daily Chronicle* denied a history of tension in the community, especially with law enforcement, as the newspaper faulted Chicana-Chicano youth with unreasonable, violent impatience. Contrary to this biased reporting, which denied the racial subordination of the ethnic Mexican community, organizational leaders of the Beneficencia Mexicana, the Mexican-American Civic Association, Chicanos de Ahora, the Brown Berets of Santa Paula, and others met regularly with city officials, such as Mayor Alan Teague and the police chief, to address the grievances and needs of youth. At one meeting Luis Espinoza of the Mexican-American Civic Association stated that the group needed to identify youth leaders to guide other young people, Mexican and Anglo alike, in the right direction.[55]

Early the next the month, on Sunday, May 1, one hundred uniformed Brown Berets gathered from noon to dusk at Las Piedras Park. Another 150 people listened to speeches and moderated discussions on the challenges that faced their community. As part of their program, the Brown Berets awed onlookers as they paraded with precision around the park in close-order drill. In his comments to the press, police captain Harold N. Barker commended them as "well disciplined," "respectful," and "cooperative." Curiously, as if terrified of Chicana-Chicano youth, the *Santa Paula Daily Chronicle* did not directly interview event leaders or participants. Instead, the anonymous reporter relayed information provided by the Santa Paula Police Department.[56]

Six weeks elapsed before another episode of civil unrest, which exploded in Santa Paula on the evening of Sunday, June 11. That night's conflict began after Gilbert Mora ran from a group of fifty youth to confront two Ventura County narcotics officers at Main and Ojai Streets at 9:45 p.m. An exchange of gunshots followed, with Mora wounded and arrested. Another hours-long "melee" developed, with the windows of many businesses shattered. In the end over thirty adults and juveniles would be arrested on this night. Chief Tull averred that the cause of the uprising was a carryover of a conflict between police the day before, when they responded to a fight at a wedding party upon which, according to witnesses, Santa Paula police officers (like the Fred Jones case detailed in chapter 2) exercised excessive force to suppress the disturbance. Wedding party guests then turned on the police. Despite the repeated fighting between his police officers with local youth, Chief Tull claimed that the June insurgency had nothing to do with the events in the month of April.[57]

In spite of such denials, these acts of resistance did not emerge in a vacuum. As far back as the early twentieth century, the ethnic Mexican community expressed an almost complete lack of trust in the Oxnard Police Department when a jailhouse fire took the lives of two Mexican nationals. Toward midcentury people rebelled against an Oxnard police officer's reckless discharge of his firearm, which had threatened the lives of bystanders, to apprehend a suspect. Infuriated by the incident, ethnic Mexican witnesses attacked the police officers in pursuit of the suspect. In response the OPD called for backup from outside the city to suppress the rebellion. There was also the expressed disdain for law enforcement when the Oxnard Police Department responded to calls in La Colonia.[58]

In the case of Santa Paula, newspapers largely failed to adequately represent the point of view of ethnic Mexican youth. For example, certain officers of the

Santa Paula Police Department notoriously harassed drivers; one was infamous for pulling over cruisers, then throwing the drivers' car keys into adjacent citrus orchards. Only when people picketed or caravanned through city streets in protest, as previously described, did newspapers provide any sort of contextual information for its readers to understand these dramatic acts of resistance on the part of Chicana-Chicano youth. Otherwise, the public, for the most part, would be led to believe that such uprisings occurred without cause or provocation, especially as law enforcement chiefs such as Owens and Tull, as well as policymakers, habitually feigned ignorance of community grievances against their departments. In the end tensions in Santa Paula decreased as civic leaders of the Mexican American generation, such as Robert Borrego, Sallie Castro, Connie Gonzales, and Al Urias, negotiated a cease fire, if you will—the eventual peaceful coexistence between Chicana-Chicano youth and the Santa Paula Police Department.[59]

La Marcha de la Reconquista

From the tension created by the incessant harassment and excessive use of force on the part of law enforcement and the U.S. involvement in the Vietnam War, the Chicana-Chicano generation took their grievances to the streets and highways of the state. The spirit of the times of El Movimiento motivated the NCMC to map out a May 1971 march, to start on Cinco de Mayo, from the border city of Calexico in Imperial County to the state's capital in Sacramento. It followed the precedent of the National Farm Workers Association's *peregrinación* (pilgrimage) five years before that raised public awareness to the oppression of farmworkers by way of starvation wages, pernicious labor conditions and housing, and the agricultural industrial complex's refusal to collectively bargain. Inspired by Chávez's courageous true believers with the shared goal to achieve dignity for all people, the central demands of La Marcha de la Reconquista (the march of the reconquest) called for the end of the Vietnam War, of police brutality, and of *migra* deportation raids. Other redresses included the full restoration of funds for Chicano studies and Educational Opportunity Programs at colleges and universities as well as welfare relief slashed under the gubernatorial administration of Ronald Reagan.[60]

At the start of a six-hundred-mile campaign, a group of seventy quickly increased to three hundred with the banners of the United States, Mexico, and the NFWA at the front. Reconnaissance teams sprang ahead of the procession to recruit community support in the form of food and lodging from families, civic groups, and churches. The scouts explained the purpose of La Marcha and park rallies to law enforcement. As the demonstrators approached the Los Angeles region, Flores lobbied Muñoz, chairman of the NCMC, to route La Marcha through the Ventura County communities of Oxnard, Saticoy, Santa Paula, Fillmore, and others. As was the case for many, it was then that Yvonne De Los Santos of Saticoy became politicized as she joined La Marcha and the larger movimiento, in which she committed herself to the end of her life in 2017.[61]

Along the way the number of the core group of marchers waned as low as 70 and surged back to 150 persons, according to news reports. Throughout the trek champions greeted them with *abrazos* (hugs), the honking of car horns, and cheers. Detractors taunted them with racist epitaphs and vehicle swerves in their direction. At other times the marchers struggled to locate lodging and ran out of food and water. As they passed the community of Coachella on May 12, police killed farmworker Francisco García in the course of a drug raid; this further validated the distrust of many marchers who personally knew of unarmed youth gun downed by the police, not uncommonly in the back. Law enforcement in some places, such as McFarland, were uncooperative with march leaders, who diplomatically explained the safety procedures and protocols they had created to discipline their peaceful demonstration.[62]

La Marcha afforded youth like De Los Santos an emotional outlet to direct their frustrations as well as develop dreams for their community while networking with like-minded activists from various parts of California in becoming Chicana-Chicano. In a joint interview with the author, Flores and Del Los Santos recalled the overall camaraderie as an esprit de corps blossomed during the La Marcha. Along the way Gilbert Cano, a leader of NCMC and a student at San Fernando Valley State (SFVS), performed faux weddings for *los enamorados* (lovebirds), as well as divorces. Chicanas also challenged patriarchal assumptions of the leadership endemic of the larger movimiento.

In one instance De Los Santos told one of the male marchers who expected to be catered to by women, "If you want something cooked, don't look at me."[63]

Men and women also performed agitprop *actos* (theater skits) along the way. At San Fernando Park in Los Angeles County, El Conjunto Aztlán played music. Others, such as Muñoz, Irene Tovar, and Corona, conducted teach-ins. Hence, La Marcha allowed youth to encounter a world beyond the agricultural and the urban environs from which they came. Shared stories underscored their distinct plight.[64] This entailed speeches that denounced the Vietnam War and the assassination of Ruben Salazar at the hands of law enforcement, as well as informed the issues behind land grant rights as articulated by Reies López Tijerina in New Mexico. De Los Santos embraced this knowledge, as it "pinpointed the Chicano experience."[65] When a combination of 1,500 marchers and other demonstrators converged in the state capital at Sacramento on Saturday, August 7, they raised the Mexican flag with emboldened hearts and minds.[66]

Takeaway

During El Movimiento people of the Mexican American and Chicana-Chicano generations fumed with *coraje* (rage) as they witnessed local and global injustices in education, their overrepresentation in the Vietnam War, and the abuse of power on the part of law enforcement. These grievances not only compelled them to action but also instilled in them a Chicana-Chicano identity. As this transgenerational cohort—of U.S. citizens and Mexican national residents, authorized and unauthorized—asserted themselves in public spaces, this not only raised the profile of the ethnic Mexican community as a whole, but also chipped away at the trope, often introjected, of their social and political passivity. To continue the legacy of struggle for social uplift, men and women who with each passing day became more and more Chicana-Chicano set their sights on the reform of the educational system. This pursuit further integrated the struggle of the two generations: Mexican American and Chicana-Chicano.

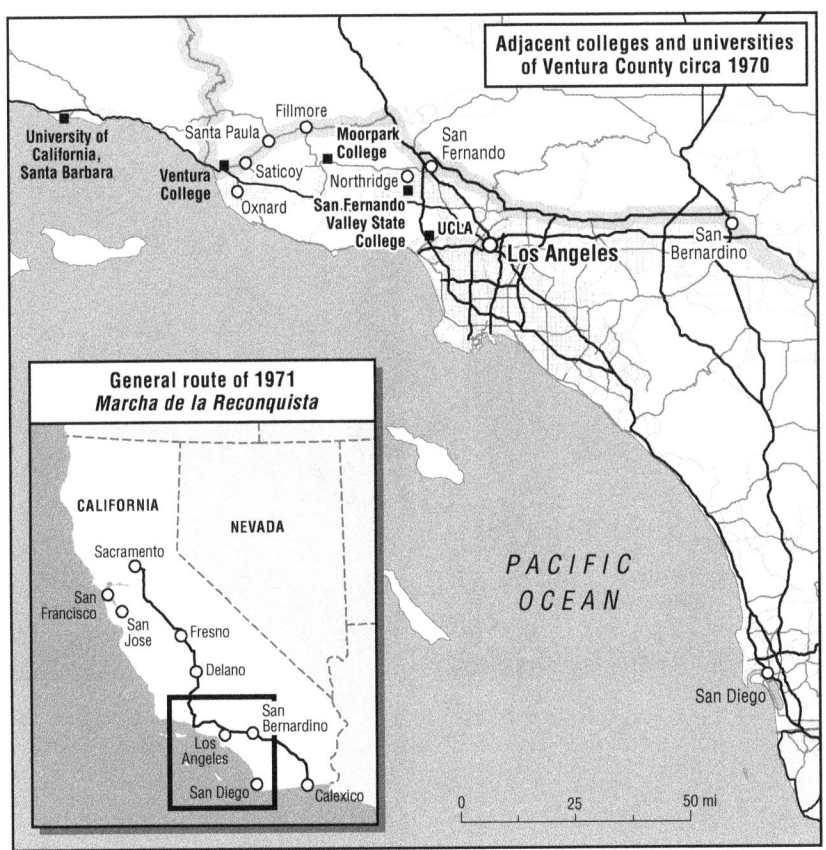

1. Map of Southern California. Created by Erin Greb.

2. Yvonne De Los Santos, *center left*, La Marcha de la Reconquista. Spring-summer of 1971. Courtesy of Rosalio Muñoz.

3. Ventura County Chapter, Community Service Organization members during the Oxnard general election of 1958. Tony Del Buono stands in the center, with Carmen Yslas and César Chávez to the right. Courtesy of the Walter P. Reuther Library, Archives of Labor and Urban Affairs, Wayne State University.

4. John Soria, assistant to César Chávez, at the Community Service Organization of Ventura County headquarters in Oxnard, 1958–1959. Soria also served in the Farm Labor Service Center and the Mexican American Political Association, as well as other organizations. He ran for a seat on the Oxnard City Council in 1960 and 1962 and championed the desegregation of students in the Oxnard Elementary School District. Courtesy of Armando Soria.

5. KOXR La Mexicana *El Pueblo Opina* radio host Javier Santana. Courtesy of Jess Gutíerrez.

6. Diana Borrego Martínez, *far left*, of Santa Paula at the Van Nuys Los Angeles Police Department jail with San Fernando Valley State College peers arrested for their participation in a campus anti–Vietnam War protest on January 9, 1969. January 10, 1969, *Los Angeles Times* Photographic Archives (Collection 1429). Library Special Collections, Charles E. Young Research Library, UCLA.

7. César Chávez speaking at a strawberry strike rally at Colonia Park on June 1, 1974. Image from the June 2, 1974, edition of the *Oxnard Press-Courier*.

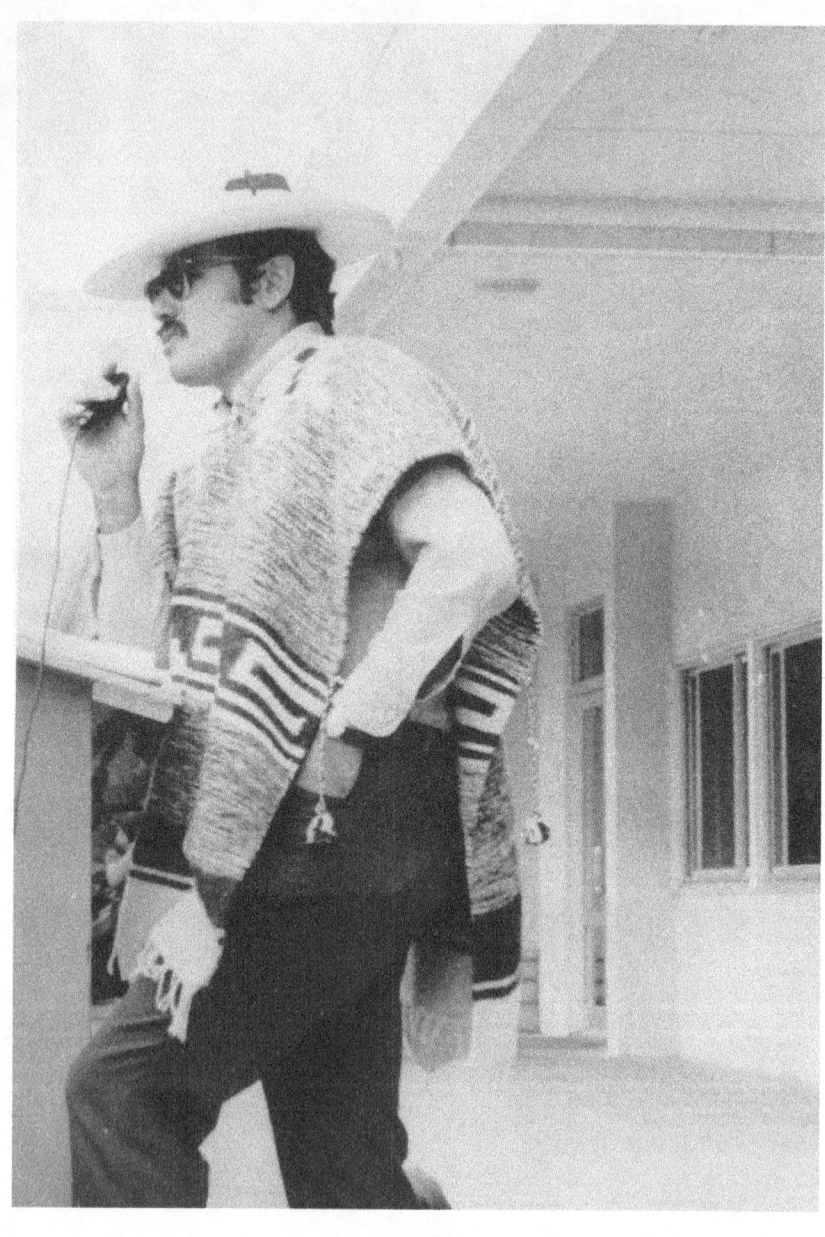

8. Ray Reyes, Ventura College faculty and MEChA Advisor. Photographer George Valle. Courtesy of Jenaro Valdez.

9. Oxnard La Raza Peace Moratorium, September 19, 1970, demonstration flyer. Created by Alberto Ordoñez. Source: https://www.flickr.com/photos/sinfronteras/5331708617/in/set-72157634272858058/lightbox (accessed November 5, 2020).

10. Bert Hammond, *third from the left*, Oxnard High School educator and community activist. Installation of Officers, National Association for the Advancement of Colored People Oxnard-Ventura Branch, 1963. John Flynn, *far left*; President Fred Jones, *second from left*; Bert Hammond, *middle of the back row*; Albert Duff, *second from right*; Jan Kelsey, *standing far right*; Assemblyman Mervyn Dymally *sitting*; Secretary May Davis *sitting*. Contributor Black Gold Cooperative Library System. Source: Calisphere. https://calisphere.org/item/ark:/13030/c8445k8n/ (accessed November 5, 2020).

RACHEL WONG
Woman of Many Hats

11. Rachel Murguia Wong served on numerous Ventura County community advisory boards and commissions and worked as a school liaison at Juanita Elementary in La Colonia. Hence, Woman of Many Hats cognomen. Image from the February 27, 1972, edition of the *Oxnard Press-Courier.*

12. Rachel Murguia Wong, Oxnard Elementary School District Board trustee (1971–1973). Courtesy of Rachel Murguia Wong.

13. Roberto Flores, a founding member of the Oxnard Brown Berets, a student activist of the 1960s and 1970s, and United Farm Workers Captains' Committee organizer. Photo taken at the Eastside Café in El Sereno, California, July 2020. Courtesy of Roberto Flores.

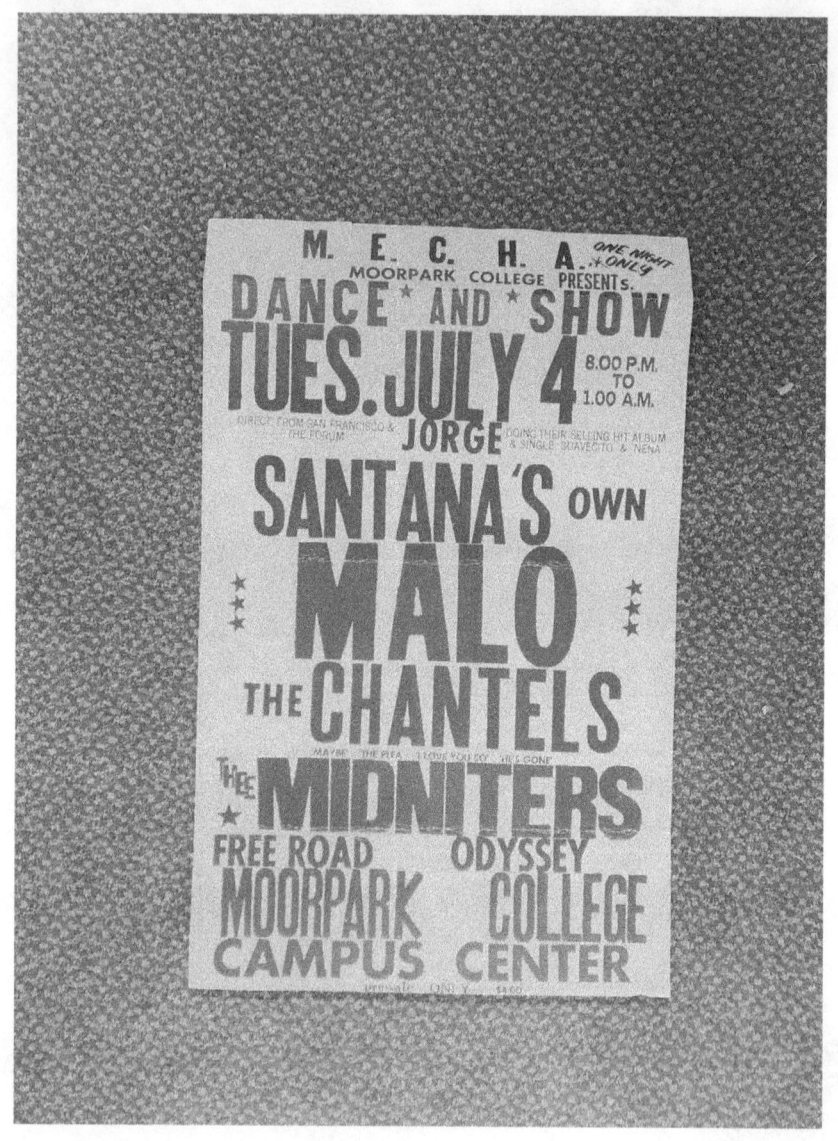

14. Moorpark College Movimiento Estudiantil Chicano de Aztlán (MEChA) flyer, ca. 1973. Courtesy of Joseph González, Moorpark College professor of history (1971–2004) and MEChA advisor (1971–1975).

15. La Colonia "cauldron of racism" cartoon. Creator Dennis Renault. From the April 13, 1969, edition of the *Ventura County Star-Free Press*.

4

Racially Segregated Schools, 1968–1971

Most ethnic Mexicans well understood the importance of a quality public school education to advance the life chances of children. Unlike many adults in the Black and ethnic Mexican community who grew up on commercial plantations and farms in the Deep South, Southwest, and Far West, parents of children from the baby boom generation sought to ensure that the grade schoolers in their community—largely La Colonia in the city of Oxnard—did not suffer the same fate. Hence, Black and ethnic Mexican activists, with the help of white and ethnic Asian allies, struggled to dismantle systems of race-based segregation. This determination, fueled by righteous indignation, found organized support in local collective bodies such as the National Association for the Advancement of Colored People (NAACP) and Community Service Organization (CSO), as the national civil rights currents propelled this fight. But, as in many struggles for equal justice and protections, reactionary forces, both in the community and within institutions, pushed back with vehemence.

This chapter illustrates the racist-normative character of school segregation in the city of Oxnard and the fight for its dismantlement on the part of ethnic Mexicans, Blacks, and other segments of the larger community. In the course of this examination, I reveal nuanced, ironic social dynamics as middle-class

Mexican American generation parents (many of farmworker provenance) who lived in predominately white neighborhoods found their children bused to Mexican schools in the barrio of La Colonia. Moreover, Black and Chicana-Chicano activists and others initially did not support busing to desegregate; they demanded an equal education in their neighborhood schools. But the more the Oxnard Elementary School District (OESD) opposed change, I argue, Blacks and people of the Mexican American and Chicana-Chicano generations called with increased fervor for an equal education for all the children, even if it entailed busing.

El pueblo para Rachel

Rachel Murguia Wong's parents met and ultimately started their family just outside the Ventura County community of Santa Paula at the company housing camp of Rancho Sespe. The Murguia family labored in the citrus industry during the 1930s up until the countywide strike of 1941, after which Rachel's father relocated them briefly to the city of Port Hueneme before they finally settled in Cannery Row in Monterey. As a young woman of the Mexican American generation, Murguia attended and graduated from the University of California, Los Angeles (UCLA), where she met her husband, Alan Wong. After a one-year stay in Hong Kong, in 1966 Murguia Wong and her young family relocated to Oxnard, where they lived in the northern, predominantly white, middle-class section of the city.[1]

As youth protests escalated nationally during the 1960s, the activism of the Brown Berets in Oxnard intrigued Murguia Wong: they contested with brio law enforcement's abuse of power, the maleducation of barrio children, and the nation's interventionist war in Vietnam. Determined to act, Murguia Wong attended Brown Beret meetings at the corner of Colonia Road and Oxnard Boulevard and, after a while, requested membership. Perhaps due to being a middle-class woman in her early thirties with a family—the organization, which was led by men, included women in their teens and early twenties—the Berets denied her request, informing her that she could be more useful to the cause independently. So she blazed her own path.[2]

Committed to the republican ethos of civic engagement, Murguia Wong volunteered her time to numerous commissions and boards, including the

Ventura County Community College District Citizen's Advisory Board, the city of Oxnard's Community Relations Commission, and the California Advisory Committee for Migrant Education, which afforded her an insider's view into the systems that oppressed the ethnic Mexican community. In 1968, at the age of thirty, she applied for an advertised position at the OESD as a community school liaison at Juanita Elementary, a federally funded Title 1 campus with a low-income student population, in the heart of the La Colonia neighborhood. As she was bilingual as well as bicultural, with a UCLA degree, the school district appointed Murguia Wong to the job. To advance a culturally relevant curriculum, she researched and ordered books for Juanita Elementary teachers and its library that centered on the history and culture of ethnic Mexican students—for example, Carey McWilliams's germinal *North from Mexico: A History of Spanish-speaking People in the United States*. For her affirmative actions, she met with contemptuous resistance from teachers, chiefly white women, who were not accustomed to taking direction from a person of color. Murguia Wong, however, was not completely isolated; she would recall how a district psychologist admonished the teachers for their insensitivity to the cultural capital of their students, over 90 percent of whom were ethnic Mexican. Furthermore, as a community liaison charged to promote parent involvement in the schools, she conveyed district news as a regular guest on Javier Santana's Spanish-language radio show *El Pueblo Opina*.[3] This support in and out of the district allowed Murguia Wong to persevere in the service of students and their parents.

As the contentious issue of busing intensified, Murguia Wong's effective outreach to the ethnic Mexican community raised the ire of teachers and administrators. Consequently, the principal at Juanita Elementary, Patrick Allen, pink-slipped her on the grounds that she was "inefficient" in her duties. As part of her regularly scheduled report on *El Pueblo Opina* that week, she announced her termination. This news jump-started the mobilization of community support to help her keep her position.[4] On the evening of Tuesday, June 2, 1970, Murguia Wong's champions jammed the district school board meeting to demand her retention. Since the regular chambers at the Wilson Junior High School on 255 Palm Avenue did not accommodate the 175-plus community members that arrived, the overflow audience stood outside the boardroom, clapping and stomping their feet in protest. To accommodate the crowd, the board temporarily adjourned the meeting to move to the auditorium of Driffill Elementary. Once reconvened, James Chambers, a member of the district's Compensatory Education Advisory Committee, informed the board that the committee had voted 14–2 to recommend Murguia Wong's retention. In fact, Waymon Wells, the committee's president, in his statement affirmed Murguia Wong's performance, saying that she did an excellent job keeping La Colonia parents up-to-date on Juanita school programs and outcomes. From outside the district, a CSO representative backed Murguia Wong as well. In regard to her effectiveness in La Colonia, Ron Govan, an officer of the Ventura County NAACP, pointed out to the board the motivated audience who were demonstrating on her behalf as proof. In his address to the board, Colonia resident Santiago Vargas warned that if the board did not reconsider Murguia Wong's termination, violence was possible. In fact, Roberto Soria, whose daughters Debbie and Doreen would later be lead plaintiffs of the 1971 *Soria v. Oxnard School District Board of Trustees* desegregation case (described in the following paragraphs), predicted that if Murguia Wong's dismissal stood that the "whole town of Colonia" would come to the next board meeting in full force.[5]

After hearing the public's commentary, the school board went into an extended executive session. Upon their return they informed the community that their decision would be subject to the recommendation of the Murguia Wong–friendly Compensatory Education Advisory Committee, based on the reconciliation of community expectations with her job description. One of the community's own had been protected. But before the session adjourned, trustee Thomas Kane introduced a resolution to the board in support of the Compensatory Education Advisory Committee's proposal of two-way busing for the "total" integration of the district's schools. This involved the busing of majority-group (read, white) children to the schools of La Colonia. The board accepted the recommendation without comment.[6]

Three months after Murguia Wong resumed her position at the school district, OESD trustee John Marshall and his wife tragically perished in a plane crash on September 13, 1970. A special election was held on January 5 of the following year to fill his seat. At the age of thirty-two, Murguia Wong ran for the position in a field of six and won, making her the first ethnic Mexican elected to the board.[7] As the local press solely used her married last name, it is likely that Murguia Wong's adopted ethnic Asian surname made her an amenable candidate, especially among a white-dominant electorate perhaps made uneasy by a dynamic ethnic Mexican woman in possession of a critical seat within the local power structure. Nonetheless, with community support, she wasted no time upon her installation in exercising her authority to challenge the custodians of the status quo in and out of the OESD board, by pursuing the ethnic and racial integration of the district's schools in terms of its students, faculty, administration, and staff.[8]

After *Brown* and Before *Soria*

Nine years after the U.S. Supreme Court's *Brown* decision in 1954, which ruled as unconstitutional the doctrine of separate but equal in public education, the Ventura County chapter of the NAACP submitted a plan to the OESD board in 1963 to integrate schools designated as racially and ethnically imbalanced. The OESD and residents of the community generally agreed that de facto (effective but not officially sanctioned) school segregation resulted from housing practices that excluded people of color from purchasing property in neighborhoods in the western and northern parts of the city. This entailed racist and restrictive covenants in deeds, mortgage lending practices, and the resistance of white property owners and real estate agents, who refused to present homes on the market in white neighborhoods to people of African, Asian, and Mexican origins.[9]

In 1963 the OESD inadvertently instigated the controversy, when it weighed the potential construction of a junior high school in the easternmost part of the La Colonia barrio, which was already home to two elementary schools isolated from the rest of the district. To avert the further segregation of Black students in particular, the NAACP proposed that the school board bus segregated east side students to white-dominant schools west of Oxnard Boulevard. Indeed, the NAACP submitted a template like the ones presented to school boards in Pasadena and San Francisco. Althea Simmons, the subregional head of the NAACP in Los Angeles, recommended that children of La Colonia be allowed to attend the Fremont Junior High School during either the seventh or eighth grade, and that all students attend the proposed new school in La Colonia the alternate year. The *Sentinel* newspaper of Los Angeles reported that Simmons's proposal was met with "heated" opposition from Oxnard's "white city and school board officials."[10]

As detailed in chapter 2, after the CSO and the NAACP simultaneously yet independently confronted the OESD with the issue of school segregation, the trustees ultimately admitted to—as it could no longer deny—the racist nature of neighborhood attendance patterns. Hence, on May 2, 1967, the OESD board of trustees adopted a resolution that recognized *Brown*'s determination of segregation as unconstitutional. The OESD also acknowledged the California State Board of Education's resolution that both de facto and de jure segregation resulted in unequal education. The district went on to admit that de facto segregation in "some" of its schools was attributable to extant housing patterns and class disparities in the community. Thus, the board resolved to work with city agencies to address the problem of segregation as well as to compensate "within the means available" minority students in the segregated schools of La Colonia. It also promised to consider de facto segregation as it moved forward with its planning of future school sites.[11]

Out of Balance

The next year an OESD report documented that an aggregate of Asian, Black, and ethnic Mexican students outnumbered their white peers in the district. At the Juanita school, 98 percent of the students consisted of children of color. The Ramona school site, less than a block away, had the same demographic makeup. In both instances ethnic Mexican students dominated the schools in population, by 84 percent and 98 percent, respectively. Black students made up the difference in both cases by 15 percent and 2 percent.[12] These facts, along with community pressure, compelled the OESD to request that the California State Department of Education's Bureau of Intergroup Relations investigate the state of de facto segregation in its schools. In its April 1969 report, the bureau commended the OESD administration and board of trustees for their "strong commitment" to examine "*de facto* [forces] and to action toward the elimination of segregation and the improvement of intergroup relations."[13] It then highlighted three legal precedents involving the issue of segregation. The first was the *Mendez v. Westminster School District* case of 1945—affirmed by the U.S. Circuit Court of Appeals in 1947—that found that the segregation of ethnic Mexican students was not authorized by California law and unconstitutional under the Fourteenth Amendment. Second, in the *Brown* decision, the U.S. Supreme Court declared unconstitutional the separate but equal clause established in the 1896 case of *Plessy v. Ferguson*. Third, and more recently, the California Supreme Court case of *Jackson v. Pasadena City School District* of 1963 connected residential segregation to that of the schools. In *Jackson* the court required school boards to take corrective action—"as reasonably feasible"—to reduce ethnic imbalance no matter the cause.[14] This meant that the pretext of de facto forces, specifically residential patterns, determining segregated neighborhood schools could not preclude districts from taking remedial action. This was a crucial finding, as district boards could no longer point to forces outside of their authority to defend the continued segregation of students.

Based on the study completed by the Bureau of Intergroup Relations and approved by the OESD board in October 1968, the California State Board of Education cited eleven recommendations to the schools of the state with the "force and effect of law." Section 2010 of the California Administrative Code held districts responsible for the creation of student centers or the assignment of students to prevent and eliminate ethnic imbalances in schools. This was to be the highest priority of a superintendent and to boards of trustees.[15] To inform remedies to "prevent and eliminate" ethnic imbalance, Section 2011 required the comparison of the district's student demographics with the attendance population in each school and grade. Imbalance at a school existed when students of one or more racial and ethnic groups differed by more than 15 percent of their makeup in a district. To determine whether imbalances existed in schools, the Department of Education mandated districts to conduct a study and develop plans of correction. It also required the district to compare the demographic makeup of "certain" adjacent schools within it; as a result, the district was to monitor closely demographic shifts in the student population in relation to each school and grade level. These data were to inform the decisions of district leaders in their creation and reformulation of school attendance boundaries and practices.[16]

The bureau's report then documented the OESD's negligent "color-blind" approach to the educational needs of all students. It admonished the district to correct the effects of de facto segregation by a "color-conscious" "cultural consciousness." To remediate systemic bias, the district needed to improve racial and ethnic balance in the schools, complemented by programs that focused on the "special" challenges of Black and ethnic Mexican students, particularly in the intermediate schools of Fremont and Haydock Junior High. The report then censured district officials in the statement:

> There seems to be a need now for a more significant, conscious, built-in, district-wide effort to include the culture and contributions of the many peoples who make up this country in the regular programs, not necessarily as separate units but as part of the total picture. Some lack of awareness or sensitivity in this area, and sometimes even surprise at the idea, exists even in Oxnard. Greater and more effective use of materials depicting and describing racial and ethnic differences, histories, cultures, and problems, and the development of such materials when they are not available, would seem essential, as would use of staff and community persons of minority background in such projects and as speakers and resource people generally.[17]

In the development of alternative plans for the desegregation of schools, the Bureau of Intergroup Relations further enjoined the district to consider the population and corollary residential development of Oxnard, characterized as the "urban center of Ventura County." In the view of the authors, extant economic, social, and demographic segregation translated to "psychological isolation." The problems of La Colonia—and the rest of the city, for that matter—would not be rectified until the city's leadership addressed this dilemma. Thus, as proposed by Simmons earlier, the bureau recommended that local policymakers integrate white pupils into the schools of La Colonia and encourage an economic diversity that promoted "greater residential integration." If this could not be accomplished, it behooved the OESD to see that all students of La Colonia be "fully integrated into the educational program elsewhere in the district."[18]

Voices of the Parents

As the issue of school desegregation heated up into a community-wide controversy, district archives indicate that OESD administrators closely followed public opinion, as expressed in the Voice of the People letters section of the *Oxnard Press-Courier*. Cloene I. Marson, a white woman originally from Florida who lived in the northside of Oxnard, boldly criticized people in the community who declared support for integration but at the same time opposed busing. Marson chided whites who refused to recognize their privilege and their own promotion of bigotry. After the citation of court decisions and directives of state officials that mandated school districts to desegregate immediately, Marson asked, "How can Anglos criticize illegal, often violent, reactions when they themselves violate the Constitution? They criticize the disadvantaged for 'no initiative,' but belittle and ignore them when they try to resolve frustrations through proper channels, such as the school board."[19] White children in integrated schools stood to benefit as more well-rounded individuals, Marson argued, from their interaction with a greater "cross-section" of classmates. This outweighed, in her opinion, the convenience of her children walking to their neighborhood school.[20]

Marson's letter responded to the published views of Kenneth L. Mytinger in Voice of the People the week before. Mytinger's message, like Marson's, provided an insight into the range of sentiments in the community regarding the notion of school busing, as he conceded the necessity and worthiness of integration to advance, in his words, "a well-rounded education." But he then pivoted to state that there existed many instances in which busing failed, at a high financial cost. As the chairman of the Oxnard Wakefield Initiative petition (authored by Assemblyman Floyd L. Wakefield of Downey, California, to amend the Education Code of the state to prohibit school boards from busing children without the consent of parents), Mytinger, in order to fashion his stance as less reactionary, pointed out that the proposed modification to extant law did not prohibit voluntary busing.[21]

As the larger community entered the debate, ethnic Mexican residents did not stand united. The Brown Berets in Oxnard, for example, doubted the necessity for integration, with the conviction that ethnic Mexican children would be best served in equitably resourced schools that implemented a culturally relevant curriculum that affirmed the distinct reality of students. This would instill an amour propre in barrio youth to face with confidence a white-dominant society. Furthermore, the Brown Berets, as well as the Black cultural organization of Uhuru in the city of Oxnard, questioned the implicit educational benefit of school integration.[22]

The perspective of the Brown Berets and Uhuru was not unusual. California's deputy superintendent of public instruction, Wilson C. Riles, a Black educator and candidate for the state superintendent's office in 1969, asserted, in relation to de facto segregation, "Our first job is to get good schools. I think the busing issue is highly emotional and not relevant. The fear is that children will be bused to an inferior school." Ironically, the Brown Berets and Uhuru generally agreed philosophically with politically conservative OESD trustee Robert Pfeiler, who pronounced in 1963 that no evidence demonstrated that a "Negro child will benefit if he rubs elbows with a child with a better background who has better aptitudes. No study has ever shown this to be true. There's a danger of just the opposite happening."[23] But who was the "child with a better background," and what was the "opposite" outcome alluded to by Pfeiler? Perhaps he had in mind middle-class students whose education would be negatively compromised by peers from poor families. Then there were the apprehensions of ethnic Mexican professionals economically able to move out of barrio communities in Ventura County in order to live in solidly white, middle-class neighborhoods such as those on the northern and western areas of Oxnard. Now, as parents, they faced the possibility of having their children bused to one of the Mexican schools in La Colonia—an irony of history.[24]

Other opponents of busing argued that racist systems of exclusion diminished to the point that all that was needed to reduce the achievement gap in education was individual initiative. In this regard, Sue Nava, who claimed to have been raised in La Colonia, characterized the parents of the plaintiffs in the case of *Soria v. Oxnard School District Board of Trustees* of 1971 as "grossly" unmotivated and lectured them to save their money in order to buy homes outside of La Colonia. For Nava, institutionalized forces of racism were of no import. The ability of people to be economically upwardly mobile would rectify pernicious dynamics of segregation.[25] Nava refused to recognize that the parents of the *Soria* plaintiffs were using the legal system to obtain justice. Nava apparently was also not aware that policies of the Federal Housing Authority alone contributed to racially defined residential patterns by way of redlining.

While this debate continued locally, the OESD followed national currents linked to school desegregation. In late October 1969 the U.S. Supreme Court in *Alexander v. Board of Education* in Mississippi unanimously and immediately outlawed the "dual system" in education. The decision directed school districts to cease tactics of delay that undermined the 1954 judgment in *Brown*. In response the *Los Angeles Times* editorialized, "While there will be practical problems in implementing this week's order, the transcendent consideration must be to give all citizens the legal and moral rights due them under the Fourteenth Amendment."[26] In essence the 1969 Supreme Court opinion eliminated the indeterminate "all deliberate speed" clause within *Brown II* of 1955 that school districts utilized to perpetually delay, if not forever postpone, school integration.[27]

No Laughing Matter

As it received the report of the Bureau of Intergroup Relations and the community's debate on school desegregation intensified, the OESD board majority harbored no intention to implement any plan to desegregate imbalanced schools beyond the 650 students bused from La Colonia to west side campuses.[28] It even rejected the bureau's conservative recommendation to close the Ramona school and bus an additional 700 students from the barrio to white-majority schools. Instead, trustee Kenneth N. Tinklepaugh, after an extensive discussion of the options in a November 1969 board meeting, proposed to his colleagues that the district petition the state for funds to upgrade the schools in place of moving forward with an integration plan.[29] OESD board president Robert Pfeiler found the matter humorous, sardonically remarking, "You'd be needling the State Board of Education, giving them a little jab.... The state might give us a million dollars." Trustee Thomas Kane ignored the comment and suggested that the district adopt the advisory recommendation in closing the Ramona school. Pfeiler then reiterated his opposition to "forced" busing.[30]

Meanwhile, in May 1969, the *Oxnard Press-Courier* acknowledged the OESD board's stance of "planned gradualism" to avoid community upheaval.[31] In addition to the racial integration of students in and of itself, perhaps the newspaper sought to avoid a backlash by residents who opposed busing as a remedy as well. The editorial board, however, held that the trustees failed in their fiduciary duty to address the issue of segregation at a time when the community sought leadership, and it called on the district to appoint a committee to create an action plan and timetable to remedy the problem.[32] In October 1969 Ventura County NAACP president Eddie London and Frank Olivares of the ethnic Mexican organization Los Amigos addressed a joint letter to the trustees for the establishment of a citizen's committee to perform what the *Oxnard Press-Courier* suggested. But the board majority, led by Pfeiler, thought otherwise.[33] This proved to many in the community that the OESD did not want to offend those who favored neighborhood schools due to the fact that the only effective way to desegregate the schools entailed mandatory busing. Interestingly, as the OESD refused to act, district director of special projects Norman Brekke admitted to the Ventura County Community Action Committee (CAC) that OESD boards had been concerned with de facto segregation, dating back to the 1930s. In contradiction to board president Pfeiler's belief, he also went on record that "all the evidence we have indicates that an integrated education is a better education, not only for minority children but for other children as well."[34]

Notwithstanding the school board's intransigence, the North Oxnard Methodist Church sponsored a November 16 forum on the topic of de facto school segregation. Brekke represented the district in an overview of desegregation proposals.[35] The next month the NAACP of Ventura County further drew the community's attention with the organization of a protest march of fifty persons to a district meeting. The group highlighted the OESD board's insincerity in remedying de facto segregation.[36] The group procession started at Colonia Park, adjacent to the Juanita School, and continued on to the district office on 255 Palm Drive, and, further, into the boardroom, carrying signs reading "Separate Is Not Equal" and "Remove Bigots from Board Room." London read a letter to the trustees that demanded that it stop delaying desegregating and that questioned why the children of white growers who lived east of La

Colonia were bused to schools on the west side when they lived closer to the schools of Juanita, Ramona, and Rose Avenue. Probably with the notion that superior resources and excellent teachers flowed along racial lines, London argued that the enrollment of white children in the schools of La Colonia would go far in addressing ethnic imbalances in the school district. Deputy superintendent Seawright H. Stewart responded that children were being bused from the east side of town in order to alleviate overcrowding, and that most students bused to west side schools were nonwhite.[37]

Persistence tipped the political balance in favor of those of who demanded action. Approximately two weeks after the NAACP demonstration, on December 16, 1969, the board of trustees adopted a thirteen-point desegregation plan that called for the reassignment of fourteen portable classrooms to campuses west of Oxnard Boulevard to accommodate potentially eight hundred Colonia children bused to white-dominant schools. To meet the overall demand for additional space, this plan also called for the creation of permanent buildings at school sites, as well as the construction of a new school.[38] In relation to busing specifically, board president Pfeiler and trustee J. Keith Mason proposed a voluntary busing program. Tinklepaugh and Kane, on the other hand, favored the mandatory one-way busing of students living in La Colonia to west side schools.[39] This plan, meant to accommodate white parents, must have angered many Black and ethnic Mexican mothers and fathers. At this point John Soria spoke openly about the need for a federal class action lawsuit to end racism in the district. In late February 1971 the case of *Soria v. Oxnard School District Board of Trustees* case was filed.[40]

Tricky Dick

The same month that the OESD deliberated on means to achieve desegregation, U.S. District Court judge Manuel L. Real ordered the Pasadena School District (PSD) to submit a plan for the complete desegregation of its high schools by February 16, 1970. A key point of Real's decision ruled that no single campus, from the elementary grades to high school, would have a majority population of students who were of a racial minority group. Judge Real also ordered the PSD to include integration plans on the assignment, hiring, and promotion of teachers. The case was not limited to school desegregation; it also encompassed the implementation of affirmative action remedies that included construction projects.[41]

On the national scene, in February 1970, President Richard Nixon articulated a woolly position that simultaneously opposed school segregation as he rejected court-mandated busing as a remedy. This stance emerged in a letter sent by Nixon's legal counsel to Pennsylvania Senate Republican Hugh Scott, author of an amendment to a bill that permitted the existence of de facto segregation in the nation's schools. The Scott Amendment, as it came to be called, responded to Mississippi Senate Democrat John D. Stennis, who called for the elimination of any distinction between school segregation, de jure or de facto.[42] It was in this context that Leon Panetta, director of the Department of Health, Education, and Welfare Office, characterized the Nixon administration's "kind of buying and selling" of civil rights policy. In fact, Panetta viewed civil rights legislation as completely endangered by the Nixon administration's appeasement of "racist" members of Congress who were determined to undermine the "tough" enforcement of antidiscrimination laws. This being the case, the administration forced Panetta to resign in February 1970.[43] Similarly, the U.S. Commission on Civil Rights criticized Nixon for his equivocation on school desegregation, expressing its disappointment with his support of the neighborhood school concept and his opposition to busing. The commission also admonished his administration for making a false distinction between de facto and de jure school segregation—in other words, as racially defined residential patterns were fundamentally knotted to "official actions" of state, local, and federal government agencies. The commission went on to dispel the fiction that busing violated a mythological national neighborhood school tradition, pointing to the busing of Black and white children for decades in the South, up to fifty miles one way, to preserve a system of racial apartheid, during which time white southerners failed to complain about the detrimental effects of busing on the well-being of students.[44]

Later in the spring of 1970, Republican governor of Florida Claude Kirk blocked a federal school desegregation busing order when he placed the Manatee County School District under his control. In response federal marshals arrested Manatee County sheriff deputies for attempting to prevent the entrance of federal agents into the office of the superintendent of schools.[45]

Before Kirk's obstructionism, in 1969 Oxnard resident Ken Mytinger expressed his opposition to school busing as the local sponsor of the Wakefield Amendment, detailed in the previous pages, authored by Assemblyman Floyd Wakefield of the Los Angeles community of Downey adjacent to the city of Compton, where school desegregation was also a hot-button issue.[46] Locally, state representatives in Ventura County split on the question: State Senator Robert Lagomarsino supported the initiative while Assemblyperson J. K. "Ken" McDonald expressed his inclination to oppose it, due to its probable violation of constitutional equal protections.[47]

Brown People v. OSD Board of Trustees

Vexed by the OESD's refusal to remedy racist inequities in the schools, Soria encouraged parents—chiefly his young brother Roberto—to file a school desegregation suit in the U.S. Ninth District Court in Los Angeles: the same juridical district of Judge Real in the aforementioned Pasadena case. The suit charged the OESD with the violation of the Equal Protections Clause of the Fourteenth Amendment of the U.S. Constitution. It also accused the OESD board of the deliberate sabotage of efforts to achieve "nondiscriminatory education."[48] As a newly minted attorney out of Hastings College of Law in Northern California, Thomas Malley of the Legal Aid Center took on the case and welcomed the assistance of Peter Roos and Stephen Kalish at the Los Angeles–based Western Center on Law and Poverty. Both centers emerged from the federal Office of Economic Opportunity's Legal Services Division, which represented low-income communities.[49] From the start Malley, Roos, and Kalish understood the historical and emotional landscape of the *Soria* case, both regional and national, as did the parents and supporters of the student plaintiffs. In the nation's southern states, there was no question that de jure (state sanctioned) segregation existed, but in the western and northern regions of the country housing patterns and the creation of neighborhood schools addled the distinction between de jure and de facto (of custom) segregation.[50]

Initially, a spectrum of organizations and individuals such as the Brown Berets, the CSO, MAPA, and the NAACP opposed the idea of busing. In the eyes of many, ethnic Mexican and Black students sitting next to white peers did not in and of itself remedy the systemic maleducation of students of color. First and foremost they demanded an equitable and culturally relevant education in their neighborhood schools. Knowledge of inferior facilities and the assignment of teachers at the Colonia schools based on race, inexperience, and ineffectiveness infuriated parents of color. If the schools of Juanita and Ramona Elementary were equally supported, transgenerational residents such as Roberto Flores, London, Soria, William Terry, and Murguia Wong had no doubt that students of color would excel no less academically than their more economically privileged white peers across town. The use of an open enrollment district policy that allowed white parents to have their children bused to white-dominant neighborhood schools on the west side aggravated matters. Added to this the idea of one-way busing that largely impacted Black and ethnic Mexicans students exacerbated tensions further.[51]

One month before the start of the *Soria* case, in April 1971, the U.S. Supreme Court unanimously reaffirmed the *Brown* decision in *Swann v. Charlotte-Mecklenburg*. In an opinion written by Chief Justice Warren Burger, the court declared North Carolina's antibusing laws unconstitutional as they barred desegregation and determined busing an appropriate remedy. Furthermore, the ruling sanctioned demographic ratios as a valid means to determine whether or not segregation existed or had been remedied. Consequently, Swann held that state law could not proscribe the promotion of a unitary educational system or advance a dual school system.[52]

The next month, on May 10, 1971, Judge Harry Pregerson of the Ninth District Court heard the case. The community could only observe as the judicial proceedings unfolded. Malley and John Childers of the Legal Services Center of Ventura County and Kalish and Roos of the Western Center on Law and Poverty in Los Angeles argued that the district's 1970–71 "open busing" policy worsened segregation, because it promoted the transportation of white students in the attendance zone of La Colonia to predominantly white campuses on the west side of the city. It also entrenched segregation with the gerrymandering of school attendance boundaries, the increased use of portable classrooms, and the selection of new campus sites. The OESD's own studies impressed Judge Pregerson: they revealed that segregation negatively thwarted the educational achievement of Black and ethnic Mexican students, as test scores and the grades of racial minority children in schools located in predominantly white neighborhoods were higher than their counterparts in the schools of La Colonia.[53]

William A. Waters, assistant counsel of Ventura County, represented the defendants, the OESD Board of Trustees. He maintained that the material question in the case was if the "distribution of students and the distribution and composition of the faculty" resulted from the policies of the district. Judge Pregerson ruled, however, that the district had an affirmative duty "to provide the plaintiffs with a racially balanced school system." The question of school segregation being de facto or de jure was irrelevant; segregation existed, so the law required the school district to remedy the problem to ensure equal protection as guaranteed by the Fourteenth Amendment. As a result, Pregerson, upon the request of the plaintiffs, based a summary judgment of relief on "the agreed-upon facts of the case, as contained in plaintiffs' proposed finding of fact with the deletions and alterations requested by counsel for the defendants."[54]

Judge Pregerson's judgment underscored the Supreme Court's tenet in *Brown*, which held that "the doctrine of 'separate but equal' has no place. Separate facilities are inherently unequal. Therefore we hold that the plaintiffs and others similarly situated for whom the actions have been brought are, by reason of the segregation complained of, deprived of the equal protection of the laws guaranteed by the Fourteenth Amendment." Pregerson went on to state that "*de jure* overtones" of segregation existed on the part of the OESD. This finding, as outlined by Kalish, consisted of policies of open enrollment that allowed white parents to transfer their children out of predominately Black and ethnic Mexican schools and the situation of new school sites and portable classrooms to maintain a segregated district. Pregerson also noted the evidence presented by Kalish of the district's refusal to adopt plans of integration. To remedy the problem, Pregerson ordered the district to submit within twenty days of his ruling a "workable plan" of remedy. It could not entail one-way busing.[55]

After adjustments were made to its initial integration plan, the OESD filed a revised version to the court, to which the plaintiffs made no major objections.

Judge Pregerson praised OESD superintendant Doran W. Tregarthen for his "steadfast, patient, and exemplary leadership."[56] A major component of the remedy paired elementary schools and children in the K–6 grades in relation to busing. For example, the Colonia school of Ramona was coupled with the Sierra Linda School in the northernmost part of the city. The Juanita school was paired with Curren Elementary in the northwestern part of the city. And the Colonia school of Rose Avenue was connected to the Marina West School in the midwestern part of the community.[57]

But, as in the case in Pasadena, Pregerson's ruling entailed much more than the demographic desegregation of campuses. The order prohibited any classroom to have a dominance of a group beyond a percentage of 25 in the district. Only a "compelling educational interest" could allow for exceptions.[58] The decision also held the district responsible for the enhancement of demographic representation at all levels of employment. The staff (i.e., administrators and teachers) was to be trained in incorporating the historical contributions and experiences of diverse groups into the curriculum, as Murguia Wong attempted to do.[59] It also prohibited a "freedom of choice" policy that permitted parents to determine what district school their children attended.[60]

Takeaway

Emblematic of a dual system of education in the region, this chapter contextualized the nature of school segregation in the city of Oxnard and struggles in the community for its dismantlement during El Movimiento. For incipient Chicanas-Chicanos, both baby boomers and those of the Mexican American generation, the issue of school segregation underscored the continuity of injustice in societal systems. The next chapter examines the OESD board's resistance to Judge Pregerson's desegregation order by way of its determination to obtain a stay on it while it sought to prove on appeal that the district was innocent of racial segregation. This only served to polarize the community further, which emboldened Mexican Americans to adopt a more militant stance as the trial exposed the forces of systemic racism. This fused two generational cohorts into becoming Chicanas-Chicanos.

5

No Way, José!

SCHOOL BUSING

Soon after Judge Harry Pregerson's decision, Oxnard Elementary School District (OESD) superintendent Doran W. Tregarthen, in a memo of May 13, 1971, to his staff, asserted that the court order was "unpalatable to most in the community," but there was no middle ground: compliance was an all-or-nothing proposition. The superintendent closed his memo by stating, "We can grumble, and we can protest. We can go about our task in a negative and complaining manner. In the final analysis, however, we are going to carry out the court's order. There is no alternative."[1] Despite Superintendent Tregarthen's icy commitment to comply with Judge Pregerson's order, the district's board majority refused to accept the mandate to desegregate its schools via two-way busing. This chapter details the determination of the board to overturn Pregerson's decision that ultimately exposed an even more insidiously racist transgenerational system of education. In the process, tension in the community continued, if not intensified. Although the demand for an equal education for all children did not take the form of school blowouts, as in East Los Angeles high schools in 1968, this struggle, I argue, on all sides of the school integration issue, contributed to an integral shared identity among the Mexican American and Chicana-Chicano generations, especially as an aggrieved class that demanded the fulfillment of the American promise for all children. This fight was carried out by lawyers in court; for the most part, the community could only observe the legal process. The court battle nonetheless further politicized the worldview of ethnic Mexicans across generational lines in Ventura County during El Movimiento.

We Demand a Trial

After the OESD developed and submitted its desegregation plan, which entailed paired busing, in the late spring of 1971 trustees Mary Davis, Ken Mytinger, and Ken Tinklepaugh voted to retain private attorney Edward Lascher, an appeals expert, to overturn Judge Pregerson's decision.[2] The crux of the appeal held that the summary judgment of an issue of such import betrayed the public's trust. The case therefore warranted a trial, especially considering the nationwide controversy caused by compulsory busing to remedy school segregation. When the district filed its petition, it also requested a stay on Judge Pregerson's order that was ultimately rejected. This made way for the busing of 2,350 students in the fall of 1971.[3]

In response to the district's appeal, the plaintiff's lawyer, Thomas Malley, in turn filed a formal notice of opposition to the school district's request for a stay on Pregerson's decision, as the school district had wrongly submitted its request to the Ninth Circuit U.S. Court of Appeals in San Francisco; Malley correctly maintained that the request for a stay should have been made to Pregerson's bench. Malley also argued that the summary judgment was issued after the court had assiduously reviewed over five hundred pages of sworn testimony and one thousand pages of exhibits. Specific to segregation, the school board contended that the question was whether the district had intentionally segregated students. In the court of public opinion, Malley stated to the press that since members of the board admitted that they built and maintained racially imbalanced schools, Judge Pregerson ruled that it didn't matter what the board intended. The facts of segregation spoke for themselves.[4]

Angered by the judge's decision, Oxnard opponents viewed mandatory busing as a violation of not only their individual rights, but especially those of their children. This, in their eyes, made them victims of federal tyranny. Resident Richard Rogers, in a June 1971 letter to the *Oxnard Press-Courier*, encouraged parents opposed to busing to sue the district for discrimination if ordered to participate. The only way that busing could be constitutional, in Rogers's asinine view, was if every child in the district was ordered to be bused; otherwise, those who were bused would be discriminated against in relation to those who were not.[5]

As board president, OESD trustee J. Keith Mason's opposition aligned with parents who regarded integration via busing as a constitutional violation of their freedom of choice, as they elected to reside in a certain section of the city for the convenience of nearby stores and the quality of homes and neighborhood schools. Understandably, many who held this perspective most likely held no prejudice toward Blacks and ethnic Mexicans. Others, perhaps, proposed a pro–neighborhood schools stance as a dog whistle, to mask an aversion to racial integration. Furthermore, as taxpayers, such parents argued that busing for integration would be an added cost to the district that would ultimately saddle them with higher property taxes.[6]

In anticipation of Judge Pregerson's ruling, trustees J. Keith Mason, Robert Pfeiler, and Thomas Kane ordered a poll to gauge support for and opposition to busing. This was carried out over the opposition of Superintendent Tregarthen and assistant superintendent Norman Brekke. Completed in June 1971, after Judge Pregerson's ruling in late May, only 636 families (23 percent) of the 2,739 polled indicated that they would voluntarily include their children in a cross-town desegregation plan that involved busing. Tregarthen questioned the validity of the poll, since many of the parents surveyed did not have children in OESD schools—or, if they did, they attended junior high schools not affected by Judge Pregerson's initial ruling.[7] Why the three trustees insisted on the poll is not clear.

Conflict with the busing issue deepened when Judge Pregerson decided in late June that it would involve kindergarten students. This further raised the ire of board president J. Keith Mason, who was also a member of Oxnard's Citizens Opposed to Busing (COB). Rather than have them bused to a La Colonia school, Mason declared to the press his intention to withdraw his children from the district by either enrolling them in private school or moving his family. At the request of attorneys Malley and Roos, Judge Pregerson also ruled that the classrooms in each school would also have to reflect the demographic makeup of the students in the district.[8]

Despite the poll, which showed that parents in general within the district opposed busing, in August 1971 Russ M. Licke and Carla M. Bard wrote letters to the *Oxnard Press-Courier*'s Voice of the People section to express their opposition to the district's decision to appeal Judge Pregerson's desegregation order. Both also detailed their dissatisfaction for COB's campaign to recall trustee Rachel Murguia Wong due to her support of Judge Pregerson's decision. In this regard Bard commended the OESD board for its public stance against her recall. In addition, on behalf of the Association of Mexican American Educators (AMAE) of Ventura County, Gilbert G. Cuevas of the Mexican American generation penned a letter to the *Oxnard Press-Courier* that defended trustee Murguia Wong, as he commended her opposition to the district's decision to retain Lascher at the expense of $6,000 to pursue the legal stay.[9]

In anticipation of the school year in 1971, tension among the school trustees escalated as COB co-chair Nancy McGrath questioned what the board would do if the petition for a stay failed. In response Mason pronounced his intent to withdraw his children (one of them a kindergartener and the other a third grader) if they were to be bused from Curren Elementary on the northwest side of town to its paired campus, Juanita in La Colonia. Mason also opined that Judge Pregerson's ruling made the district a "ward of the court."[10] Trustee Murguia Wong, who had three children of her own, two designated to be reassigned from Sierra Linda Elementary on the northernmost side of the city to Ramona in La Colonia, proclaimed her compliance. She then challenged Mason's statement by enquiring when the district had been placed in "receivership."[11] In a board meeting on September 21, Mason again announced the district's pursuit of a stay on Judge Pregerson's order, which he indignantly characterized as a betrayal of the rights of parents and their children. When the Ninth Circuit refused to hear the motion filed by Lascher for a stay of the busing order pending an appeal, Mason charged the two-judge panel with dodging the issue on technical grounds and negligence in the conduct of its duties. COB members in the audience added their voice of opposition to busing, but also expressed their continued compliance with the district's desegregation plan.[12]

After COB members and the trustees voiced their dissent against Judge Pregerson's ruling, William Terry of the city's Community Action Commission rebutted that when the system maintained the status quo, the opponents of busing lauded the democratic process, but when change occurred in terms of remedies to address racial injustice, the system somehow no longer suited them. He then implored opponents to the desegregation order to move "away from this façade of antibusing." For Terry, the controversy was rooted in segregation and racism.[13]

What's Behind the Fuss?

Two years prior to the contretemps at the September 21 board meeting, on December 10, 1969, the Compensatory Education Advisory Committee (CEAC), which was composed of residents and OESD staff, convened. Of the thirty-seven committee members who participated, four had Spanish surnames. One question was asked as part of a conversation on desegregation alternatives: "For what reasons do people oppose integration?" Members suggested that people largely opposed two-way busing because Colonia schools were inferior to those on the west side. It was also stated that some in the community opposed integration due to "their deep-rooted concern for 'cultural contamination,'" followed closely by their "concern" for the encouragement of interracial marriage. The minutes of this meeting, however, do not specify if these views were held largely by whites in the community or equally shared among Blacks, ethnic Mexicans, and people of Asian ancestry.[14]

Another topic addressed by CEAC pertained to the convenience that neighborhood schools afforded families and the troubles associated with children being bused. According to the CEAC discussion, many people did not oppose—at least openly—busing if it only involved students of La Colonia. Black and ethnic Mexican parents as well as other groups that lived outside of La Colonia opposed the practice as a remedy if it solely entailed their families. Therefore, parents opposed busing for different reasons. For many Black and ethnic Mexican parents who supported busing, they believed it would only work if it consisted of two-way busing, so that the white community was equally "burdened." Armando López, as one of the Chicano generation leaders of the Brown Berets, had expressed this to assistant superintendent Brekke a year earlier, in October 1968. López also shared with him, as did CEAC, that both Black and ethnic Mexican people in La Colonia valued their neighborhood schools, as they felt that these campuses could best provide their children a culturally relevant education that would inculcate a strong sense of self to equip them to face a white-dominant society as adults.[15]

In an undated document in the Oxnard School District archive titled "Common Fears Related to Integration," Neil V. Sullivan, superintendent of schools in Berkeley, California, and author of the Berkeley Plan, which mandated two-way busing, posited that there were often coded motivations behind the opposition to desegregate, especially when it involved mandatory busing. The first entailed the notion of the presumed sanctity of the mythical neighborhood school. Even as they existed at the time, Sullivan argued that this model should change, as other societal institutions—such as agriculture changing from small farming to agribusiness, and the obsolescent "corner grocery store" to supermarkets. Sullivan wrote, "In an era of greatly improved transportation, why should not our schools keep pace in altering their organizational patterns to meet new educational needs."[16]

From a white, Black, and ethnic Mexican middle-class perspective, integrated "erstwhile Caucasian schools" were associated with the diminution of scholastic achievement. Standardized test scores defined schools; therefore, parents, regardless of their race and ethnicity, for the most part, did not want their children's education potentially compromised by the lower performance of students of color, who were victims of a systematically racist educational system. This was the case despite evidence presented by James S. Coleman et al. in his "Equality in Educational Opportunity Report" of 1966, which concluded that desegregated schools did not harm the performance of white students. I must editorialize here, that even today in 2021 many ethnic Mexican parents, especially solidly middle-class professionals, like their ethnic and racial white counterparts, will undergo extreme sacrifice and inconvenience to yank their children from Latina/o-majority schools and transfer them to predominantly white blue-chip schools. Sullivan conversely argued that Black students benefited performance-wise when they attended integrated schools—however, at a price. Sullivan was alluding to life-damaging white supremacy more generally when he wrote, "It has been the Negro rather than the Caucasian who has generally felt the harmful results from interracial contacts over the hundreds of years in our country's history."[17]

Ultimately, while it supported the "total integration" of the district, in June 1970 CEAC recommended that this be accomplished by relocating fourteen classroom portables from the Colonia schools to sites on the west side. This meant the one-way busing of some three hundred students of La Colonia to "fully-integrated classes" in the schools of Harrington, Elm, Curren, and Sierra Linda.[18] In an attempt to alleviate enmity in the city as well as promote an appreciation for the sociohistorical condition of ethnic Mexican students while celebrating a new identity, AMAE—which consisted of individuals of the Mexican American generation such as Cuevas, mentioned previously, and Joe Mendoza, discussed in chapter 3—formulated a speakers' bureau that embraced the Chicano label. The presentations consisted of "What Is a Chicano?" by Mendoza (head of migrant education in Ventura County schools), "The Schools and the Mexican-American" by Alex Pulido (a counselor at the Oxnard Union High School District), "The Barrio, an Analysis of a Powderkeg [sic]," by Donato Ventura (a Moorpark College counselor), "The Acculturation of the Chicano?" by Virginia Oaxaca, and "The Chicano Studies Program in Our Schools" by Nicholas Ochoa (a Ventura College counselor). Trustee Murguia Wong was also listed in the program as making a presentation titled "The Responsibilities of Our Public School Boards."[19] But this series did more than just educate the public; it was a means by which to affirm the grievances of the plaintiffs and the ruling of Judge Pregerson in the *Soria* case.

In its own attempt to advance reconciliation and truth in the schools, the OESD introduced the film *Chicano from the Southwest* to five fourth-grade classes of Sierra Linda Elementary, in the northern, predominantly white section of the city. This, however, became an "explosive" matter at an OESD board meeting in October 1971. "In nose-to-nose, heated confrontations," as characterized by an *Oxnard Press-Courier* reporter, ethnic Mexican residents defended the film on the grounds that it represented the experience of the Chicano in the Southwest; whites at the meeting, however, felt it represented them in a negative light—perhaps similar to the racist Texans portrayed in Edna Ferber's 1952 novel *Giant* and the 1956 motion picture by the same title. In another exchange, between trustees Murguia Wong and Mason, Murguia Wong accused the board president of attempting to skirt the controversy. She stated that *Chicano from the Southwest* was ostensibly banned in the schools, so she wanted the board to decide whether the schools could screen the film. Ultimately, the board voted to allow the film to be shown with advance notice to parents—like sex education—so that they could prohibit their children from the viewing, if desired.[20]

Wheels on the Bus Go . . .

The day before school buses rolled out of the district yard to transport children to their paired schools, the *Oxnard Press-Courier*, in a Sunday editorial on September 12, 1971, recognized the magnitude of the local controversy within a national context. Apprehensively, it questioned whether acquiescence to the desegregation order (as was the case in Pasadena, California) or ugly resistance (as demonstrated by the emergence of the Ku Klux Klan in Pontiac, Michigan) would prevail. To encourage the former, the newspaper lauded the lawful resistance of COB as well as the OESD's compliance with Judge Pregeson's order while it pursued an appeal.[21]

The newspaper's concern for peace was warranted, as COB-sponsored former Florida Republican governor Claude Kirk's visit to Oxnard to forge its cause. In speaking to an audience at the Oxnard Community Center on September 1, 1971, Kirk argued that the OESD had been denied its constitutional right to a trial. He continued ad hominem that the issue of segregation legally involved Blacks, not Mexicans, and then singled out trustee Murguia Wong for having a Chinese surname but actually being of Mexican ancestry, shamelessly conflating her married name and actual ethnicity with mandated busing to frame the issue of desegregation as false as well as un-American. Kirk further stoked division by crassly equating busing in Oxnard to the atrocity of the My Lai massacre in Vietnam. If these histrionics were not enough, Kirk misogynistically predicted busing accidents at the hands of women bus drivers. Adding on to Kirk's bluster, board president Mason attributed the controversial issue of busing to the work of "guilt-ridden social do-gooders willing to trade dime store sensitivity training for a good education."[22]

A month and a half prior, on July 20, 1971, a bomb threat forced the suspension of an OESD board meeting that had been held in the Driffill Elementary auditorium to accommodate three hundred members of the community. After the police cleared the building for explosives, the meeting reconvened. COB spokesperson Patricia Willoughby claimed that threats had been made toward members of her group. She also expressed concern for the safety of students bused to the La Colonia schools of Juanita and Ramona, considering the consecutive Sunday-evening revolts of July 11 and July 18 (discussed in chapter 3). Dallas Holverson, an Oxnard resident who also addressed the school board, faulted the city council for the structural implementation of segregated, low-income residential developments that primarily housed people of Mexican origin. What Holverson did not mention, however, was that middle-class residents invariably opposed low-income developments in their vicinity. This was in addition to other forces of exclusion of the past and the then-present that entailed redlining of the Federal Housing Authority, lenders, realtors, and white neighborhood councils. When the community asked for the position of the OESD administration, as an at-will manager who served a board majority staunchly opposed to busing, Superintendent Tregarthen replied that, although he favored integration, he did not agree with Judge Pregerson's order, even though his staff designed the court approved plan.[23]

As opposition to busing fomented, COB leaders McGrath and Willoughby mobilized an unsuccessful recall of trustee Murguia Wong, as she opposed the board's retainer of Lascher to place a stay on the case on appeal. As others who disagreed with Judge Pregerson's summary judgement, COB emphasized that it did not oppose integration—only busing to achieve it. But COB did not propose alternative remedies. As a result of the public debate, COB member Bill Lattrell postulated at the board's meeting on July 17, 1971, that court decisions did not uniformly agree on the issue of racial balance within districts and, certainly, busing as a remedy. This was particularly true in Oxnard, as the OESD never maintained a dual school system, Lattrell insisted, despite the agreed-upon facts of the case, which proved otherwise. At this moment an unidentified person in the audience, as if seizing an auspicious opportunity, projected a loud riposte by reading from a booklet created by the League of Women Voters with excerpted OESD board minutes of 1936 and 1938.[24] As printed in the *Oxnard Press-Courier*:

> Minutes from the Nov. 9, 1936 meeting state that the board then presiding... "agreed to the recommendation about the removal of the American children from Haydock (separating them from Mexican classes)" but not to other suggestions such as staggered release times. On Sept. 13, 1938, the minutes read: "All children south of Fifth Street to attend Haydock with separate classes for white and Mexican children. Combine grades of white children to make sufficiently large classes, using some of the 'brightest and best' of the Mexican children in the white classes if the class was too small."[25]

This revelation clearly flummoxed the audience, as the newspaper did not report any response to this bombshell information, which debunked the putative discrete relationship of de facto (of action) segregation from that of the de jure (by policy) on the part of the OESD. Sans any commentary of its own, the newspaper report simply moved on to the topic of employing aides to ensure the safety of children to be bused to a paired school.

Evidence in the OESD archive suggests that by late 1969, if not earlier, executive district administrators, staff, and most likely the trustees themselves were privy to board sanctioned segregation in the 1930s. As a result of inexorable community pressure from people and groups such as Eddie London of the National Association for the Advancement of Colored People (NAACP) of Ventura County and Frank Olivares of the Oxnard civic club Los Amigos at the district's October 7 board meeting, a document was later created titled "School Integration: Why? How? and When?" With a November 1969 date and probably authored by acting superintendent Seawright H. Stewart, the report began by referencing the July 17 board meeting. The disquisition explained the legal basis for integration and educational benefits. Subsequent to the characterization of integration as "morally right" and the reference to a 1968 board resolution in support of ethnic balance, as well as a document titled "Alternative Plans for the Elimination of De Facto Segregation in the Oxnard School District," the report ended with a coda that pointed out the requirement for reconciliation on the part of the district in light of school board minutes of November 1936.[26]

Despite public knowledge of a history of de jure segregation on the part of the district, the OESD board continued its appeal. The district first challenged Pregerson's denial of a stay to the Ninth Circuit Court of Appeals, which ruled on August 21, 1972, that the Broomfield Amendment (proposed by Senator William Broomfield, Republican of Michigan, within the Education Act passed earlier that year that suspended busing orders on appeal) did not apply to integration plans in effect.[27]

The National and Local

Earlier, in January 1972, Attorney Lascher petitioned and won the support of the Justice Department under the Nixon administration to have Judge Pregerson's order quashed. This fell in line with President Nixon's two-faced politics, which maneuvered through contrary sides of an issue for maximum political advantage, all the while pandering to the fantasies of reactionary conservatives, particularly segregationist. In fact, in August 1972 Nixon undermined the Department of Health, Education, and Welfare's compliance with recent Supreme Court decisions when he barred the direction of federal funds to finance busing. The Nixon administration also ordered attorney general John N. Mitchell to appeal a busing order by U.S. District Court judge Jack B. Roberts in Austin, Texas.[28]

Meanwhile, the passage of the Broomfield Amendment within the Higher Education Act in June 1972 and the Nixon administration's duplicitous stance on integration emboldened the OESD board majority to press forward with its opposition. Further encouragement arrived when the Justice Department's Civil Rights Division filed an application with the San Francisco Court of Appeals to join the *Soria* case on the side of the OESD.[29]

As division continued in the community over busing, the OESD persisted in its pursuit of a stay, filing an appeal to the U.S. Supreme Court that the justices unanimously denied without explanation on October 24, 1972. And, doggedly, in the summer of 1973, the OESD placed its hopes in the high court's decision in *Keyes v. School District No. 1, Denver, Colorado*, which was anticipated to define de jure segregation for northern and western states. On June 21, 1973, the U.S. Supreme Court ruled in *Keyes* that a district could be held "liable for intentional segregation." It also designated ethnic Mexican students as an "identifiable class" eligible for protection under the Fourteenth Amendment and *Brown v. Board of Education*.[30] Ron Sabo, assistant Ventura County counsel and also one of the lawyers for the OESD, optimistically interpreted *Keyes* to mean that deliberate intent must be proven in a trial in regards to the determination of racial imbalance subsequent to the *Brown* decision of 1954.[31]

In view of the *Keyes* decision, the OESD board focused on the demand for a trial to reverse Judge Pregerson's summary judgement. On November 27, 1973, the Ninth Circuit granted the board's wish when it vacated Pregerson's decision and remanded the case back for a full trial. But, to avoid disarray in the district, the ruling allowed paired school busing to continue.[32]

Between Judge Pregerson's summary judgment in May 1971 and the start of the trial in late September 1974, Thomas Malley left the Legal Aid Center to start a private practice. Peter Roos moved on to Harvard's Center for Law and Education, where Stephen Kalish accepted a fellowship. Herb Nowlin stepped into the case for Legal Aid, as did Joel Edelman for the Western Center. Tony Waters reassumed the case on behalf of the district after Sabo separated from the county.[33]

On September 24, 1974, the trial coveted by the OESD board of trustees and COB commenced. Edelman presented the plaintiff's opening statement, arguing that, up to 1971, the OESD board continued a policy and an intentional practice of segregation set by trustees in the 1930s. In following up Nowlin wasted no time in presenting crucial new evidence, reading excerpts from the board minutes of the mid-to-late 1930s previously mentioned, which documented the OESD board's direction to segregate ethnic Mexican schoolchildren. Ted Neff of the California State Department of Education and consultant for the OESD then took the witness stand. The *Oxnard Press-Courier* reported that, in response to Judge Pregerson's questions, "Neff testified that the Oxnard School District was made aware there was ethnic and racial imbalance in the schools and that the state regulations were in effect to correct the imbalance." Yet from 1969 to 1971 the board took no corrective action.[34]

On day two of the trial, the attorneys for the plaintiffs presented evidence of how housing patterns and the practices of the real estate industry forged racially exclusive neighborhood schools.[35] One document presented to the court was the May 1949 covenant declaration made by W. C. and Bessie Watt Stroube for a property in the Vineyard Estates in the unincorporated community of El Rio adjacent to Oxnard, contracting "that no person any race other than the White or Caucasian races shall use or occupy any building on any lot in the subdivision, except such as are in the employ of the owner or tenant of said building." In his incisive *Strategies of Segregation: Race, Residence, and the Struggle for Educational Equality* (2018), David G. García methodically traces the financial investment of OESD trustees in a racialized residential geography that entrenched an insidious scheme of segregated schools since the early twentieth century. Over decades this chauvinist system became tantamount to a putative race-neutral policy in the determination of attendance boundaries. Therefore, "strategies of segregation" on the part of city, school district, and county officials advanced the interests of a white supremacist project dating back to the first half of the twentieth century. To accentuate this point, García highlights the ownership of racially restricted property by Ventura County superintendent of schools Blanche T. Reynolds, whose tenure was defined by a public resentment toward the presence of ethnic Mexican children in schools. In short, racially exclusive white neighborhoods translated into systemically racist school boundaries and classrooms.[36]

Over time OESD trustees cemented this institutionalized racism. After World War II, this system to advance white supremacy in the schools progressed on autopilot. Neighborhoods with restrictive real estate covenants largely barred ethnic Mexican families, as well as Asians and Blacks, from purchasing homes in the western and northern areas of the city. White neighborhood committees (as portrayed in the classic 1959 Lorraine Hansberry play *A Raisin in the Sun* and its 1961 film adaptation) as well as real estate agents steered potential buyers of color away from such neighborhoods.[37]

Chronologically more approximate to the trial itself, from 1961 to 1965 the OESD board's intransigence perpetuated racial and ethnic imbalance, testified Harold R. De Pue, superintendent of the OESD during these years. When questioned by Judge Pregerson, De Pue answered that board members, specifically Robert Pfeiler, "without equivocation," maintained segregation by not acknowledging the problem. De Pue favored school desegregation, but the plans and agendas set by the board defined it a "no-no subject."[38] Los Angeles County superintendent of schools Richard Clowes, who served as OESD superintendent from 1949 to 1961, testified to the OESD's racist tradition of segregation in both halves of the twentieth century. He stated that segregation defined rural communities in California, which Oxnard was, for the most part, while in transition to a more miscible economy of agriculture and commerce. He also confessed to his own complicity in the perpetuation of a segregationist "residue." If he had known then of its impact on children, he would have performed his duties differently, Dr. Clowes testified.[39]

On the third and final day of the trial, the defendants presented their case. Attorney Waters maintained that the policies of the 1930s and 1940s were irrelevant, since segregation was lawful prior to the *Brown* decision of 1954. As for segregation in the 1960s, Waters argued that the district opposed its continuation, as it decided not to construct a middle school at the Culbert site and lobbied against the further establishment of low-income housing in La Colonia. Furthermore, he contended, the district devoted considerable federal money in compensatory education. In a deposition of April 16, 1974, former trustee Mason (1969–71) insisted that the board did everything feasible to integrate the schools prior to the court order. He also declared his philosophical opposition to busing when he stated, "I think it doesn't accomplish anything. I think it is an expense that isn't warranted.... It hasn't accomplished anything since it has been instituted"—only antagonism in the community. Upon repeated questioning by the plaintiffs' lawyers, he emphasized that he supported the idea on a voluntary basis. The social climate in Oxnard, in his estimation, did not warrant court-mandated busing, as in the case of Watts in Los Angeles County; the city of Oxnard was more racially and ethnically integrated, although, he admitted, barriers and forces of discrimination did exist.[40]

Former trustee Thomas Kane (1963–71), when asked by Waters if a segregationist mindset existed on the board, responded, "Absolutely not, nothing could be farther from the case."[41] But he was more conflicted regarding the question of school integration in terms of the district's devotion of resources to "complete integration" by way of "mass busing" over the best interests of children within the neighborhood schools of La Colonia. He expressed in his April 16 deposition that his goal, and that of the district, was to provide the "best possible education" that met the specific needs of students. Kane also testified that the neighborhoods schools of La Colonia were making progress in the delivery of such an education, with the help of the community. Kane alluded to voluntary tutorial programs on the part of high schoolers, such as those initiated by the Brown Berets in 1968 (discussed in chapter 3) and El Movimiento Estudiantil Chicano de Aztlán students (to be discussed in chapter 8) that validated the superior value of well-supported neighborhood schools over integration by way of mandatory busing when he stated:

> I will have to say that in my mind, I'm sure that I ultimately resolved that question by feeling that the education program that we were rendering was more important than a mass bussing situation that would give complete integration.... I used to spend a lot of time visiting the program over in Juanita, and I was very, very proud of it. I loved to see the high school kids coming over in the afternoon and given [sic] their time to the children. I loved the attitude

of the staff that we had. I was thrilled with special programs, sesame street [*sic*] on the television. I couldn't help but feel that this was more important than breaking that school up and mass bussing these children all over the district and putting them in a situation where they may be very uncomfortable.⁴²

As to the Culbert site question, however, it was the inexorable activism of the Community Service Organization (CSO) and the NAACP of Ventura County (as demonstrated in chapter 1), which opposed this plan, that precluded the further segregation of students in the district. It was disingenuous for the defense to contend that the district, by its own volition, stymied the perpetuation of segregation. And, although the board may have opposed low-income housing in La Colonia, no evidence existed that it pressed such developments in middle-class areas of the town. To take credit for the dismantlement of segregation prior to the filing of the *Soria* case, the trustees could have implemented one or a combination of the numerous plans presented to the district prior to 1970, such as those by its own advisory board and Althea Simmons, field secretary of the NAACP in Los Angeles.⁴³

More brazen yet less grumpy than Mason, trustee Pfeiler, when questioned about segregation in the district, confirmed in a sangfroid manner Clowes's testimony when he admitted that he was aware of its existence in the 1950s but not bothered by it.⁴⁴ Similar to Kane and Mason, in his deposition Pfeiler likewise emphasized his opposition to busing and his focus on the provision of "proper" programs and teachers at neighborhood schools in relation to the education and specific needs of students throughout the district.⁴⁵

The Decision

In his December 10, 1974, verdict, Judge Pregerson reiterated that his summary judgement found that de facto segregation violated equal protections of the laws under the Fourteenth Amendment; the question of intent "did not raise a genuine issue of material fact" in the case. Consequently, the plaintiffs warranted the remedy of "a racially balanced elementary school system."

However, as ordered by, and in deference to, the Ninth Circuit Court of Appeals, Judge Pregerson acknowledged the necessity of a trial to find if the OESD purposely pursued a policy of racial segregation. In his adjudication of oral testimony, exhibits, and post-trial briefs, he found that the evidence proved that the OESD board since the early 1930s initiated and maintained the segregation of school children. To preempt another appeal of his ruling, Judge Pregerson quoted "deplorable" and "odious" school board minutes: "August 7, 1934: Trustee Dockstader also brought up the matter of the segregation of Mexican children. After discussing the matter at some length it seemed to be the general opinion that complete segregation was impossible at the present time and that the matter was being handled in perhaps as satisfactory a manner as could be expected. November 4, 1934: President Dockstader stated that the Board was in favor of the principle of segregation, although it might not be entirely practical at this time."[46] To fully exploit segregation, the OESD board then "established and maintained" schools, as well as classrooms, that separated ethnic Mexican and Black students from their white peers. Within schools, district officials created staggered attendance and playground schedules. When untenable, district administrators allowed the "brightest" and "cleanest" of ethnic Mexican students (as detailed in the minutes of September 13, December 12, and December 21, 1938) to share classroom space with white students. But as the student population expanded and diversified the stratagems of the board and its complicit at-will administrators, who could be summarily terminated, created byzantine policies, such as these of September 13, 1938:

> The attendance of all children in the first, second, third, fourth and fifth grades living south of Fifth Street at the Haydock School.
> The placing of white children of two grades in one class room when the classes are small and the combined classes would not be too large.
> The retention of Mexican classes as such.
> The placing of Oriental children in white classes that are not too large.
> The placing of some of the brightest and best of the Mexican children in white classes when the white class is small and the Mexican class is too large.[47]

In addition to the physical segregation of students, the district withheld quality resources from the schools that educated ethnic Mexican and Black students. When it opened, in 1940, the lighting, sanitation, and flooring of the Ramona school were grossly inferior to that of Brittell Elementary, which opened nine years later. In 1951, to address impaction, the district ordered the building of the Juanita school the next block over from Ramona rather than locate a middle-ground site in which white, ethnic Mexican, and Black students could attend together, as in the case of Wilson Junior High School, sans the school-within-a-school scheme.

Ostensibly to bulletproof his verdict from an appeal, after the review of the new evidence that proved de jure segregation, Judge Pregerson revisited the facts presented by the plaintiff's lawyer, Stephen Kalish, in May 1971. He characterized the evidence presented that year as having "de jure overtones" that consisted of open enrollment policies (which allowed whites to freely remove their children from schools predominantly attended by ethnic Mexican students, such as Ramona and Juanita), the busing of students from a Mexican school to a predominantly white campus, the location of new schools in segregated neighborhoods, and the rescission of resolutions to relocate portable classrooms to promote integration. Although there was no written smoking gun of explicit and intentional board policy to segregate in 1971, the actions of the district spoke for themselves.

Perhaps mindful that documents and data alone would not shield his decision from criticism, Judge Pregerson overviewed the testimony of past OESD superintendents Richard M. Clowes and Harold R. De Pue. Clowes testified that OESD schools were segregated during his tenure and that the board "took no action" of remedy. De Pue, whose service to the OESD trustees had ended just nine years before the trial, testified that the same mentality that compelled racial and ethnic segregation in the 1930s and 1940s existed on the board in the 1960s, despite his efforts to implement reforms. Instead, Pregerson pointed out, the district "took positive action to aggravate segregation" by constructing the neighborhood schools of Rose Avenue, Sierra Linda, and Marina West—the latter two campuses on the west side of the city and the former in La Colonia.

Due to the new evidence in the trial and the agreed-upon facts by the plaintiffs and defendants three years before, Judge Pregerson "ordered, adjudged, and degreed" that the desegregation plan of July 21, 1971, continue in "full force and effect."[48]

Integration beyond Students

An important component of the desegregation plan of 1971 included the integration of staff at all levels, as the number of teachers of color, in particular, did not reflect the diversity of the student body. Incremental progress was made in the hiring of diverse faculty between 1971 and 1975.[49] In addition, Judge Pregerson ordered that the curriculum be inclusive of the history and culture of the student population. Consequently, the district created an in-service agreement with the University of California, Santa Barbara (UCSB), and California State University Northridge (CSUN, formerly named San Fernando Valley State College).[50] The year before the trial, the OESD and CSUN's Chicana/o Studies Department agreed to have Professors Fermín Herrera and Carlos Navarro instruct district teachers in two courses: Chicano Culture and The Student of Mexican Descent and the Schools.[51] Herrera was an excellent choice for the appointment as his family's history of activism dated back to the early 1960s, when his father was a CSO member. Later in the decade, he, along with his brother Andrés and friends Roberto Flores and Armando López, spearheaded the formation of the Brown Berets in Oxnard. As a student at UCLA, he continued his activism in the Berets and presented student lectures along with Flores and López in a course taught by Rodolfo F. Acuña (a Mexican American turned Chicano) via extension classes at UCSB. Now, as a tenure-track university professor of Chicano studies, Herrera continued empowering the ethnic Mexican community, particularly youth, by way of education and the performing arts.[52]

To racially diversify its faculty, the OESD divvied up regions of the nation to recruit teachers, particularly those of color.[53] Trustee Murguia Wong tapped into the support of her CSUN network, Professors Rodolfo Acuña and Jorge García. In 1968–69 Acuña met Murguia Wong when she was a Chicano studies student. Acuña also conducted in-service workshops for the OESD; as teachers and administrators assailed him for his counterhegemonic perspectives, Murguia Wong defended him. Because the OESD personnel director charged with the recruitment of faculty claimed he could not locate ethnic Mexican teachers, Acuña suggested to Murguia Wong that the Chicano Studies Department had many majors and double majors it could train into excellent, culturally competent teachers. She presented the idea to the board, which it supported. Brekke then devoted his full authority to the plan.[54]

With CSUN's Chicano Studies Department's recruitment of students, Murguia Wong moved the plan forward from within the district.[55] García and Acuña, both of the Mexican American generation, ingeniously developed a program to produce Chicano teachers in the counties of Los Angeles and Ventura audaciously named Operation Chicano Teacher (OCT). The two then submitted a grant application to the Ford Foundation for $346,000 over three years to train 150 prospective teachers on the history and culture of Chicanos, linguistics, and educational theory. OCT covered the cost of stipends (an attractive financial incentive for working-class students), curriculum development, and operational expenses. Appointed staff vetted cohorts of seventy-five students each year of the grant's life to serve in the schools of Ventura and Los Angeles counties.[56]

Specific to the OESD, García, Acuña, and Murguia Wong obtained eight guaranteed slots for OCT students out of a total of twenty-eight teacher district intern openings. The director of OCT ensured that their candidates would have the cultural competency to instruct ethnic Mexican students. Selection committees that screened OCT applicants consisted of Chicano studies faculty, MEChA students, and community members.[57] After their acceptance OCT students participated in an intensive summer program to prepare them for the fall term that consisted of the teaching of culturally relevant art, festivals, and *baile folklórico* (folkoric dance). To qualify them for a teaching certificate, their training continued throughout the school year. In a statement to the *Oxnard Press-Courier*, William Berzman of the district administration attributed the groundwork for this innovative program to Murguia Wong, largely due to her rapport with the Chicano Studies Department of CSUN.[58]

Takeaway

Although antibusing opponents who remained in the city did not boycott the schools of the Oxnard Elementary School District under Judge Pregerson's desegregation order, many parents who resisted mandated busing did so by relocating their families to the neighboring white-enclave cities of Ventura or Camarillo. But, overall, in comparison to the aggressive protests, both rhetorical and physical, that arose in places such as Boston, Detroit, and Louisville, school integration in Oxnard moved forward without anyone being physically harmed. As superintendent of the district, in September 1975 Brekke attributed the board's steadfast legal opposition as an action that moderated the response of residents against busing, making extreme tactics of resistance such as the employment of a boycott unnecessary.[59]

This same year the OESD submitted its fourth annual report to Judge Pregerson, which examined five schools that were ethnically balanced and would remain so without busing. As a result neighborhood attendance boundaries were reinstituted for these schools. Much of this integration was due to an increase of residents with Spanish surnames having moved into more working-class neighborhoods once dominated by whites.[60] As the OESD enrollment of Spanish-surnamed students grew from 4,349 (48 percent) in 1971 to 5,361 (55 percent) in 1975, the white student population, conversely, dropped from 3,553 (39 percent) to 3,230 (33 percent). Superintendent Brekke, in the *Oxnard Press-Courier*, attributed the decrease of the white student population in the OESD to flight instigated by busing. Indeed, the enrollment of white students dropped by 318 the first year the desegregation plan went into effect in the fall of 1971.[61]

Although little support existed in the city of Oxnard to remedy segregation in the OESD via busing, the community polarized along racial lines when it became clear that white residents, predominantly on the west side of town, fiercely opposed their children being transported to schools in La Colonia that had a reputation of not only being inferior to their own neighborhood schools, but were also populated with children of color who academically performed at lower levels due to systematic racism.

Despite this resistance, district administrators such as Norman Brekke, Seawright H. Stewart, and Doran Tregarthen and their staff, as at-will employees, successfully advocated for the institution of compensatory reforms and remedies to better educate students of color. In fact, documents and oral history testimony given by Oxnard residents, plaintiff lawyers, and Judge Pregerson himself commended OESD administrators for their full cooperation in accessing district records, complying with the integration order, and seeking funds to provide compensatory educational programming. This was especially the case of Brekke, whom participants in this study recalled as a person of rectitude who cared for the provision of a quality education to all students. Unfortunately, such administrators of the OESD became the face of the board's recalcitrance.

6

Laying the Groundwork

By way of a measured militancy that entailed pertinacious civic engagement as well as direct action campaigns, activists of the Mexican American generation role-modeled for an incipient social movement of young men and women a savoir faire that manifested as an outwardly exhibited moxie. This chapter demonstrates how Ventura County organizations advocated on behalf of farmworkers—domestic and migrant, authorized and unauthorized—after César Chávez's departure in 1959 with the establishment of initiatives funded by President Lyndon Johnson's war on poverty. As part of paid job training programs, the curricula of these projects developed leadership skills in men, women, and youth. In the process, organizers and civic activists of the Mexican American generation and their allies served as role models for Chicanas-Chicanos in the continuance of a tradition of resistance with a barrio brio.

The connection between Chicana-Chicano participants of El Movimiento to *la causa* of farmworkers was that the former consisted of a transgenerational amalgam that included folk who toiled in the fields and orchards alongside their parents, *abuelitos* (grandparents), and *tías y tíos* (aunts and uncles), as well as other families of their barrios and colonias. *Chicanitos* (ethnic Mexican grade schoolers acculturated largely in the United States) too young to work in the *campos* (agricultural fields and orchards) often entertained themselves as others labored under the brutal heat, in rains, or bitter cold, at times witnessing heads of family bear the verbal abuse of *mayordomos* (field bosses), who were often ethnic Mexican themselves. Siblings old enough to carry a fruit sack or load a tray worked alongside their guardians and friends in the harvest of crops. Then there were Chicanas-Chicanos a generation away from a life in the factories in the field but often living among Ventura County agricultural workers who, to use sociologist Tomás R. Jiménez's deft definition, "replenished" the ethnic Mexican identity of individuals in and out of barrio communities. At home, during the predawn hours, Chicanas-Chicanos coming of age lay in bed, local Spanish-language radios audible, while family members got ready for their daily slog. The Chicana-Chicano generation also saw members of their community return home in crop-stained clothes and soiled footwear.[1] Family vehicles smelled of in-season produce—broccoli, chilies, lemons, and strawberries. The workers on these farms were not exclusively ethnic Mexicans; others included ethnic Japanese landowners and field managers as well as Filipino men, many *los maridos* (husbands) of *mexicanas*. Thus, agricultural life in Ventura County galvanized a transgenerational identity prior to El Movimiento Chicano.

Against Poverty

As a community crusader of the Mexican American generation, John Soria advocated on behalf of the interests of ethnic Mexicans. Subsequent to the creation of the Farm Labor Service Center, as detailed in chapter 1, Soria devoted his energies to funded war-on-poverty projects such as the Emergency Committee to Aid Farm Workers (ECAFW), the Farm Worker Opportunity Project (FWOP), and Operation Buenaventura. He also organized a local chapter of the Mexican American Political Association (MAPA) that was focused on electoral politics. The work of these organizations—like the activism of ethnic Mexicans in Salinas to the north—nurtured a benevolent base in Ventura County for Cesár Chávez's organizing of the United Farm Workers (UFW) in the 1970s.

Illustrative of a tradition of cross-cultural succor for farmworkers, Katherine Peake, the daughter of a Colorado mining industrialist and former wife of Clive Knowles, the director of the United Packinghouse Workers of America union, continued to collaborate with ethnic Mexican leaders of Ventura County as well as politically connected individuals and celebrities including Steve Allen, Max Mont, Dore Schary, John Anson Ford, and Rod Serling. In early 1965 Peake and Daniel Lund, executive director of the ECAFW in Los Angeles, recruited Peter Lauwerys of Visalia in the San Joaquin Valley to direct the FWOP from an office at 128 Colonia Road in Oxnard. ECAFW worked in partnership with the U.S. Manpower Development and Training Agency (MDTA), the California State Departments of Employment and Education, and the Oxnard Union High School District. These entities jointly received a $600,000 grant to recruit and train six hundred lumpen citrus workers for year-round employment. The project paid cohorts of forty students to learn tree pruning, fumigation, and other technical skills to address the wants of growers who complained about the labor shortage following the expiration of the Bracero Program.[2]

Lauwerys, a self-described "professional agitator," in 1969 actualized the FWOP mission to integrate farmworkers into the civic life of Ventura County as it enhanced the agency of the farmworker and nonfarmworker alike in the conduct of know-your-rights instruction. The FWOP also led Community Service Organization (CSO)–styled house meetings to discuss issues that impacted their lives. Subsequently, collective reflection led to the formulation of action-based solutions. Moreover, FWOP students split their time between vocational training and classroom instruction in civics, English, and other academic subjects.[3] This same year, under the FWOP umbrella, Lauwerys implemented Operation Harvest Hand, an initiative to train and hire counselors to advise farmworkers on locating employment and collectively bargaining for improved work conditions. Meanwhile, the leadership of the ECAFW, under which the FWOP existed, stayed in contact with Chávez to coordinate its efforts with his union. In this regard Operation Harvest Hand was an essential component in laying the foundation for the development of a farmworker union movement in Ventura County.[4]

The next year the Office of Economic Opportunity (OEO), headed by Sergeant Shriver in Washington DC, authorized $95,431 to fund Operation Buenaventura, an additional war-on-poverty project that focused on migrant workers. Peake, as the program's director, situated its office at 506 Cooper Road in Oxnard's La Colonia quarter. Like ECAFW, Operation Buenaventura functioned as a service center and leadership program for migrant agricultural workers and residents, instructing non-English-speaking heads of households (both men and women) on how to navigate bureaucracies in relation to filing taxes, attaining driver's licenses, and searching for work. With the provision of stipends, the program also educated students in locating public and private housing as well as improving their residency status.[5]

To inform Operation Buenaventura's work in the community, Peake formed an advisory committee, half of which consisted of farmworkers; a cross-cultural group of allies made up the other half.[6] The paid counselors largely consisted of a transgenerational cohort of ethnic and nonethnic Mexican residents, among them Armando López and his mentor Tony Del Buono. The counselors recruited agricultural workers as clients, among whom they selected aides to find additional people to provide guidance in relation to employment and social services. The counselors also accompanied clients to help resolve problems with public and private agencies. Through this process the counselors identified farmworkers to train in community organizing.[7] Each registered farmworker received forty-five dollars for thirty hours of instruction each week, plus mileage, to attend the classes conducted at Oxnard High School. The pay increased by ten dollars after the completion of the first week of class. Workers with children could receive up to seventy-five dollars a week.[8]

The education of farmworkers, however, threatened both the agricultural industry and the bosses at the *Oxnard Press-Courier*. In May 1966 the newspaper ran a three-part exposé on Operation Buenaventura, the FWOP, Peake, Lund, and Lauwerys. Sans any pretense of journalistic objectivity, the newspaper headlined the lead story "Farm Worker Programs—Success or Waste?" and characterized the attainment of the OEO grant by the trio as a sales job. Creepily, to encourage indignation and community acts of intimidation, the newspaper listed the home addresses of the three as well as their marital status and the amount and sources of income for each. The article, written by John McCormick, labeled them as interlopers, do-gooders, and agitators.[9] Another report audited the proposal of the OEO grant application to the actual outcomes. For example, where the proposal focused on farmworkers, the newspaper criticized the programs for servicing nonfarmworkers and providing nonvocational paid academic instruction. Tacitly, the exposé condemned the financial and educational uplift of the ethnic Mexican community to be civically engaged as well as free from the economic grips of growers. The newspaper demonstrated its interlocked interests with the industrial complex of agriculture when it published the following:

> Whether the operations have been successful during their first year with federal financing is something that is difficult to determine. In the eyes of the three heads, each is a success story.
>
> Farmers and many laborers disagree violently. They claim the money has been poured down the tubes, a complete waste and a blot against government leadership in financial management.
>
> Mrs. Katherine Peake, Dan Lund and Peter Lauwerys are the three who have guided and planned every move of the two ventures.
>
> All three share the same desire to elevate the farm laborer in mentality, education, and social position. They have each been active in farm strikes in California before their respective programs were ever financed by the government.[10]

Read inversely, as projected by the *Oxnard Press-Courier*, "farmers" and unspecified "laborers" condemned the work of Operation Buenaventura and the FWOP because they agreed with the satraps of the agricultural industry who wished to maintain farmworkers in a complete state of dependency. The agricultural regime also found the socioeconomic mobility of farmworkers intolerable; in this, Peake, Lund, and Lauwerys had sinned. Criticism toward the three for their involvement in labor strikes, if accurate, failed to contextualize the causation behind such acts: wage slavery, inhuman work conditions, the lack of health insurance and pension benefits, and the continual importation of labor to mercilessly depress extant wages.

After the exposé McCormick interviewed growers and managers of farms to publish what they thought of the work of Operation Buenaventura and the FWOP. James Lloyd Butler, a resident of the city of Camarillo and the superintendent of ranches for Ventura Farms, viewed the social services provided by the two programs as redundant to the work performed by CSO that he admitted served its clients with dignity, without the assistance of state and federal agencies. Butler also resented how the programs of Lauwerys, Lund, and Peake, in his opinion, transformed persons into dependents of the state. Howard Peto, proprietor of the Peto Seed Company, took issue with outsiders such as Steve Allen for their interference in his business. Citrus grower Ed Friel shared Peto's view and added that people such as Allen, Peake, and Lauwerys only sought to agitate agricultural workers to protest.[11]

Overall, McCormick's reports registered the vexation of the agriculture industry toward war-on-poverty projects. Their cri de coeur echoed the sententious states' rights posture of social justice critics in that they opposed federally funded interventions on the part of perceived outsiders. Since growers and related interests did not financially control war-on-poverty programs of the likes of Operation Buenaventura and the FWOP, they dog-whistled their reproach in a language of fiscal responsibility and efficiency. Meanwhile, proxies for the industry refused to admit to agriculture's acceptance of state and federal subsidies in the form of publicly funded university research, tariffs, irrigation projects, and social services that maintained a fluid supply of labor during the off season.[12]

Farmworker Verities

In addition to the delivery of services and training, in 1965 FWOP counselors chronicled farmworker realities that neutralized fictions propagated by growers' associations, ranch managers, and media that was friendly to the industry. A recurrent narrative shared by farmworkers detailed how the industry slashed wages soon after their recruitment and assigned their jobs to newly imported people from Texas or Mexico subsequent to the coup de grace of the Bracero Program in 1964. To scrounge a livable household income, farmworkers, from the elderly to the young, toiled collectively as families. But the agricultural industry's persistent recruitment of migrant workers to saturate the labor market undermined their economic viability. Hence, resident farmworkers (a.k.a. locals or domestics) of Ventura County quit rather than endure an ever-depressed wage rate. This system allowed functionaries of the agricultural industry—spokespersons and advisory board members for federal and state employment agencies appointed by elected officials—to espouse the notion that labor shortages plagued food production.[13]

When workers called grower-owned labor camps home, they and their families lived under the threat of arbitrary eviction. Indeed, company housing agreements contained an "ouster clause" that stipulated, according to one 1966 *Oxnard Press-Courier* report, that "the occupancy of the house 'after cessation of employment,' or 'during any labor dispute,' was at the discretion of the ranch."[14] The probable threat of eviction was particularly ominous, as rent at many labor camps was significantly lower compared to the open market. For example, in 1965, at the Oak Village camp in the Rancho Sespe community outside the city of Santa Paula, Roberto Soto paid ten dollars a month to live in a unit. The fact that workers like Soto were paid miserable wages made it nearly impossible for them to afford housing independent of their job sites. Hence, they survived as virtual serfs.[15]

The oppressive wage rate set by growers associations stood as another stress factor in the life of the farmworker. Interviewees such as Ramon Magdalena of Santa Paula, who worked at the Burpee Seed Company, detailed pay cuts from $1.40 to $1.25 an hour. Such wage reductions often occurred after employers successfully recruited additional migrant workers from the diasporic streams of Texas and Mexico, at which point employers culled "locals" from job sites with the ultimatum to accept the newly depressed wage rate or leave.[16]

This was the case in the orchards of Ventura County. For example, in July 1965, Frank Guzmán of Saticoy, who worked for the Briggs Lemon Growers

Association in Santa Paula, told an FWOP counselor that he had worked for Briggs since 1957. Prior to the recruitment of Texas migrant workers, the piece rate for the harvest of lemons ranged from forty-eight cents to fifty cents per box. As growers' associations inundated its pool of workers with new recruits, the wage rate dropped to thirty-nine cents. To sweat workers further, the picking of citrus intensified as yields diminished toward the end of the harvest season. When Guzmán and about forty of his co-workers complained, the company responded that if they did not like the situation they could always quit. As previously mentioned, this was a particularly dire choice if a worker and his family resided in company housing.[17]

In an interview with FWOP counselor Del Buono, Ann L. Martínez recounted how she had been recruited by an agent of Action Farm Labor to work in the packinghouse of the Santa Paula Lemon and Orange Growers Association. The headhunter promised Martínez a wage of $1.40 to pack, label, and spray citrus at a shed. Upon arrival, however, she found herself in an orchard picking citrus at a rate of $1.25 an hour. To harvest enough citrus to subsist, Martínez's thirteen-year-old son worked with her. Then the *mayordomo* charged each of them $2.25 for picking gloves that he never delivered. Since she was a seamstress in San Antonio, Texas, Martínez left the orchards after a week to return to her trade.[18]

Labor contractors, often ethnic Mexicans themselves, charged migrants from Texas and elsewhere the cost for their transportation and food. For example, a prospective employer advanced Antonio Cano of Mathis, Texas, thirty-five dollars to pay for his transportation to Ventura County and six dollars for subsistence. Once in Ventura County, many employers placed them in company-controlled—and frequently substandard—housing. Compelled to work off their debt before being set free to labor elsewhere, this was indeed a form of indentured servitude.[19]

In the strawberry fields, growers paid at a piece rate. In this scheme the average worker found themselves pitted against nimbler pickers. According to one person identified as "MY," a white male from Texas's Rio Grande Valley, field supervisors fired workers unable to keep apace. Pickers also found themselves laboring in the fields and orchards of Ventura County nine hours a day, six days a week. In the final phase of a harvest, when there was less of a crop, families struggled to sustain themselves as employers cut the piece rate.[20]

Like the testimonials documented by FWOP counselors, the June 2, 1966, edition of *El Malcriado*, the newsletter of the National Farm Workers Association (NFWA, later rebranded as the United Farm Workers) published the experience of Santa Paula citrus worker Pablo Izquierdo. One brisk morning Izquierdo and twenty-eight co-workers reported to work at an orchard of the Lemon and Orange Growers Association in Santa Paula. They believed they would be paid the prevailing wage of the previous season: thirty-five cents for each box of oranges harvested. At the conclusion of two weeks, however, they discovered to their dismay that they were paid a rate of twenty-four cents for each box. Subsequently, the workers demanded to know in advance the wage rate in a different grove. The supervisor directed them to continue their work, saying they would be informed of the rate at the completion of the harvest. The pickers refused and demanded to speak to the association's manager, Eddie Beason. At the association's headquarters at Campo Nuevo in Santa Paula, Beason, according to Izquierdo, shoved him and accused him of being a striker. The *mayordomo*, a Mr. Bob, assured Izquierdo and his crew that the wage question would be sorted out and instructed them to return the next day. They did and were arrested by the Santa Paula Police for trespassing. Ultimately, the district attorney's office dropped the charges. *El Malcriado* declaimed at the story's conclusion that the experience of Izquierdo and his co-worker was not uncommon, as growers filed false charges with law enforcement to intimidate monolingual Spanish-speaking workers that stood up for their rights.[21]

Another inequity—if not iniquity—that surfaced in the interviews entailed the conditions of housing provided by the employers. Martínez described the Santa Paula Lemon and Orange Growers Association's Grant Street residence in La Colonia of Oxnard as indecent. Rent ranged from sixty-five dollars a month for a small, one-room studio-like residence to eighty dollars a month for a larger four-room house. Each dwelling housed six to ten persons. They were also located in barrios with unpaved and unlit streets and without sidewalks or indoor plumbing. Penurious due to miserable pay, farmworker families had little to no choice than in residing in company housing offered below the market rate. Not only did growers enjoy an added stream of revenue as landlords, company-controlled housing undermined the independence of workers to freely protest not only the conditions in which they lived but also in which they worked. In one instance, however, the circumstance was complicated.[22]

The Rancho Sespe Affair

As part of the Tejano diaspora throughout the nation, in May 1965 Mario Soto and his family of eleven migrated from Mathis, Texas, to work in the citrus orchards of Ventura County's Santa Clara River Valley. The family resided in what *Oxnard Press-Courier* reporter Bob Denman characterized as a "five-room shack" at Rancho Sespe's Oak Village labor camp. At forty years of age, Mario quit his job in September to further his education in the FWOP. His family remained eligible to remain in the Oak Village camp as his wife, Anita, and son Robert continued to pick fruit in Rancho Sespe's orchards. After Anita suffered a shoulder injury from a ladder fall, the family received a notice of eviction. The Sotos' eldest son, nineteen-year-old Robert, became the family's main breadwinner and continued to work as a picker until his induction into the U.S. Army in December. This resulted in a second eviction letter, due to the fact that no one in the family worked any longer for the company that owned the camp. Anita, as directed by her doctor, asked to be reassigned to work in a packing shed. The company claimed no such job existed.[23]

With Lauwerys as their representative, the Soto family asked Rancho Sespe if they could remain at Oak Village for a year; they could pay the monthly thirty-dollar-a-month rent if Anita could work. The family's other expenses could be met by the seventy-five-dollar weekly stipend that Mario earned as an FWOP student as well as by the income of Mario and Anita's seventeen-year-old daughter Rosita, who worked in a laundry. Company officials refused the request, stating that the housing was needed for workers recruited for the peak of the next harvest.[24]

The controversy garnered the attention of members of Citizens Against Poverty (CAP) and the Oxnard Legal Aid Association. The *Oxnard Press-Courier* reported that employees of the Rancho Sespe Company worked as casuals, on a day-to-day basis, and that the end of employment constituted grounds for residents to be evicted.[25] Ultimately, the Soto family moved out of the Oak Village camp to live in the neighboring community of Santa Paula; Mario could not chance court costs if he contested the eviction and lost. But the Soto affair demonstrated the precarious nature of farmworkers' life and work, which offered little security and little freedom.

At an OEO conference in Washington DC, in January 1966, Peake, who represented Operation Buenaventura, and Lauwerys, who represented the FWOP, underscored the larger import of the Soto–Rancho Sespe dispute, as it signified the serf-like status of farmworkers. In a further restriction on their independence, farmworkers at sites such as Oak Village could not join a labor union without the threat of termination and concomitant eviction. In turn, the children of farmworkers experienced instability as the security of their residence rested on their parents' good standing with the company.[26] To remedy this modern form of feudalism, Peake and Lauwerys recommended that the federal government's Farm Home Administration (FHA) establish grants to public and nonprofit agencies to develop farmworker housing. Free from the threat of eviction by their employers, farmworkers that lived in these developments could negotiate improved work conditions or seek employment elsewhere. Lauwerys and Peake further suggested a federal program to allow farmworkers to acquire land to develop housing communities of their own. To make this happen, they proposed that the FHA provide loans and grants to families to construct or purchase residences that private lenders refused to finance.[27]

For the People, by the People

Josephine Marquez and Al Rojas accompanied Peake and Lauwerys to the OEO conference. In one of the workshops, twenty-seven-year-old Rojas spoke as the leader of CAP. He also served on the Ventura County Community Action

Commission (CAC), which was responsible for the pursuit and management of OEO funds. In his address to the audience and Sergeant Shriver, who led the OEO, Rojas expressed the need for initiatives to develop civic leaders at the grassroots level who would advocate for the poor.²⁸ After his expression of appreciation for war-on-poverty programs, Rojas stated to Shriver that the poor "don't want you to take us by the hand and lead us. Just give us the opportunity and the means to lead ourselves."²⁹

Rojas transplanted his wife and young son from Tulare County in the San Joaquin Valley of California to Oxnard in 1959. He toiled in the fields of Ventura County before he found employment in the city's sanitation department.³⁰ While working in and out of the *campos* (fields and orchards) of the Oxnard Plain, Rojas witnessed the division between domestic farmworkers (a.k.a. locals) and braceros. In fact, as a bicultural and bilingual person, at one job site the *cuadrilla* (crew) that Rojas worked with designated him their spokesperson when they shared a celery field with a discrete outfit of braceros. The locals' grievance was that the supervisor of the field provided Rojas's *cuadrilla* with damaged slickers and rubber boots during a week of rainshowers as they spied from afar their bracero counterparts, who enjoyed brand-new raingear. After one day Roja's compeers urged him to visit Chávez at the Ventura County CSO office. Once there Chávez admonished Rojas to organize his crew and make the demand for the same functional equipment issued to braceros; if the farm supervisor refused, they should stage a sit-in. Chávez also informed them of the consequences: termination and arrest by law enforcement for trespassing. In the end Rojas and his co-workers followed Chávez's advice, and the field boss met their demand.³¹

After Rojas's departure from the fields to work for the city of Oxnard, in 1963 he attended a community meeting organized by Soria, who worked for the ECAFW—at the time affiliated with the Quaker organization the American Friends Service Committee—to mobilize the community to demand that city officials desegregate its schools. It was at this event that Soria befriended Rojas. Ultimately, Rojas became one of twelve FWOP community aides. Over time, Lauwerys, a talented grant writer, obtained war-on-poverty funding for the creation of CAP.³²

As the leader of CAP, Rojas countered Rancho Sespe president T. A. Lombard's contention that a labor shortage of farmworkers existed in Ventura County. To debunk the industry's recurrent lies about worker shortages, Rojas dispatched twenty-eight men from FWOP headquarters in La Colonia to apply for jobs at the Lombard Ranch. They were turned away due to a lack of openings. Rojas's claim was further supported by a report on February 2 by John V. Newman, president of the Ventura County Citrus Growers Committee, who documented an oversupply of citrus workers in the county.[33] This surplus labor pool worked to the benefit of the industry, as it allowed growers to depress the wage rate to expand their profit margin.

The United Farm Workers Omen at Egg City

On the cool morning of Thursday, July 13, 1967, 100 workers walked out of Egg City, one of the nation's largest egg producers, near the unincorporated community of Moorpark. The plant employed a total of 250 people. Led by Oscar Gonzales, the strikers demanded recognition of the United Farm Workers (UFW)—an independent union not associated with Chávez's relabeled organization by the same name—as their bargaining agent. Julius Goldman, the company's owner, downplayed the severity of the action when he declared that only 20 of his workers originally walked out; another 80 followed upon the coercion of outside agitators. Goldman also labeled the strike illegal under the Taft-Hartley Act of 1947, which proscribed job actions that left livestock unattended. In a riposte that exposed the division among ethnic Mexicans, Gonzales accused Goldman of employing "wetback" (unauthorized migrant Mexican national) workers.[34]

As the strike intensified, Rojas joined Gonzales, with the title of UFW vice president. The two organized picket lines at Egg City and the State Employment Office in Oxnard. The picketers in Oxnard protested the agency's delay to certify the strike, since this would stop the office's referral of workers to the plant. Rojas also planned the establishment of picket lines at the Border Patrol office in Oxnard and the Department of Immigration in Ventura to expose the Egg City plant's employment of undocumented migrants.[35] On the sixth day of the strike, Rojas contacted the U.S. Department of Justice to further ban

Egg City's use of unauthorized migrant workers. He then led twelve picketers to the office of Congressman Charles M. Teague.[36]

The fact that the racist "wetback" label was used so freely by U.S. citizens and longtime resident ethnic Mexicans evidences the tension that existed among workers. Many local ethnic Mexican workers who were U.S. citizens and authorized residents reviled the presence of unauthorized migrants, as they often replaced them at work sites at lower wage rates. But they also loathed the fact that employers, via labor contractors, exploited their unauthorized co-ethnic brethren at their economic expense. This divisive reality was so normalized that ethnic Mexican U.S. citizens and longtime migrant residents (e.g., Chávez and Ernesto Galarza, respectively) utilized the "wetback" epithet in a frank manner similar to how white characters in Mark Twain's *The Adventures of Huckleberry Finn* voiced the racial pejorative toward slaves.[37]

The Santa Barbara Committee to Aid Farm Workers donated food and monetary support to the Egg City workers on strike. In an address to the group, former Democratic congressional candidate Stanley Sheinbaum stated, "These people get as little as $1.15 an hour. They are trying to do something for themselves. They are desperate. There is no such thing as a strike fund. You can't save much for a rainy day on $1.15."[38] The strikers received other translocal and intraethnic support. The Ventura Organizations Council for Agricultural Labor, a self-described humanitarian group, raised money and acquired foodstuffs and clothing for the strikers. Educator John Flynn, chairman of the group Kay Senior, and other teachers called upon civic organizations to donate. Ventura County MAPA chapter president Vincent Godina sponsored the attendance of sixty strikers at the organization's annual meeting in San Bernardino, where MAPA passed a resolution of support for the workers as well as contributions for a family relief fund. Rojas and Gonzales also spoke to a group at a Santa Barbara coffee house that resulted in additional donations.[39]

The emphasis that the UFW placed on Egg City's employment of unauthorized immigrant workers gained traction. In an *Oxnard Press-Courier* report of July 19, 1967, titled "5 'Wetbacks' Arrested at Egg City," assistant chief inspector of U.S. Border Patrol in Oxnard Dale Swancutt announced the arrest of five unauthorized migrant workers as part of a "routine check." This same day the State Employment Office certified the strike.[40] In defense of his plant, Goldman held that the law did not require employers to demand proof of legal residency upon employment.[41]

As events unfolded the Superior Court of Ventura County granted Goldman a temporary injunction that prohibited the UFW entry into his plant but not from picketing the facility.[42] Nonetheless, with the injunction in place, Goldman further attempted to undercut the efforts of Rojas and Gonzales by elevating the wage rate. Goldman faulted Rojas and Gonzales with not allowing the strikers to accept his offer.[43] Based upon both a discussion between Goldman and a seven-member "grievance committee" of Egg City workers, on July 26, 1967, the two sides reached a settlement. With Moorpark merchants Ruben Castro and Abe Menashe serving as mediators, Goldman agreed to raise the minimum wage at the plant to $1.45. The agreement also entailed the establishment of a recognized grievance committee and the workers' rejection of the UFW.[44]

In response to the settlement, Rojas and Oscar Gonzales organized a two-day protest march from the streets of Oxnard, to and through the communities of Saticoy, Fillmore, and Santa Paula, concluding in Moorpark. The mediated agreement, however, ended the labor dispute.[45]

"An Anathema to Some Men, Hero to Others"
Since 1958, when Chávez created a CSO chapter in Ventura County to assist the United Packinghouse Workers of America combat agribusiness's corruption of the Bracero Program, he remained connected with civic activists such as Del Buono, Soria, and, later, Rojas. During the election season in particular, he stumped for favored local and statewide candidates friendly to the interests of ethnic Mexican communities. In Oxnard he addressed audiences at either Juanita Elementary or the adjacent Colonia Recreation Park. In the community of Santa Paula, he spoke to fans at La Casa del Mexicano. Farmworkers and their supporters (many of whom graduated from ranch-related work to careers in the public sector and the unionized trades of construction and commerce, among other industries) traveled from around the region to listen to Chávez's updates on the struggle of *campesinos* (agricultural workers).

In 1966, for example, MAPA of Ventura County, headed by Soria, organized an electoral rally in Santa Paula. At this event Chávez stirred the audience with an account of the NFWA's challenges and victories. One report consisted of Governor Edmund Brown's refusal to meet with him after the NFWA's March to Sacramento that year. He also explained how Bert Corona, MAPA's statewide president and a Mexican American generation confrere, subsequently mended affairs between Governor Brown and himself. Chávez praised Corona's ability to convey the issues and demands of farmworkers in a manner that convinced Governor Brown ultimately to support, in his words, "the first farm labor election in the history of the country." In the achievement of this milestone, Chávez hailed the transgenerational support for his union, declaring, "We were successful because we had justice on our side. We were faced by a solid opposition from every community agency and force—chambers of commerce, city council, boards of supervisors. Only two elements fought for us—the churches and students."[46] As an example, Chávez shared how, when he spoke at the University of California, Berkeley, on the steps of Sproul Hall, he asked students to contribute their lunch money to *la causa*. In one hour students contributed $5,000 to post bail for jailed picketers in the DiGiorgio fight of September 1965. After Corona's appearance in Santa Paula, Del Buono introduced him to a group of one hundred people in Oxnard. Corona explained the history and work of MAPA before introducing Charles Storke, candidate for Congress. Like the previous speakers, Storke articulated the Democratic Party's platform entirely in Spanish. He concluded with an imprimatur to Chávez's cause: "I am solidly behind the farm worker."[47]

Two years later, in April 1968, Chávez addressed an overflow crowd at Juanita Elementary in La Colonia. In a report on the event, the *Oxnard Press-Courier* described him as an "anathema to some men, hero to others," as well as physically haggard, due to his recent conclusion of a twenty-one-day fast. As a member of senator Robert Kennedy's California delegation, Chávez announced that Republicans did not support the cause of farmworkers. He then went on to endorse Kennedy for the Democratic presidential nomination. To mobilize supporters, as he did as a CSO organizer, he announced a drive to register one hundred thousand voters in California. He also stated his opposition to the Vietnam War, as it was inconsistent with his belief in nonviolence.[48]

Chávez went on to remind the community that he stood by domestic workers in the struggle against the preferential hiring of braceros in 1959, but he admonished the crowd that Ventura County farmworkers were not prepared to walk out of job sites. As he articulated the NFWA's aversion to striking, however, he recognized the capacity of a union to embark upon other job actions to compel employers to negotiate. His union, moreover, would only strike against large growers; small operations would not be targeted, Chávez declared, as their problems were worse than those faced by workers. And, like Lauwerys and Peake, Chávez called for union, governmental, and grower cooperation in the development of programs to train workers so they could work year-around at a given locale. Chávez then promised that, when a labor dispute occurred in Oxnard, "we will win—or will keep coming back until we win."[49]

Takeaway

Prior to the rise of the farmworkers' movement in Delano, California, with the grape strike of 1965, immigrant and domestic agricultural laborers in Ventura County had been primed for action by the groundwork laid by intrepid organizations such as CSO, the FWOP, and Operation Buenaventura. Cross-cultural allies aided the efforts of ethnic Mexican activists of the Mexican American generation to advance the rights of workers in Ventura County. As they challenged industry abuses, people such Tony Del Buono, Peter Lauwerys, Katherine Peake, and John Soria served as role models of leadership for youth of the Chicana-Chicano generation. And, as César Chávez led the campaigns of the National Farm Workers Association into state, national, and international prominence, Ventura County activists both young and old were further inspired to improve the status of agricultural workers in their own communities, especially as he had been one of their own since the late 1930s. So, even though Chávez did not identify himself a Chicano, he articulated the *coraje* (indignation) that compelled youth and many ethnic Mexican adults to adopt this label as they resisted the abuses of institutionalized power.

Chapter 7 will show how the farmworker movement in Ventura County paralleled the strikes of the NFWA in the San Joaquin Valley and other parts of California. These job actions energized the activism and support of the Chicana-Chicano generation, who understood the struggles of family, neighbors, and friends who toiled in the grounds of Ventura County.

7

¡Que vivan las huelgas!

As César Chávez's National Farm Workers Association won international attention for the grape strike and boycott that it ignited in 1965, labor protests germinated in Fillmore, Moorpark, Oxnard, and Santa Paula. Although the fight in the fields of the San Joaquin Valley encouraged these struggles, the groundwork laid by the Community Service Organization (CSO), Operation Buenaventura, and the Farm Worker Opportunity Project cultivated for it a transgenerational leadership. The strikes that ultimately erupted in Ventura County benefited from the wisdom of veteran activists of the Mexican American generation as well as the exuberance of Chicana-Chicano youth. This fueled direct actions not only against the mighty interests of the agricultural industry, but also the law enforcement agencies that encompassed the border patrol, courts, police, and sheriff. This collective resistance invited media coverage that in turn provoked the spread of protests across the county. Therefore, in this chapter I argue that agricultural labor struggles in Ventura County, as part of a larger national movimiento, stirred the passions of ethnic Mexicans of the Mexican American and Chicana-Chicano generations in defense of a largely migrant-Mexicanist population of workers in terms of their national identity.

The Fillmore Citrus Strike of 1970

On the balmy Friday night of July 17, 1970, César Chávez addressed a crowded room of devotees at Our Lady of Guadalupe Church in the city of Santa Paula to announce the enlistment of Ventura County citrus workers as dues-paying members of the United Farm Workers Organizing Committee (UFWOC). Local union organizers, led by its president, Pablo Izquierdo, a founder of Santa Paula's CSO chapter, accomplished this after two years of covert efforts in the county's orchards and fields. Subsequently, upon the pleas of residents to start a union movement in Ventura County, local Friends of the Farm Workers member Arthur S. Gómez mentioned the intention of Chávez to return Sunday to the community at Santa Paula's La Casa del Mexicano at 218 South Eleventh Street to thank the community for its "moral and material" support during the five-year grape boycott and listen to the grievances of citrus workers in Fillmore.[1]

In the *Oxnard Press-Courier*'s reportage of Chávez's Friday visit, it noted his CSO history in the county. Chávez's myth expanded in a July 26 report of the *Ventura County Star-Free Press* that claimed he held his first picket sign as a twelve-year-old, in an Oxnard labor dispute. Similarly, residents involved in the bitterly fought 1941 Ventura County Citrus Strike reminisced about the participation of their own families. Even Ivan McDaniel, a Los Angeles attorney for the growers of Ventura County, recalled his work on behalf of Charles C. Teague, president of the Ventura County Fruit Growers Exchange in 1941 and founder of the notorious violent union-busting organization the Associated Farmers.[2]

A day before the assembly at Our Lady of Guadalupe Church, on July 16, approximately five hundred citrus pickers left in protest the orchards of the F and P Growers Association in Fillmore. As insisted upon by other workers previously, they, too, demanded the announcement of the pay rate before the start of each workday and a raise in the existing wage by five cents. The workers added to their demands a $2.50-per-hour base wage, health benefits, and lower housing rents as the citrus harvest season winded to a close. Due to the variation of the size of the trees as well as the grade and quantity of fruit from orchard to orchard, manager of the Ventura County Citrus Growers Committee Warren F. Wegis alleged it virtually impossible for the growers to determine the wage rate in advance.[3]

At a harvest season's height, 4,000 citrus workers—mostly men, but also women and youth able to fill a sack with lemons or oranges—toiled in the groves of Ventura County. But, this time, they struck. Gómez, in the role of spokesperson for Friends of the Farm Workers, informed the press that pickers of Rancho Sespe and Rancho de los Campanos deserted the orchards in solidarity. Hence, the number of strikers grew from approximately 350 to 500 throughout the Santa Clara River Valley. By July 19 an estimated 2,000 citrus workers in the county had walked out of the citrus orchards.[4]

To raise the profile of this labor struggle, 180 people picketed the entrance of the Fillmore Citrus Association before sunrise each day. On July 22, starting at 4 a.m., Chávez marshaled a procession of 50 men, women, and children from the F and P Growers labor camp in Fillmore to an orchard in the neighboring community of Piru to draw out *esquiroles*, or scab workers. This steadfast group enticed 5 pickers to leave a Piru orchard with their bags as they shouted, "Viva la huelga!"[5]

The home of the Aparicio family in Fillmore served as strike headquarters. A young Ben Aparicio, the eldest son, worked alongside his parents and seven siblings in the orchards and fields of Southern California. And, as his parents stressed the importance of an education as a pathway for a better life, in 1970 Benjamin attended Moorpark College and worked part-time as a picker in the orchards of the F and P Growers Association. As the chosen representative of citrus workers who demanded advance written knowledge of an orchard's wage rate, the ranch manager fired Aparicio on May 29. His brethren walked out with him and declared a strike. Subsequently, in consultation with UFW leader Gilbert Padilla in Delano, the pickers organized themselves into the Santa Paula Farm Workers Committee (SPFWC). Ben's sister, Manuela, drafted leaflets that pronounced the demands for union recognition, improved housing, increased pay, and the statement of the wage rate prior to the start of a day's work. Moreover, the SPFWC called for improved communication between white managers and workers, since many of the former did not speak Spanish. The strikers also charged growers with wage thievery and refused to return to work unless they provided porta potties in the orchards for the workers. The latter demand was critical, as crews often consisted of families. As far as conditions outside the orchards, the SPFWC protested the high rents charged by the citrus associations for substandard room and board at labor camps.⁶

As Chávez rallied supporters throughout Ventura County, the intransigence of the capos of the citrus industry began to falter. President of the Fillmore Citrus Association Russel Hardison declared the growers' decision to grant a paid annual vacation benefit to citrus workers as well as establish the pay rate at orchards before the start of each workday. He then went on to contest the charge that the camps charged exorbitant rents for substandard residences. Area growers, he argued, created twenty-eight new residential units and remodeled fifty-five existing homes. Newer units rented at fifty-five dollars a month, and the older homes ranged from thirty to thirty-five dollars.⁷

The strikers rejected the concessions of the Fillmore Growers Association, which had not included in a written contract their demands for UFWOC recognition as their bargaining agent, improved sanitation at job sites, and the appointment of bilingual personnel to facilitate communication between field bosses and citrus workers.⁸ Although the workers desired UFWOC representation, extant labor law under the federal National Labor Relation Act did not apply to field or orchard workers—only those in agriculture's packing sheds. But, after thirteen days, the strike ended on July 29, 1970. In exchange for paid vacations based on the hours worked during a year and the statement of wage rates at orchards before the start of picking, the citrus workers surrendered the demand to have the UFWOC recognized as their bargaining agent. Without a written contract, this led to the resumption of the orange harvest in the orchards of Fillmore, Moorpark, and Piru. To save some face, field bosses claimed no crop losses due to the walkout, but the partial labor victory in Fillmore shook industry leaders. Consequently, toward the end of August 1970, the Matilija Growers Association in the county's Ojai mountains announced its decision to grant forty hours of paid vacation after the completion of nine hundred hours of orchard work in a year.⁹

Notwithstanding the concessions made to the workers, sans a written contract or the recognition of a bargaining agent, the conclusion of the Fillmore citrus strike vexed Ventura County's agricultural industrial complex as Chávez's union claimed victory in the five-year-long grape boycott in the San Joaquin Valley. New walkouts then erupted in places such as the Salinas Valley, one of the nodal points on the migrant worker circuit along the California coast, approximately 250 miles north of Ventura County. The idea of a similar tide of unionism in their fiefdom panicked the wealthy grower class. To inoculate themselves against imminent strikes, the citrus industry announced a plan to survey its employees to find out if they wanted to "remain independent" workers and to have the "freedom of choice" to consider a bargaining agent to represent them. Even though a tradition existed of bitter labor disputes resulting in modest wage increases minus the recognition of a collective bargaining agent or contract, Warren F. Wegis, manager of the Ventura County Citrus Growers Committee, paternalistically maintained that growers were "not opposed to their field harvest employees joining a union of their own choice as long as their choice is free of undue influence, threat or other coercion by any labor organization or for that matter, a grower." The county's citrus barons claimed that both the Teamsters union and the UFWOC incurred upon the jurisdiction of labor contractors absent the consent of the workers as well as formal elections. In the minds of the leaders of the agricultural industry, workers were mindless pawns to be protected from union agitators. Furthermore, amid the 1970 Fillmore citrus strike, the grower class created a declaration of independence for workers to "voluntarily" sign. Employers contended that this right-to-work document protected workers, since no elections were held about the representation of UFWOC or the Teamsters.[10] County citrus growers also held that,

> for many years, citrus harvest empolyes' [sic] earnings in Ventura County have been constantly increasing to the point that our growers pay among the highest annual agricultural wages in the state. At the peak of our harvest in the county, nearly 4,000 field harvest employes are covered by fringe benefits, such as medical and health insurance, life insurance and annual paid vacations, which few agricultural employes receive in the state or nation. The majority of our growers have been providing these benefits to their harvest employes before

any of the growers in the state signed contracts with the Teamsters Union or the United Farm Workers Organizing Committee.[11]

The growers created and disseminated the independence document to ensure that agricultural workers remained un-unionized, even though they claimed it was a private "informational letter" to be signed by their employees when "asked." But, if a worker refused, and their families lived in company housing, they risked termination and eviction. Moreover, before the citrus industry publicly rolled out its survey and declaration of independence, the *Ventura County Star-Free Press* published on September 7, 1970, a letter written by Gonzalo R. Casillas, who viewed the declaration as another example in which the agricultural industry oppressed the ethnic Mexican community.[12] Three days later the newspaper published the reaction of V. H. Graig Jr., general manager of the Limoneira Company in Santa Paula, who accused Casillas with misinterpreting the private letter distributed to the company's employees.[13]

Let Them Have Lettuce

Four months after the contretemps between Casillas and Graig, in January 1971 Chávez returned to Ventura County to lead a UFWOC picket line at the U.S. Naval Construction (SEA BEE) Base Center in the city of Port Hueneme, adjacent to Oxnard. The protest involved the Bud Antle Lettuce Company, a federally contracted supplier that enjoyed a sweetheart labor agreement with the Teamsters. Chávez's participation in the picketing nationally publicized the military's purchase of Salinas-produced lettuce boycotted by his union.[14] Three months later, in April 1971, the UFWOC signed a contract in Oxnard with the Mel Finerman Company, which produced lettuce on three thousand acres of land on the Oxnard Plain worth $3.9 million. The preemptive contract established a $2-an-hour minimum wage, or a 40.5-cents-per–lettuce box piece rate. In addition, Finerman contributed 10 cents for every hour of work to the UFWOC's medical fund as well another 5 cents per hour to an economic development account. The two sides consented to a grievance process, as well as health and safety procedures for workers, especially those who came in contact with pesticides. Under the written bargain, Finerman agreed to hire workers out of a UFWOC hall as well as to mark boxed lettuce with the UFWOC label. With this victory Chávez declared a moratorium on the lettuce boycott to allow growers who had signed contracts with the Teamsters to switch over to his outfit, since the two unions decided to have the UFWOC represent workers in the fields while the Teamsters organized workers in the canneries.[15]

The Finerman agreement represented a major victory for the UFWOC as the company—with operations in Arizona, California, Colorado, New Mexico, and Texas—shipped some 160 million heads of lettuce annually. This contract set an hourly wage of six dollars for 5,100 cabbage and lettuce workers' forty-five-week harvest season. The pact breached the collusion of the agricultural industry that hypocritically espoused antiunion right-to-work rhetoric. As a result, the Free Marketing Council, the public relations arm of the vegetable industry, howled that other lettuce producers would not be intimidated by a UFWOC boycott.[16]

Five months later, on September 16, 1971, Mexican Independence Day, to encourage a work stoppage the UFWOC in Oxnard booked a mariachi band to perform at 6 a.m. at a bus pickup for pepper and tomato fieldworkers while the union catered them breakfast. Perhaps to suggest the rebirth or awakening of workers as conscious agents resisting oppressive economic systems, the mariachis played "Las Mañanitas" for those disembarking from the buses. While enjoying food and song, four hundred men and women ignored the queued buses ready to transport them to job sites. William Manking, an organizer charged with the advancement of the union's efforts in Ventura County, averred to the press that the job action demonstrated the UFWOC's ability to recruit new members. With the transport of workers to the fields on the Oxnard Plain stymied, the UFWOC led the men and women on a march through the city's streets. The procession stopped in front of the offices of known labor contractors. As the protesters paraded past the agricultural fields that surrounded Oxnard High School, students of farmworker lineage scaled and squeezed through campus gates to join the demonstration. These students also convinced the protesters to circle the high school before heading toward the city's east side. Once at Colonia Park, the campesinos, students, and community feted Mexico's holiday and their protest action with barbecued food, more mariachi music, and dance.[17]

No follow-up media reports on local activities of the UFWOC surfaced between September and early April 1972. But on April 17, 1972, the UFWOC established a picket line of approximately sixty people at the Finerman office at 300 East Third Street in Oxnard. Gale Ray Ortiz, a UFWOC leader of the demonstration, his wife, Barbara, and twelve lettuce workers barricaded the building's entrance. Discomfited, Finerman claimed to the press that he did not know the reason behind the protest, as his company had honored the pact signed in 1971 that was not due to expire until 1973.[18] But apparently the UFWOC was protesting the company's use of casuals to fill the gap between the number of workers needed and those provided by the union for the lettuce harvest at a Saticoy site. The union also objected to speedup harassment by one of the field supervisors. The work stoppage affected one thousand acres of lettuce and cut production by 50 percent. To end the dispute, union representatives and Finerman met in private at UFWOC La Paz headquarters in Keene, California, and in Oxnard. The two sides focused on nine undisclosed points of dispute. One accommodation that leaked to the press was the removal of the field supervisor in question. In the end the two parties attributed the controversy to poor communication and different interpretations of agreed-upon work conditions as stipulated in the 1971 contract.[19]

It behooved industry bosses to promote peace in the fields and groves, as the labor of campesinos fueled a multimillion-dollar economy. In January 1974 the *Ventura County Star-Free Press* reported the value of the crops for 1972: lemons, $64 million; tomatoes, $17 million; strawberries, $16 million; celery, $25 million; sugar beets, $1.3 million; and the production of lima beans, $2.1 million. Concurrent harvests of avocados, citrus, strawberries, and other produce throughout the county in large part caused a shortage of five hundred workers with 85 percent of the product still in the fields.[20] The citrus marketing cooperative known as Sunkist enjoyed $381 million in sales in 1973—a 9 percent increase from the fiscal year of 1971–72, which brought in $349 million. In 1972–73 agricultural sales rose 31 percent above the average in the previous five years.²¹ But the boom in corporate profits failed to translate to a commensurate increase in farmworker wages.

The Strikes of 1974

A year and a half after the dispute in the lettuce fields, two hundred citrus pickers walked out of Santa Clara River Valley orchards on January 23, 1974. Despite the record incomes listed in the previous paragraph, rapacious citrus magnates slashed workers' pay. Prior to the strike, pickers earned one dollar per box, the equivalent to a sixty-pound sack of citrus. The SP Growers Association dropped the piece rate first to eighty cents per box, then to sixty-five cents. And, as in 1970, pickers were not privy to what they would earn at a site until noon the next day. In addition to the cut in the wage rate, the workers protested work conditions of harassment, as well as workweeks that exceeded forty hours without overtime.²²

Head of the Ventura County Citrus Growers Association (VCCGA) Lee Chancey called the labor dispute a misunderstanding and said that the piece-rate schedule confused the workers.²³ As in 1970 the SP Growers and the VCCGA argued that the wage rate could not be determined before the start of a workday due to the discrete nature of each orchard. The rate of pay based on this criterion could only be set after the workday's start. However, to settle the labor dispute, the VCCGA abruptly promised to set and post the piece rate for each orchard within three hours of each morning.²⁴

The citrus workers rejected the concessions made and added the demand for the establishment of a grievance committee at all SP Growers Association sites. But the growers refused to negotiate. To plan their next move, the strikers, their families, and community allies congressed at Las Piedras Park in Santa Paula. Here the strikers accepted food and other donations from organizations such as El Movimiento Estudiantil Chicano de Aztlán (MEChA; the Chicano Student Movement of Aztlán) at the community colleges of Ventura and Moorpark, the American Federation of Teachers, and La Casa del Mexicano. Even a Jeep loaded with food arrived, compliments of the Friends of the Farm Workers chapter at the University of California,

Santa Barbara. In this meeting the citrus workers decided to petition Chávez's union to spearhead their fight.[25]

The strikers then formed El Comité de Campesinos de SP (the Farm Workers Committee of Santa Paula) Growers Association. Steve Harvey and Richard Weinstock of the Legal Aid Association of Ventura County, George Castañeda (proprietor of Gil's Market in Santa Paula), Father Duncan McDonnell, and citrus workers Juan Gonzales, Juan Barrios, and José Baez served as El Comité's representatives. The ag bosses' representatives were attorney Leon Gordon, Lee Chancey, Jim Beekman of the Briggs Lemon Association, an unnamed translator, and growers Keith Barnard and James Sharp. The two sides met at Las Piedras Park. The growers offered to raise the piece rate per box by 3 cents, and the pickers accepted. The growers also agreed to fully pay the unemployment insurance premiums of the workers as well as augment the hourly minimum wage from $1.65 to $2. The pickers rejected this wage rate and countered that the piece rate must translate to $3 an hour for experienced pickers. Additional demands entailed a 20 percent increase in the piece rate on muddy days, since such conditions hampered the productivity and safety of pickers, who performed their work on ladders. This also applied to hilly orchards. Poorly pruned trees warranted a 15 percent increase.[26]

Meanwhile, citrus workers in the area consulted with Chávez and UFWOC representatives, and in early February they obtained an 8 percent increase in the piece rate. The SP Growers Association also promised not to increase housing rents for at least one year. To help offset the economic hardship endured by the strikers over the two weeks of the strike, the growers agreed to extend a fifty-dollar advance to each worker and to defer unpaid rent.[27] But, again, the farmworkers failed to obtain the recognition of the UFW as their bargaining agent. Despite the platitudes they issued, the plantation bosses refused to make this concession.

Two months later, on May 24, 1974, pickers of a different sort walked out of the strawberry fields of Ventura County.[28] Months in advance they clandestinely collaborated with peers from the Salinas Valley within and outside of ranches, organizing workers in meetings and passing out mimeographed flyers. On May 29 Cecil Martínez, owner of the Martínez Berry Company, applied for a preliminary injunction and a restraining order against the picketers. He claimed $15,000 in losses for every day the strike continued and an additional $1 million in overall damages. That same day Manuel Chávez (erroneously reported by the local press to be César Chávez's brother; he was his devoted cousin) spoke to a crowd of five hundred at Juanita Elementary in La Colonia. At this meeting, Manuel Chávez pledged $500,000 in UFWOC aid for the strike. Roberto García, the leader of the Salinas strawberry strike, revealed a translocal network of agricultural workers when he informed the audience that this victory to the north earned a sliding pay scale tied to field conditions. For example, at the start of the harvest season, when the fruit serried strawberry plants, the contract set a pay rate of 90 cents a box. Toward the end of the crop, however, workers earned $1.10 a box, due to diminution in production. At this point of the harvest season, pickers struggled even more, as this class of strawberries was designated frozen food, which required the labor-intensive removal of stems from the fruit. During this phase Salinas pickers earned $1.60 an hour after June 1 and $1.80 after August 1.[29]

After Roberto Flores's arrest for his alleged lethal dirt clod assault upon a sheriff's department helicopter, the UFWOC posted a $1,000 bail bond for his release. To cull a key leader in the strike, the sheriff's department swiftly rearrested Flores at a work site after he refused court documents served by Deputy Bill Hunt. When a fellow striker took the restraining order and placed it in Flores's car, Flores retrieved the document and placed them at Hunt's feet. The deputy then arrested Flores for littering.[30]

To protest law enforcement's collusion with the strawberry plantations, UFWOC organized a march through the city of Oxnard on the evening of Saturday, June 1, 1974. César Chávez joined in and vowed to get over 2,000 persons arrested, in order to overwhelm the county jail. With an initial crowd of over 300 that quickly expanded to 1,500, Chávez likened law enforcement's practices in the county to that of the terroristic Texas Rangers. Meanwhile, UFWOC picketers caravanned from ranch to ranch to implore the strawberry pickers who remained in the fields to join their cause. Accompanied by 100 strikers, UFWOC attorney Ellen Lake later petitioned the Oxnard City Council to direct the Oxnard Police Department (OPD) to cease its suppression of strikers' activities. Lake further informed the council that in order to check such police actions, the UFWOC recruited the support of white clergy and attorneys to serve as observers. In this regard, Lake stated, "it's a sorry reflection on the motives and tactics of the police that only when white-faced people are present can they treat brown-faced people with dignity and respect." Lake then balanced her reproach with the commendation of OPD officers for their low profile throughout the procession on June 1.[31]

In early June Tony Guilen of the State Department of Employment Development estimated that 40 percent of strawberry pickers of the Oxnard Plain participated in the strike and questioned the effectiveness of the job action, as it was already late in the harvest season. Furthermore, the court sanctioned proscriptions that continued to divert the energy of strawberry strikers. On June 19, 1974, the UFW conceded the struggle.[32]

At the conclusion of the strawberry strike, the *Ventura County Star-Free Press* resurrected from the shadows of the agricultural industry Hector Zamora, Chávez's nemesis in the CSO's Bracero Program protest of 1958–59. As the manager of the Ventura County Agricultural Association (VCAA), Zamora attributed the failure of the strawberry strike to two forces that undermined UFWOC's effectiveness. The first entailed the firebombing and vandalism of farm equipment. Growers accused the strikers of setting the camp housing of workers on fire as well as packing sheds. UFWOC protesters conversely accused the growers of torching their own sheds to malign the union's moral authority, especially as Chávez espoused a commitment to nonviolence. But there were members of the UFW that went out on their own to commit arson to intimidate the strikebreakers. Other members confronted them for these actions and told them to cease and desist.[33]

The second point that split the unity of strikers, Zamora contended, was Chávez's decision to cull grower-exploited, unauthorized migrant workers from the strawberry fields by way of their deportation. This infuriated people such as Flores, and many other ethnic Mexican families with loved ones with mixed-residency status: some U.S. citizens and authorized migrant Mexican nationals, as well as unauthorized residents. The deportation tactic further divided the strikers, as many of them and their supporters witnessed violent deportation raids that traumatized many in the larger ethnic Mexican community. It was not unusual for authorized residents—U.S. citizens and Mexican nationals alike—to be swept up in the process of such dragnets. Hence, many UFWOC supporters resented Chávez's use of this stratagem. In fact, people viewed Chávez's denunciation of the brutality of law enforcement as hypocritical, since he had unionists survey farm operations that exploited unauthorized migrant workers to alert *la migra* (the border patrol) for their deportation. To make matters worse, Chávez isolated UFWOC members such as Flores who called him out on this practice.[34]

A couple of weeks after the conclusion of the fight in the fields, superior court judges issued decisions in the favor of the UFW. In one case a judge granted the union's request to restrict the enforcement of an Oxnard ordinance that prohibited the use of neighborhood sound trucks. Furthermore, a trial confirmed the union's contention that law enforcement exercised its authority to defeat the strike. And on July 5, 1974, a jury acquitted Ramiro Ahuamada, who was charged with the battery of a police officer that involved a thrown rock. Similarly, a judge dismissed the charges against Flores for the rock assault on a sheriff's department helicopter.[35]

After the conclusion of the strawberry strike of 1974 and its concomitant legal fights, Zamora announced on July 21, 1974, the VCAA's elevation of the minimum wage for row-crop farmworkers from $2–$2.15 per hour to $2.55. Parroting face-saving pronouncements in past labor disputes, Zamora emphasized that the recent strikes did not influence the decision of the VCAA. This claim does not ring true, however, as the wage increase not only followed two significant strikes but also a caravan demonstration conducted by Friends of the Farm Workers. During this audacious act of community solidarity, vehicles filled with UFWOC supporters traveled from community to community in Ventura County. At its height eighty automobiles joined the convoy, which included supporters from other unions besides the UFW—interestingly, the Teamsters among them. And, despite the minimum wage increase announced by the VCAA, Flores, who was identified by the press as the spokesperson for Friends of the Farm Workers, stated that the

UFWOC would continue to work for the improvement of conditions of row-crop workers.[36]

Labor peace in Ventura County did not last long. A month later, on August 20, 1974, 120 pickers blew out of the orchards of the Santa Paula Citrus Association (SPCA). Many of the strikers participated in the labor dispute against the Briggs Lemon and Mupu Citrus Associations that ended that February. José Rodríguez, the strikers' spokesperson, informed the press that the workers demanded a 25 percent wage increase from the February settlement.[37]

Apparently, supervisor De Wayne "Buck" Basolo instigated the new strike when he switched a crew from a lemon orchard to an orange orchard at a reduced pay rate. This translated to approximately a weekly minus in take-home pay of $60 to $70. As the strike continued, José Rodríguez, spokesperson for the strikers, clarified that the pickers earned $8.33 for each seventeen-box bin of lemons, per the February agreement of 1974. Picking oranges, on the other hand, garnered only $4.96 per bin. Tired of being ripped off in one way or another, the pickers demanded $10 for each bin of lemons harvested and $8 for oranges.[38]

As the strike progressed, Rodríguez appealed to Ventura County students of the Chicana-Chicano generation in the creation of picket signs and food drives for the families of the strikers. Many answered his call. At the behest of their Mexican American generation professors and advisors, students also joined strikers on the picket line to convince approximately forty pickers that remained in the orchards of Santa Paula to walk out. At this time the citrus pickers also claimed that their employers repeatedly violated the conditions set in the February agreement, which entailed the growers' promise to hire bilingual field bosses, particularly from within the associations so that interested employees could apply. The agreement further promised compensation for wet time; otherwise, pickers would not have to report to an orchard until after a morning's dew had evaporated. The rate of pay was supposed to be announced three hours before the start of work, and the growers had also agreed not to blacklist leaders of the January strike. Growers, however, permanently fired one such person and distributed the names of others to the ranches of other growers.[39]

Barnard responded to the charges. First, if workers had a "legitimate grievance," the growers sought to address them. He also denied the firing of any worker due to their participation or leadership in the previous citrus strike. The two sides also could not agree on the rate of pay per hour and the worth of bins.[40] Consequently, the number of pickers who walked off the job grew from 150 to 180. Pruning crews joined the strike as the UFWOC embarked on an aggressive recruitment campaign. The workers met at the home of George Castañeda, owner of Gil's Market in Santa Paula. Castañeda participated in the negotiations of the previous walkout. In addition to the creation of a mechanism to address grievances, Rodríguez stated to the press that the strikers demanded that their cost-of-living wage be raised, Basolo removed as their supervisor, and growers honor the agreement of February 1974.[41]

On September 4, 1974, as negotiations stalled, Chávez met with the strikers, their families, and supporters at Santa Paula's La Casa del Mexicano. He warned the audience to "be prepared to go hungry," as a protracted battle loomed. Chávez then pointed to the specter of the Citrus Strike of 1941. Perhaps in respect to an antipathy toward workers who remained in the strawberry fields in the last strike, which manifested in confrontations and the arson of camp housing, Chávez advised the audience to reach out to the workers that remained in the orchards to convince them to join their cause. "You do this by talking to them, not beating them up," Chávez stated.[42]

To settle the strike, president of the Santa Paula Growers Association Ives Vanoni announced on September 6 Basolo's removal and replacement by Ralph DeLeon, formerly an assistant manager of the Oxnard-based Coastal Growers Association, as well as the SP Growers Association's desire to restore harmony. Despite this overture, the next day, Saturday, September 7, 1974, a transgenerational march of two hundred citrus workers and their supporters, some as young as two years old, participated in a twenty-mile protest march from the city of Oxnard to Santa Paula. Three days later the two parties agreed to a settlement at Las Piedras Park in Santa Paula. The accord entailed an 8 percent wage increase, changes in rental housing agreements, renegotiated vacation time, and, as previously mentioned, the banishment of "Buck" Basolo.[43]

Beat the Teamsters

As strikes swelled in Ventura County, the Teamsters promoted their presence. In the first week of December 1974, Art Chavarria, secretary and treasurer of Teamsters Local 186 in Carpinteria, announced the union's membership goal of six to seven thousand agricultural workers between the counties of Santa Barbara and Ventura.⁴⁴ Four months later, on March 29, 1975, the Teamsters signed contracts with three vegetable growers on the Oxnard Plain to represent five hundred workers: the Tanaka Brothers, United Celery Growers, and the Dave Walsh Company. The contracts, however, largely failed to raise the pay of most fieldworkers, at $2.55 an hour. Specific to strawberries, in May 1975 Dave Walsh and G & T Berry Farms in Oxnard also signed contracts with the Teamsters. As part of the agreements, the two companies tacitly admitted to larceny, with the disbursement of $38,000 in worker back pay for their failure to honor a piece rate agreed upon in a prior contract.⁴⁵

To contest the inroads made by the Teamsters, UFWOC dispatched its crackerjack organizer, Eliseo Medina, to Ventura County in mid-June of 1975. But, before his arrival, another strike of two to three hundred workers erupted earlier in April, again at the Egg City plant. The company's use of temporary workers, particularly Vietnamese war refugees, aggravated the dispute. As the walkout continued in Moorpark, this was where Medina focused his attention. The Friends of the Farm Workers of Ventura County quickly supported the Egg City strikers, and its spokesman, Leopoldo Urias, expressed to the press that the workers voted not to have the Teamsters represent them after the current contract expired. Soon after the start of the walkout, Ventura County Superior Court judge Richard C. Heaton issued a restraining order against the workers, as a "no strike" clause existed within the 1970 contract. Judge Heaton's decision also prohibited the establishment of pickets no closer than a mile from the plant as well as the barricade of its entrances. The workers defiantly shredded Heaton's order upon receipt and carried on an around-the-clock picket line. Meanwhile, Egg City management confirmed that nearly all its workers joined the walkout. Each day of the work stoppage cost the company $30,000.⁴⁶

In marked contrast to the actions of his agency in the strawberry strike of 1974, Ventura County sheriff Al Jalaty decided, with the imprimatur of district attorney C. Stanley Trom, not to enforce Judge Heaton's order, to avoid the criticism of bias in the favor of the Egg City plant. He also instructed his deputies to intervene only when they witnessed acts of violence and the destruction of property. Barring this litmus test, Jalaty declared that the strikers in the labor dispute enjoyed a wide berth in their freedom of speech and right to assemble.[47]

In late June and early July, Medina and the UFW organized a demonstration march throughout the Oxnard Plain. At this event Medina witnessed Chávez's popularity. In fact, at a July 12 rally in Moorpark Chávez's presence attracted three hundred strikers and supporters. As the picketing continued in Egg City, in defiance of the restraining order, the strikers publicly issued their demands to both Julius Goldman, the owner of Egg City, and the Teamsters, which entailed the reinstatement of four hundred fired workers involved in the strike at the salaries they enjoyed before they walked out. This was in addition to back pay and the termination of replacement workers. And, although the Egg City strikers favored UFWOC representation, they expressed their readiness to resume work and negotiate, temporarily, as an independent bargaining unit.[48] Since Egg City management rejected the demands, individuals and groups in and out of Ventura County, such as Friends of the Farm Workers, offered their support to the strikers. El Teatro Campesino of Santa Barbara entertained supporters at a fundraiser in Moorpark as the Ventura County Community Action Commission (CAC) collected food donations.[49]

Meanwhile, hostility grew between local workers—both citizens and long-term residents—Vietnamese refugees, and unauthorized Mexican migrants. In response to his employment of the latter two groups, Goldman expressed his empathy toward the Vietnamese in Ventura County as a German Jew who had escaped the horrors of Nazi Germany. The question then arose if the Agricultural Labor Relation Board (ALRB) would allow the replacement workers to vote in an election. As Medina criticized Egg City's use of strikebreakers, he funambulated his point to avoid alienating public opinion, which was sympathetic to a people seeking sanctuary from the ravages of a civil war: he characterized the Vietnamese replacement workers as a captive group. Reverend Wayne "Chris" Hartmire, Chávez's devoted attendant, did not hesitate, however, to characterize the fenced company housing at Egg City afforded to Vietnamese refugees as a "concentration camp."⁵⁰ As to unauthorized Mexican migrant workers, the Friends of the Farm Workers, led by Urias, picketed the U.S. Border Patrol office to pressure agency officials to raid job sites and deport such persons.⁵¹

As the labor dispute stretched into July, Medina telegrammed Goldman to formally demand an election to determine the collective bargaining agent at the plant under the anticipated Agricultural Labor Relations Act (ALRA), to be in effect that August. This raised the question of whether the strikers would be allowed to vote under the new law. The managers of Egg City and the Teamsters argued against it, due to the no-strike clause in the extant labor contract. Furthermore, the strikers had been fired and replaced since the walkout.⁵²

Chávez reemerged in Ventura County on Saturday, July 12, where he gave a speech to the strikers and their supporters in which he defined the contract between Egg City and the Teamsters as a sweetheart deal. That Sunday he traveled to Oxnard, some forty minutes southwest of the plant, to address a thrilled audience of two thousand that hung on his every word. Chávez encouraged the community to organize and be prepared to take advantage of the enactment of ALRA on August 28. To connect with his audience at even a deeper level and dispel rumors that he never worked in agriculture, he shared that he had gone to school in Oxnard from 1938 to 1939 as his family traveled California's migrant circuit. He went on to detail his involvement in the battle against the industry's exploitation of braceros to depress the wage rate and displace domestic workers in 1958–59.⁵³

Before the initiation of the ALRA, with a board to settle labor disputes, Egg City and Teamsters representatives agreed to a three-year labor contract. As another example of wonted wage embezzlement in agriculture, the agreement offered $20,000 in back pay to July 1 to the current workers, as well a new rate of $2.95 an hour. The contract also afforded a 60 percent increase in insurance benefits and an additional week of paid vacation. Another concession entailed ten-minute breaks and a thirty-minute lunch (which perhaps suggests no breaks and even a shorter lunch before the contract). The remaining workers at Egg City approved the contract in a vote of 207 to 36.⁵⁴

The fight at Egg City intensified as Medina and Benjamin Chávez, a fellow UFWOC organizer, along with strikers Ermina Becerra of Fillmore and Trinidad Villa of Moorpark, attempted to enter the plant on July 28 to speak to workers. In response plant managers called law enforcement to press charges for trespassing. But district attorney Trom refused to prosecute in order to avoid the accusation of favoring business interests over that of labor. In anticipation of the implementation of the ALRA, Judge Robert L. Shaw granted the strikers more latitude in relation to demonstrations at the plant. On September 2, moreover, he allowed fifteen UFWOC organizers into the Egg City plant to recruit support in the anticipated election. Urgency set in for the UFWOC as the ALRA mandated the conduct of an election seven days after the filing of a petition for such a vote, which the Teamsters had done on September 2. Hence, the UFW needed to obtain authorization cards from 20 percent of Egg City employees to be on the ballot by September 9. In addition to the question of the eligibility of replacement workers to participate in the vote, both sides differed on whether the strikers would be considered as part of the total number of employees. To buy additional time to gather the required signatures to be on the ballot, the UFW cunningly filed its own ALRB petition.[55]

ALRB Elections

On September 11, the vote was held to determine if the Teamsters would continue to represent Egg City workers or if UFWOC would be their new bargaining agent. Before the election Medina announced the intent of his union to challenge every ballot cast by workers hired after April 10, the date of the start of the strike. In the case of the UFWOC's defeat, if the number of challenged ballots potentially affected the outcome of the vote, the union would appeal the results to the ALRB in Sacramento. As Egg City workers prepared to cast their votes, Chávez visited them and other agricultural laborers in the county who faced imminent elections of their own, to drum up turnout. After traveling up and down the two-lane roads in the citrus communities of Fillmore, Santa Paula, and Somis, Chávez concluded his visit in Oxnard, where he addressed an audience of 1,200 at the city's civic auditorium. Ultimately, however, the tally at Egg City did not favor the UFWOC: the Teamsters won 189 votes to the UFWOC's 114. UFWOC lawyer Deborah Peyton, however, did not concede the election, as she challenged ballots that potentially could turn the vote.[56]

The official result of the Egg City election remained undetermined as of November 1975, as two principal questions held up ALRB certification. The first involved the board's delayed definition of a striker. Since the Teamsters refused to endorse the wildcat strike at the plant, the question remained of whether the Egg City employees that walked out enjoyed the right to participate in the election, or had they given up that status when they left their jobs without the support of their bargaining agent. Second, the UFWOC—the entity that adopted the cause of the Egg City strikers when the Teamsters refused to back them—also filed charges of unfair labor practices. In addition to these two points, all sides awaited the decision of the ALRB defining an "economic striker" in relation to a vote at Gallo wines in Merced. State officials initially allowed strikers to vote. Ironically, a Teamster protest held up the certification of the election at Gallo as well as at Egg City. Therefore, the question was if 166 votes cast in favor of UFWOC at Egg City would count.[57]

Three years elapsed before the ALRB decided to include the 165 votes in the original tally cast by the strikers. To add to the intrigue, before the recount could take place burglars stole the ballot box of the Egg City election on September 9, 1975, from the ALRB office in Oxnard. Nonetheless, spokesperson for UFWOC Marc Grossman responded to the press that that his union would file a motion to certify the UFWOC's victory. Management of the Egg City plant, on the other hand, viewed the company as caught between a battle between the UFWOC and the Teamsters.[58]

In the end UFWOC won the election to represent the 400 workers at the world's largest egg production plant. The ALRB reported that the 131 workers that had been on strike in 1975 voted for the UFW and 13 for the Teamsters. ALRB officials added these votes to the original vote count of September 1975 that recalculated the total to 245 votes for UFWOC and 202 for the Teamsters.[59]

As the strike at Egg City in Moorpark continued, Medina recognized an organic *coraje* (rage) that existed in Ventura County, particularly that of the vegetable workers on the Oxnard Plain. Consequently, as UFWOC director for Ventura County, he developed a strategy to unionize vegetable and citrus workers simultaneously via elections throughout the area. To this end Medina filed five petitions to have union elections under a new secret ballot law against West Foods in Ventura, Hiji Brothers Farms in Oxnard, K. K. Ito Farms in Camarillo, Watanabe Ranch in Oxnard, and the Brokaw Nursery in Saticoy. To verify UFWOC authorization cards, Ralph Perez of the ALRB matched them with an employers' list to see that 50 percent plus 1 of workers favored a union election. Medina stated to the press that UFWOC had gathered seven thousand cards at 275 farms throughout Ventura County. Due to this effort, one month after the passage of the passage of California's Agricultural Labor Relations Act in June 1975, Ventura County agricultural workers made up UFWOC's largest contingent of members.[60]

By late September the UFWOC had defeated the Teamsters union in an election to represent strawberry workers in the fields of the Tanaka Brothers Company. The ALRB Office reported that the UFWOC garnered 121 votes to the Teamsters' 43. Eighteen workers voted for no union. As a result of this victory—the seventh for UFWOC in a three-week span at a ranch formerly represented by the Teamsters—Medina claimed to represent over 1,000 farmworkers, making his outfit the largest agricultural union in the county.[61]

Takeaway

The strikes in the orchards and fields and the Egg City plant evinced the bond of ethnic Mexican labor resistance in Ventura County with that of César Chávez's fight in the fields all over the state. At the same time, the poised struggle of campesinos for improved life conditions for themselves and their families emboldened youth of the Chicana-Chicano generation to take actions of their own with the support of faculty and staff advisors at high school and college campuses in and out of Ventura County.

Although Chávez did not self-identify himself as a Chicano, he did empathize with the struggles of the Chicana-Chicano generation as they vehemently supported *la causa*. So, as his union—with the support of such acolytes—fought for the dignity of the farmworker in the pursuit of just wages and improved work conditions, including housing and fringe benefits, Chicana-Chicano youth followed this example in their communities as they witnessed elders and peers in the fields resist with brio the might of bosses and law enforcement who were largely white. As in the case of the UFW's fights in the field, they understood that the realization of an American ethos of justice for all would have to be fought for intrepidly, with the help of a wide spectrum of allies like those who supported the union of César's dreams.

8

Chicana-Chicano Agonists

Raised in a community culture of collective resistance, youth of the Chicana-Chicano generation—ranging from children old enough to recall earlier events to men and women in their early to mid-twenties—observed, if not participated in, the insurgencies of outfits such as the Community Service Organization (CSO), Farm Worker Organizing Project, and United Farm Workers throughout the 1960s to mid-1970. Such groups role-modeled struggle, often militant, largely to realize just work conditions. With this community memory Chicana-Chicano agonists made their presence known on school and college campuses as news spread of student walkouts and protests throughout the Southwest. They also heeded the direct actions of peers in organizations such as the Students for a Democratic Society (SDS) and the Black Student Union (BSU). This compelled many of the Chicana-Chicano generation to ask, "What are we doing?" As a result they embarked upon gutsy actions of their own. This chapter argues, in this regard, that the Chicana-Chicano generation of Ventura County exerted its collective agency on campuses and in their communities to mobilize campaigns of self-determination with a moxie all their own.

The World of the Chicana-Chicano Generation

Like their Mexican American generation predecessors, many Chicanas-Chicanos dreaded school, where in their early lives they suffered or witnessed violent punishments, both physical and psychological, at the hands of callous educators for using the language of their Spanish-speaking parents—an experience that destroyed their ability to excel. Such was the case for Yvonne De Los Santos from the unincorporated Ventura County community of Saticoy. Injured by such assaults, and the associated slings of poverty, the self-esteem of Del Los Santos and many of her peers deteriorated with each school day.[1] The school system instantiated the inferiority of ethnic Mexicans with the curricular erasure of their historical presence in the nation as well as by systematically tracking them away from pathways to college to vocational shop classes for boys and home economics for girls.[2]

While ethnic Mexicans lived in rural citrus communities such as Fillmore, Rancho Sespe, and Saticoy, their experience also encompassed the suburban and urban. At Ventura County's northeastern edge, the metropolis of Los Angeles was less than an hour's drive away. Families traveled regularly to the big city and were visited by kin from places such as Boyle Heights, Compton, and the San Fernando Valley. So not all Ventura County Chicanas-Chicanos were yokels, at least completely. Having a rurban consciousness of the town and city, many of the Chicana-Chicano generation understood the spectrum of material deprivations of working-class people, having often accompanied family and neighbors to harvest *chabacanos* (apricots), *nueces* (walnuts), *fresas* (strawberries), *ciruelas* (plums), and other specialty crops up and down the state. While on the migrant circuit, they lived in varied accommodations from the standard to the inhumane—for example, cashiered Quonset huts, barns, stables, and leaky tents.[3]

Ironically, the poverty of ethnic Mexican families was underscored when family breadwinners—both men and women—obtained often unionized or public-sector jobs that provided not only adequate wages to cover food, shelter, and clothing but also unemployment, pension, health, and vacation benefits. When these heads of household were so employed, Chicana-Chicano children experienced the smell and feel of new clothes, shoes, and toys. Such work also made possible enrichment opportunities in organized sports and the performing arts. Indeed, De Los Santos recalled how her family enjoyed such comforts when her father had the good fortune to obtain a job as a unionized construction worker. As a result of the incremental elevation in their quality of life, Yvonne's mother made sure her husband stayed current in his union dues, even when no work was to be had.[4]

Elders relayed to youth historical acts of collective resistance as children eavesdropped on the conversation of their parents and relatives. Unionism that organized all people provided ethnic Mexicans and their families with a system of recourse to challenge arbitrary dismissals, wage theft, and oppressive work conditions, as well as to fight for the prized benefits of health and unemployment insurance, vacation, and retirement. From these stories Chicanas-Chicanos internalized a sense of group dignity.[5] Other families who may not have been directly connected to organized labor were involved in service organizations such as the Unión Patriótica Benéfica Mexicana Independiente, Las Guardianes de la Colonia, and CSO. Therefore, when Chicana and Chicano youth refused to tolerate injustice, they consciously or unconsciously referenced examples of the collective action of prior generations.[6]

Storms Brewing

The righteous indignation of Chicana-Chicano student clubs in Ventura County—which ranged and fluctuated in membership from ten to seventy students—stemmed from the overall subordination of the ethnic Mexican community. The diversity of club labels signified the pursuit of students to define themselves not only in terms of their ethnic identity but also in relation to their citizenship and political temperament. For example, before the creation of El Plan de Santa Barbara in the spring of 1969, many ethnic Mexican student clubs in Southern California named themselves, commensurate with the mentalité of the generation before them, United Mexican American Students (UMAS), as was the case at Oxnard High School. At Ventura High a similar club was labeled La Alianza Latino Mexicano (the Latino Mexican Alliance), which alluded to the organization's pan-Latino outreach, with the simultaneous recognition that the ethnic Mexican student population was its core constituency. In the northeast plain of Oxnard, Rio Mesa High School formed the Mexican American Youth Organization (MAYO) while Moorpark High formed the Mexican American Youth Club. Many group's cognomens fluctuated as members weighed and debated labels based on their mission, member disposition, and the way they wished to be understood by people from the outside.[7]

No matter how student clubs of Ventura County identified themselves (although many ultimately adopted the MEChA epithet, the acronym for El Movimiento Estudiantil Chicano de Aztlán), they shared a commitment to support peers and those that followed them in the K–12 system. The evangelic promotion of education by Chicana-Chicano student clubs signifies the failure, if not the refusal, of educators to communicate high academic expectations for ethnic Mexican students or to support their aspirations. Chicana-Chicano youth also questioned their societal status as they defined their identity. To counter racist assumptions, Chicana-Chicano students embraced and publicly promoted their Mexican heritage as an iteration of Americanism. To bridge intraethnic differences, some clubs sought to support teachers with monolingual Spanish-speaking students.[8]

Indeed, the right to express themselves in the language of their community unimpeded served as a means by which Chicana-Chicano students asserted their amour propre, given that educators for decades prohibited ethnic Mexican students from speaking Spanish. This proscription entailed violence, to use Chicano studies professor Roberto D. Hernández's definition, that entailed being forced to wear dunce hats as well as having their hands struck with rulers and their mouths washed out with soap.[9] To resist these assaults, which were grounded in settler colonial notions of white supremacy, in the spring semester of 1969 UMAS at Channel Islands High School in South Oxnard, with a membership of about seventy-five, drafted a constitution that restricted, irrespective of race and ethnicity, its membership to Spanish-speaking students. This bold attempt to centralize their ethnic Mexican heritage, however, disqualified the club from school recognition, as the state's education code mandated that clubs be open to all students. This compelled a faction of UMAS students and their supporters totaling about forty to picket the campus administration building in February 1969. UMAS protesters also sought redress in relation to instructor racism and the lack of ethnic Mexican teachers.[10]

In 1970 Oxnard High School (OHS) students protested racist practices on the part of teachers and the absence of support services. Part of the conflict involved the refusal of students to accept advisors from within the district, since they found the faculty and staff unsympathetic to their interests. To quell the controversy, officials of the Oxnard Union High School District (OUHSD) reached out to the Association of Mexican American Educators (AMAE) to appoint a volunteer advisor from the community. The issue of racism in the schools on the Oxnard Plain reemerged the next year when chairman of the Oxnard Community Relations Commission Wallace Taylor reported that one OUHSD teacher allegedly had been asked to resign or face dismissal for calling students "n——" and "dumb Mexicans." Fellow commissioner William Terry announced that this was an example of the hostility that students faced. Terry also referenced how campuses restricted UMAS from becoming an official club and suspended students who wore such buttons.[11]

On September 16, 1971, Mexican Independence Day, OHS Mechistas joined farmworkers of the United Farm Workers Organizing Committee (UFWOC) in protesting working conditions. Familiar with the staff at the UFW Office in La Colonia off Cooper Road, MEChA president Peter Martínez suggested that the protestors march around the school site. When they did so, he and other Mechistas yelled to their peers on campus and in class, "Walk out! Walk out! Walk out!" And many did. High school administrators subsequently punished 40 student participants with detentions and suspensions. The next week half of OHS's 2,100 students blew out. As this took place, Black and brown students fought white peers. After the initial outbreak, other brawls flared later that afternoon. Pent-up frustrations united those who walked out. The situation then escalated to the point that campus officials shut down the school at 1 p.m. on Thursday, September 23. Later that evening a free-for-all erupted at a football game between Channel Islands High School and Simi High. Consistent with other instances of social unrest that involved disaffection with white-dominated institutions, Principal Clifford Powell told the press that he was clueless as to the cause of the uprising.[12]

In early October 1971 a contingent of Black and Chicana-Chicano students of La Colonia barrio formed the Minority Affairs Committee (MAC) to address grievances of racism in the schools and the lack of teachers, staff, and administrators who were reflective of their community. Their demands also included the institution of Black and Chicano studies in the curriculum. MAC met at the Juanita Elementary and protested the establishment of a district committee of students, teachers, district administrators, and community representatives that did not include them. They viewed the involvement of Oxnard City councilperson Salvatore Sánchez as an accommodationist who undermined the interests of minority constituents.[13] Sánchez responded to MAC's opposition to his inclusion on the OUHSD committee by stating, "I consider it an honor to be considered a threat to the real enemies of our community. . . . I feel these people are not only hurting the image of the Mexican-American but are bringing disgrace to those who are truly trying to become a part of our mainstream."[14]

A month after the conflicts at OHS, the campus administration office was firebombed on the evening of Saturday, October 30, 1971. The persons responsible marked the walls with "Racist Pigs" and "We Declar [sic] this a racist school," initialed with "CLF," assumed to stand for the Chicano Liberation Front.[15] On November 2, 1971, the *Oxnard Press-Courier* published an editorial on the arson attack. In a tone of condescension, the newspaper faulted district officials for the adoption of a "rap-session approach" to address tension within its schools.[16] In this dialogue, however, participants aired their grievances on topics of racist teachers throughout the district, arbitrary and unequal discipline meted out to minority students in comparison to their white counterparts, and the lack of minority faculty and administrators.[17]

Go to School, Stay in School

Chicana-Chicano students, however, did not limit their agency solely to the redress of grievances. In 1973 Channel Islands High's MEChA—composed of 140 members, the largest campus club in the district—sponsored service activities in the community such as a clothing drive for the needy in Mexico's border city of Tijuana. It also held car washes for the recreation center of La

Colonia. To raise additional funds, the organization sponsored a semiformal *tardeada* and *jamaica* (a late afternoon social and charity sale, respectively). To fill the vacuum of a culturally relevant curriculum, the club produced a literary magazine titled *Nuestra Raza* that advanced ethnic pride by way of the arts.[18] In the course of these activities, MEChA organizations networked with each other across the district. That same year MEChA at Rio Mesa High School launched its third annual tutorial program at El Rio Elementary and sponsored an annual Christmas food drive.[19]

Many students of these high schools graduated to continue their activism at universities and community colleges in and out of Southern California. In numerous instances the pipeline of barrio students to academic institutions involved an advance guard of students. Once on campus a consciousness of ethnic Mexican scarcity hit them hard. Indeed, when Diana Borrego Martínez of Santa Paula spotted Chicana-Chicano students at San Fernando Valley State College (SFVSC) in the late 1960s, she waited in front of their classes to introduce herself. In other instances, first-generation college students from the barrios and colonias of Southern California as well as afar congressed at de facto sanctuary spaces near student unions and cafeterias. Once Chicana-Chicano students discovered each other, often via restorative organizations such as UMAS and MEChA, they embarked upon recruitment drives in their home communities to cajole—if not shanghai—friends into college; such was their mission. Yvonne De Los Santos credited students active in Moorpark College's MEChA for her matriculation. Once on campus, De Los Santos enjoyed the organization's esprit de corps. Alienated, even traumatized, by the K–12 educational system, MEChA and Chicano studies courses cultivated a rich awareness of the worlds from which they came. Prior to the widespread institutionalization of Educational Opportunity Programs in California colleges and universities, such organizations also served as the support structure for the recruitment, retention, transfer, and graduation of students.[20]

As a Vietnam veteran wounded by a land mine while on patrol, Jess Gutiérrez returned to Oxnard and found employment as a salesperson at a local car dealership. High school classmate and fellow veteran Armando López visited him one day at his work to recruit him for Moorpark College. At first Gutiérrez rebuffed the idea: he was older than most college students and had a family to support. But López was persistent, and he eventually convinced Gutiérrez to enroll after explaining that he could receive more income as a full-time student with his veteran benefits and other financial aid than at his current job.[21]

A snowball effect of matriculation resulted. Once politicized, Chicana-Chicano college students recruited friends in and out of Ventura County. Many that enrolled did not survive academically for a number of reasons: some (especially men) due to a severe lack of preparation, confidence, finances, and the inability to envision the rewards of a higher education. However, success stories did emerge. The first wave of Chicana-Chicano students ultimately turned the corner scholastically with the committed support of not only their peers but also empathetic faculty and staff mentors from all backgrounds who were sensitive to the debilitating harm of interlocked white supremacist systems of education, labor, and politics. Students considered by many to be academic throwaways went on to become public and private sector professionals, which afforded them and their progeny improved life chances in terms of health, superannuation, the accumulation of assets, and the life of the mind.[22]

The Community College Connection

In the fall of 1967, Moorpark College opened its doors. To promote enrollment, officials of the Ventura County Community College District contracted a vendor to transport students from the communities of Fillmore, Piru, Santa Paula, and Oxnard to both Moorpark College and Ventura College. Chicana-Chicano students from Oxnard nicknamed the service the "barrio bus." A cohort of youthful and politically liberal faculty at the new campus—many of them recent graduates of the University of California, Los Angeles (UCLA), to the south, and the University of California, Santa Barbara (UCSB), to the north—embraced all students, especially the historically underserved.[23] Once out of their provincial environs, Chicana-Chicano community college students interacted to an extended degree with peers from a spectrum of ethnicities and economic backgrounds.

By the start of 1968, Oxnard Brown Berets López and Roberto Soria, the brother of Oxnard school desegregation advocate and community leader John

Soria and father of the principal plaintiffs of the desegregation case, engaged peers in the formation of culturally relevant programs at Moorpark College. The Berets and Mechistas invited UCSB professor of economics and Democratic candidate for Congress Stanley Sheinbaum to speak on campus.[24] In October 1968 the Berets attended a conference on poverty hosted at Ventura College. López, as the group's prime minister of education, organized a peaceful demonstration to protest neglect on the part of county social workers in relation to the needs of ethnic Mexican communities. As López spoke, fellow Brown Berets held placards that read "Less Talk and More Action" and "Viva la Raza." The Berets also presented a slideshow complemented by music and narration that detailed the Chicano perspective on poverty in Ventura County.[25]

As one of its main goals, high school and college MEChA organizations promoted as well as reinforced a sense of ethnic Mexican pride to extirpate any stigma internalized in some of its members by way of settler colonial perspectives in schools and a popular culture that not only erased the historical presence of ethnic Mexicans but also portrayed them in the present as outsiders, and often criminal at that. The provenance of self-negation, moreover, stemmed from decades of institutionalized racism and violence. Mechistas bolstered the promotion of amour propre with community-building programs in and outside their campuses. Toward this objective, Ventura County MEChAs embarked upon tutorial programs to serve grade school students. In an interview with Moorpark College's student newspaper, the *Raiders Reporter*, López described MEChA's goal as "to develop the child's self-concept and identity." Soria, in turn, asserted the importance of bilingual education to maintain and reinstate pride in young ethnic Mexican students.[26]

Raising consciousness of the challenges historically faced by ethnic Mexican communities served as another goal of MEChAs in Ventura County.[27] In November 1969 the *Raiders Reporter* spotlighted the student activism of Soria, who had suffered the loss of a brother in the Vietnam War, experienced economic deprivations associated with migrant life, and who dropped out of high school to work in the fields to support his family.[28] Soria's life lessons, coupled with his activism, ballasted a constructive indignation and motivation to challenge societal injustices. Given that Moorpark College was a startup campus that supported curricular innovation with few-to-no faculty with academic training in the Mexican American experience, the administration afforded Soria, López, and other students opportunities to formally teach classes and deliver lectures to their peers on the history, culture, and politics of the Chicano community.[29]

Be One, Bring More than One

El Plan de Santa Barbara (drafted by students, faculty, and staff from different institutions at UCSB in the spring of 1969) served as the manifesto for Chicanas-Chicanos of all ages, as it delineated the goals and objectives of MEChA. A central tenet of El Plan guided all in academe with the advancement of education in the community. Ventura County Chicanas-Chicanos actualized this mandate by visits to elementary schools to volunteer their time as tutors. For example, Oxnard Brown Berets Francisco DeLeon, Roberto Flores, Andrés and Fermín Herrera, and Armando López visited the elementary schools of Juanita and Ramona, in the heart of La Colonia, to conduct culturally relevant puppet shows. The Brown Berets of Oxnard also implemented a tutorial program in the district. The Berets then worked with the administration of Moorpark College to establish a program of recruitment and support services. In an era of a white, middle class–focused curriculum that featured "Janet and Mark" and "Dick and Jane" narratives, the Berets created curricula that spotlighted the ethnic Mexican experience.[30]

Even before the creation of El Plan in 1969, Chicana-Chicano students at the colleges and universities of Moorpark and Ventura, SFVSC, UCLA, and UCSB also went back to the barrios and colonias from which they came to encourage family and friends to become activists and obtain a higher education—not only for the sake of their own edification and empowerment, but that of their communities. In February 1969 López, while a student at Moorpark College, spoke at Rio Mesa High School to share with students the goals and objectives of the Brown Berets, an agenda that consisted of social change by way of the promotion of Mexican American studies, the establishment of a citizens' police review board, and the promotion of better communication with the community. In relation to direct action, López stressed the organization's commitment to a nonviolent philosophy.[31]

Later in November 1969, UCSB Mechistas Daniel Castro, Castulo de la Rocha, and Javier Escobar drove forty-five minutes south to meet with the members of Ventura College MEChA to discuss, among other challenges, the state's high school dropout rate among ethnic Mexicans. The three guest speakers also noted that of those that managed to graduate, many were academically ill prepared, particularly in comparison to their Black and white counterparts. The next year Tim Vásquez of UCSB's MEChA visited Ventura College to recruit Mechistas to join him in Coachella Valley to assist the United Farm Workers in stopping scabs from picking grapes during the strike. Vásquez also urged the Mechistas to participate in the moratorium march to be conducted in Santa Barbara that May.[32]

To motivate Chicana-Chicano students to stay in school and ultimately obtain degrees from the systems of the California State College and the University of California, Flores, as an Oxnard Brown Beret and UCLA premed student, worked with a newly established Educational Opportunity Program (EOP) to create in 1968 a nonprofit work-study project titled the University Study Center (USC). Based in Oxnard, USC placed approximately thirty high school and college students within public agencies. This had two functions: first, to provide students with incomes while they obtained on-the-job training in professional environs, and, second, to introduce students to white-collar careers that required college degrees. In some cases Chicana-Chicano activists virtually ushered family and friends off barrio streets to enroll them in such programs. EOP slots had opened up at universities and colleges as a result of protests such as the walkouts in East Los Angeles that year; it was now incumbent upon activists who demanded this inclusion to fill them. A number of the individuals who had no plans of going to college due to a multitude of challenges (e.g., school tracking, preparation, maturity, economics, family obligations) failed to succeed, while others initially struggled to survive and then flourished as they created social networks of support on campus.[33]

But the USC project was not just for the college-bound. It also served professionals who sought to enhance cultural competencies to effectively serve the ethnic Mexican community. For example, UCSB offered an extension course in the summer of 1969 titled Mexican-American: Past, Present, and Future, conducted at the Juanita school by Brown Beret members Fermín Herrera, Flores, and López along with Professor Rodolfo F. Acuña of SFVSC.[34]

A Space for Chicano Studies

In April 1969 MEChA, with a membership of approximately forty, met with Moorpark College president John Collins to propose the implementation of a curriculum relevant to the experience of ethnic Mexicans as well as recruiting and admitting more students from their communities. To retain students MEChA called for the college's employment of ethnic Mexican faculty, staff, and administrators. Students would endorse the appointment of candidates and recommend their termination if they failed to serve students.[35] President Collins supported MEChA's proposals. His actions contrasted with that of campus presidents at Ventura College, California State College Los Angeles, California State College at Fresno, and San Diego State College who rejected Chicano studies. Many campus presidents labeled this new field as ideologically particular in scope as opposed to universal and therefore not a legitimate academic course of study, due to its perceived Marxist radical politics.[36]

Nonetheless, in the fall of 1969, Moorpark College recruited its first director of the Mexican American Studies (MAS) Program: Amado Reynoso, who held degrees from San Diego State and San Francisco State.[37] Moorpark College Mechistas and Reynoso, as their faculty advisor, wasted no time making its mark within El Movimiento in Southern California. In November 1969 they organized a one-day conference of workshops and lectures. People from other community colleges, private and public four-year institutions, and high schools attended. In addition to establishing a support network, conference organizers strategized how to cultivate Mexican American studies while increasing the matriculation and graduation of ethnic Mexicans in high schools and colleges.[38]

President Collins, with his newly appointed MAS director, opened the program with a welcome to attendees and an introduction of the conference schedule. Jesus Chavarria of UCSB and Dr. Acuña spoke on the relevancy of Chicano studies. Raquel Montenegro of the Association of Bilingual Educators made an address on "The Broken Promises of the American Dream." After the first round of speeches, workshops addressed topics regarding the recruitment of ethnic Mexican staff and students, financial aid, support services, and curriculum development.[39]

The event, however, did not escape controversy. Campus food services erred in their catering by including table grapes at a time when César Chávez's National Farm Workers Union imposed an international boycott of the product to pressure growers for a collective bargaining agreement. Students from Los Angeles rebuked Moorpark Mechistas for the gaffe. Later, East Los Angeles College MEChA wrote a scathing open letter to President Collins expressing the offense taken. The letter pointed to the failure of "white society" to join the effort of protest of the time. Instead, the letter continued, "white society" issued an insult.[40]

Despite the table grape goof, Moorpark College MEChA pulled off a successful conference, and the succor that President Collins extended did not go unrecognized. In April 1970 the Mexican American Political Association (MAPA) of Ventura County saluted President Collins at its annual awards banquet for doing more for the Chicano than anyone else. This was a well-deserved honor, as President Collins, judging from the reports in the *Raider Reporter*, consistently supported the advancement of Mexican American studies and the hiring of faculty and staff of Mexican origin and was sensitive to the needs of students.[41]

¡Despierta! (Wake Up!)

The recognition of a gracious campus president such as Collins was of particular import, as Chicana-Chicano students did not enjoy such help at the sister campus of Ventura College with Ray E. Loehr as president. Moreover, the direct actions of Black students awakened many students unaware of, or initially unconcerned with, broader national currents of protests. At the Area IX Junior College Student Association Conference in October 1968, for example, Black students accused the association of failing to address unnamed problems important to their minority peers, then stormed out in protest. Two months later Black students presented President Loehr with a petition bearing 280 student signatures that demanded the recruitment of Black faculty. A meeting resulted after a rumor circulated that Black students planned to stage a protest at the college's homecoming football game if their demands were not met.[42]

In the following spring of 1970, BSU spokesperson Larry Ellis presented President Loehr with a list of demands that not only called for the hiring of Black professors but also instituting an independent Black studies department with a curriculum transferable to four-year colleges and universities. As part of the campus's overall infrastructure, the students called for a Black studies section in the campus library. And, to support the success of students, the BSU listed the need for Black counselors, financial aid administrators, and staff employees.[43]

The next year at Moorpark College, in October 1971, thirty Black students cleared the library's bookshelves in protest of the campus's refusal to hire a Black secretary for an open position. Like Chicana-Chicano students at Moorpark College earlier that March, the BSU held an on-campus conference with the goal "to create a black awareness within the community while encouraging young blacks toward higher education." Oxnard resident, activist, and founding member of the cultural organization Harambee Uhuru (Swahili for Freedom Fights), William Terry was one of the several speakers at the conference.[44]

As the BSU took direct action, Chicana-Chicano students endorsed their demands. Witnesses of broader protest movements in support of farmworkers and against the war in Vietnam, as well as of the student blowouts in East Los Angeles, Ventura County Chicanas-Chicanos reflected upon the needs within their communities. Like the Ventura County CSO and National Association for the Advancement of Colored People earlier, the BSU and MEChA exerted independent, yet parallel, pressure upon the administration of Ventura College to meet the needs of their students. This resulted in the appointments of Isaiah "Bubba" Brown and Ray Reyes as counselors at the Minority Student Center (MSC) in the winter of 1971.[45]

Networks in the Southern California region tethered together the activism of Chicanas and Chicanos at various high schools, colleges, and universities. Young men and women traveled roads and freeways to visit campuses, cruised lowrider cars on main streets, socialized at parks, and dated love interests in other communities. They voraciously read alternative newspapers and magazines that spoke to their experience: *Con Safos, El Chicano, La Causa, El Gallo, El Grito, El Malcriado,* and *La Raza Magazine,* to name a few. These publications, and others similar to them, established translocal, shared experiences.[46]

Other students participated in landmark protests and conferences such as East Los Angeles's Chicano Moratorium, La Marcha de la Reconquista, the Santa Barbara Conference of El Plan that was named after it, the protest marches of the United Farm Workers, and the Denver Youth Conferences. As Chicana-Chicano students listened to the speeches of anti–Vietnam War protestors such as SFVSC student Gilbert Cano, César Chávez, Dolores Huerta, Rodolfo "Corky" Gonzalez, and others, they were inspired by the defiant messages that contextualized their sense of history, mythology, and status. People who participated in or observed these events found their own experiences with racist systems of oppression affirmed; in other words, they discovered that their grievances were not imagined or individualized. This in turn inspired them to invite iconic figures of El Movimiento to their own campuses. And if they could not attract big-name movement people, Mechistas at Moorpark and Ventura College brought in local academics and activists to interpret and comment on the events of their time.

In oral history interviews, Manuela Aparicio Twitchell of Fillmore, Yvonne De Los Santos of Saticoy, and Roberto Flores and Jess Gutiérrez, both from Oxnard, expressed with pride the work they had performed in programming Cinco de Mayo and Mexican Independence Day celebrations. Collectively, organizers developed their leadership skills, which entailed the formal submission of proposals for campus authorization and funds as well as the logistical navigation of bureaucratic systems. In the process Mechistas developed cross-cultural alliances with other students to support peers on Associated Students boards for the sponsorship of their events. And, on the day of a program, Mechistas enhanced their talents at public speaking by serving as emcees and, at times, filled in for no-show guests.

For the campus's Cinco de Mayo Celebration of 1971, Moorpark College MEChA hosted Reies López Tijerina Jr. (the son of the land grant activist in New Mexico) and Rodolfo "Corky" Gonzales. The pair were part of a two-day program of speeches and performances that included Chicano poet Alurista, guitarist-folklorist Suni Paz, and Mariachi Uclatlan from UCLA. An evening concert featured the music of the Thee Midniters and Dark Corner.[47] The next year MEChA successfully booked Reis López Tijerina himself. But, that time, the organizers would add a twist to the celebration. Instead of a two-day program, the event took place over three days. And, in the spirit of El Plan de Santa Barbara, of bringing barrio communities to colleges and universities and vice versa, Moorpark College MEChA scheduled events on campus and in the communities of Oxnard and Santa Paula. The program entailed talks by, again, Alurista, and movement leaders of the Mexican American generation such as labor and immigrant rights activist Bert Corona, Armando Morales of UCLA and author of the book on police violence *Ando sangrando*, as well as Sal Castro, who mentored student leaders in the East Los Angeles blowouts. Teatro Aztlán of SFVSC and the college's own Teatro Quetzalcoatl performed *actos*, or short plays.[48]

It was at Moorpark College that Gutiérrez became further politicized, both by the zeitgeist and the knowledge he learned. Coupled with the counterhegemonic perspectives espoused by movement speakers and that of his peers, the inchoate body of Chicano studies literature expanded his worldview. And although Moorpark College did not have a Chicano studies degree, MEChA served as the focal point of support for first-generation college students.[49] Gutiérrez had been so inspired by his involvement in Moorpark College's MEChA that he ran for a seat on the politically conservative OUHSD Board of Trustees.[50]

Minority Student Center

Once matriculated on college campuses, Chicanas-Chicanos noticed BSU's demand for the curricular inclusion of their own experience and support services. This prompted them to develop similar petitions. At Ventura College, for example, both Black and Chicana-Chicano students made one demand in a parallel manner, for a minority students center. Their call converged in a meeting with the college's administration in May 1970. BSU and MEChA also pushed simultaneously, yet separately, for tutorial services to advance the retention of first-generation college students.[51]

Starting in 1972 the two organizations also collaborated each year in a Christmas charity fashion show. The proceeds from the event went toward the distribution of food baskets for the needy. Once the campus established its Minority Student Center, the two clubs jointly planned other programs. In one case they sponsored a weeklong series to educate the campus about the history and culture of their respective heritages. Spokespersons from each club articulated two outcomes. For example, in relation to space, counselor and MEChA faculty advisor Reyes stated, "We will convert the [patio] area into a Mexican marketplace in an effort to reproduce the festival that is held in Huachemango (a Mexican city) each year at this time." And in relation to the analogous experiences of Blacks and Chicanas-Chicanos, Larry Ellis stated, "The black and brown peoples are deprived culturally and educationally here and this is our chance to do our own thing and we want people to know what we are and can do."[52]

But the existence of the Minority Student Center unsettled Louis Zitnik, who felt that it segregated people and compromised notions of racial equality. For Zitnik inequities among racial groups were financial. As a result he called for unity among the economically disadvantaged, as race, he thought, only served to disunite people with common interest.[53] Vietnam veteran and student Arnulfo Casillas offered a response that complicated the notion of people of color being a minority in Ventura County, pointing out that several communities did not have white-majority populations: for instance, Moorpark, with 60 percent of its residents of Mexican origin, and both Fillmore and Santa Paula, with 50 percent of its residents as such. To appreciate the true character of segregation, Casillas referenced the spatial isolation that ethnic Mexicans experienced in the barrios of La Colonia in Oxnard, the Avenue in Ventura, Grant Avenue in Santa Paula, El Campo of Saticoy, and El Campito of Fillmore. It was in such places that people failed to enjoy the services they paid in taxes that white-dominant communities enjoyed. Casillas highlighted that this contributed to Chicana-Chicano students not graduating from or dropping out of high school at a rate of 50 percent. This exclusion also evidenced itself in the Vietnam War, where Chicano military servicemen consisted of 20 percent of the casualties when they only made up 5 percent of the population in the Southwest.[54]

The Minority Student Center gained greater visibility when MEChA, with the support of the Associated Students, convinced President Loehr to permit the installation of a mural on the building in the spring of 1973 in time for the campus's annual Cinco de Mayo celebration. Created by Blas Menchaca, the mural consisted of a gendered mosaic of tiles with images of patriarchal icons of Mexican history Joaquin Murrieta, Father Miguel Hidalgo y Costilla, Benito Juárez, Jose María Morelos, Cuauhtéhmoc, Pancho Villa, Emiliano Zapata, and Che Guevara below the rain god Tlaloc.[55]

Veni, Vidi, Vici Chicana-Chicano Style

Once a critical mass of Chicana-Chicano students found their way to college, they struggled to create a conducive campus culture. Ultimately, with the guidance of Mexican American generation mentors such as Reynoso and Reyes, they accomplished this. One objective entailed the promotion of Mexican culture on campuses. Another sought to create additional structures of support like the Minority Student Center, as many Chicana-Chicano students did not have the scholastic preparation and financial means to sustain their retention on campus. Then there were students that did not understand the connection of a higher education with improved life chances in employment, housing, health care, as well as the intergenerational transfer of social capital. This being the case, it was critical for Chicana-Chicano students—with the support of faculty, staff, and administrators who, in effect, served in loco parentis—to create systems that holistically developed students.

On March 19, 1969, the *Raiders Reporter* published an unsigned essay titled "Chicano Speaks: The Mexican Fiesta—a Chance to 'Discharge the Soul.'" The anonymous writer (or collective) described cultural events as the expression of the community's soul in an oppressive society that sought the eradication of the ethnic Mexican presence. The essay went on to proclaim, profoundly, that "the fiesta is a revolt, a revolution. . . . The fiesta unites everything: good and evil, day and night and the sacred and profane."[56] Therefore, music, theater, and lectures promoted by MEChA in Ventura County middle schools, high schools, and colleges enabled Chicana-Chicano students to declare a restorative cultural pride. This often occasioned the blare of trumpets and the strum of string instruments (violins, *el guitarrón*, and *vihuela*) as mariachi sang the songs of Mexico in the heart of campuses during the midday, when students walked to and from class. Within a hegemonic context in which all that was Mexican was subordinated—if not at best considered mediocre compared to the standards of European culture—the open-air reverence for Mexican traditions by ethnic

Mexican students born or raised in the United States was, as the unsigned *Raider-Reporter* letter of March 19 proclaimed, a revolutionary act.

At Ventura College music professor Frank A. Salazar and his Spanish faculty colleague Francis X. Maggipinto worked with Chicana-Chicano students in 1968 to develop a Mexican-style Christmas program that would, in the words of Salazar, "totally immerse" the campus in the traditions of Mexico. The Mexican American generation professors and students invited children from the Ventura barrio of the Avenue and Santa Paula to instill in them not only a unique sense of Chicana-Chicano culture but also to sow *semillas* (seeds) on the importance of a college education.[57]

The promotion of *música mexicana* included songs of the 1950s. This finessed the inclusion of intergenerational ethnic Mexican cohorts of migrant provenance. It also integrated others equally influenced by the sounds of Motown and R&B. Raves encompassed all students attracted to this genre of music, as the mellifluous Brown sounds demanded attention. As this took place, Mechistas recruited members and won over intergroup supporters. Mechistas of Ventura College took this one step further when they obtained an hour of weekly airtime on KACY radio, hosted by Bernardo Larios, titled *La Hora del Chicano*. By way of the sponsorship of such programing, Mechistas not only developed culturally responsive environs, but also advanced the goodwill of their institutions in the barrios and colonias from which they came, making their schools truly "community" colleges.[58]

The promotion of Mexican cultural expressions also served as a praxis of restoration. Celebrations of El Diez y Seis de Septiembre (Mexican Independence Day), Cinco de Mayo, and Día de los Muertos (Day of the Dead), for example, contested the dominant cultural view that depicted ethnic Mexicans as perpetual "aliens." In the spring of 1973, Casillas expressed this perspective when he stated, "When we go into the celebration of Cinco de Mayo, may we remember that this is not a foreign culture, but one that is very much a part of all that we have seen and experience during our lifetime, in our history."[59]

Renascent celebrations in Ventura County schools and colleges elevated the profile of ethnic Mexican students, particularly those active in MEChA. This not only attracted a steady cycle of new members but also inspired Mechistas to pursue campus leadership opportunities. Two such instances involved the election of representatives. The first consisted of the campus election of homecoming queens at Moorpark and Ventura College; the second entailed the election of Associated Students (AS) board members at both campuses.

In 1969 Manuela Aparicio ran for homecoming queen at Moorpark College and was voted the runner-up. When Chicana-Chicano peers asked why she entered the competition, she answered why not. In the fall of 1970, Jeanette Velasco represented MEChA as a candidate for homecoming queen at Moorpark College. She ran against Luedora Wallace. Interestingly, the newspaper was silent on who won this race. Two years later Aurelia Aparicio, Manuela's sister, won the title of homecoming queen. At Ventura College, in the fall of 1969, MEChA successfully campaigned for Betty Luna to be homecoming queen. The next year Jayne Lopez of Santa Paula was one of three elected by the students as finalists. The other two were BSU candidate Debbie Shelton and Maureen Cooney, sponsored by the Associated Men's Student club. The football team made the final decision, and, again, the campus newspaper was silent on who the team chose.[60] But the actual outcome of who won was secondary to the candidacies of Chicanas and Black women to run for elected positions—putatively the privilege, if not the right, of white contestants.

In 1969 MEChA member Richard Hernandez served as president of Moorpark College's ASB. At the end of his term, he endorsed the candidacy of fellow Mechista Angel Luevano, who won, as his successor. In 1972 Zeke Ruelas was elected speaker of parliament at Moorpark College.[61] But the most pronounced expression of the actualization of power by Chicana-Chicano students took place at Ventura College. At the behest of their Mexican American generation advisor, Ray Reyes, who mentored them to be a politically active and savvy organization that administered budgets, as opposed to just being a social club, Ventura College MEChA students held tremendous influence over the AS board for much of the 1970s. But in 1975 it achieved its zenith as the school newspaper focused on MEChA's representative majority on the AS board. A Crystal City moment, however, occurred that spring semester, when MEChA members and MEChA-endorsed candidates swept the AS election. In addition, nine other nonexecutive posts were held by MEChA members. Graciela Casillas, the younger sister of Arnulfo, won the position of ASB president. Pleased by the result, Casillas graciously expressed her appreciation for MEChA's support and promised to represent the interests of all students. But fellow Mechista and Casillas's predecessor as the outgoing ASB chair, Manuel Razo, was not so politic; he brazenly stated to the school reporter, "Just put 'MEChA wins, honkies lose.' . . . It's only obvious that MEChA is the strongest organization on campus. We are the power structure of the college." Similarly, Jesus Hernández proclaimed after winning the seat of ASB vice-president, "My number one priority is MEChA members needs. . . . Mi raza primero. We came, we saw and we conquered." Like Casillas, though, Lupe Razo, who won the post as ASB secretary, more inclusively expressed her appreciation for MEChA's support and vowed to work on the behalf of not only Chicanos but also all women.[62]

In response to the subsequent backlash, MEChA embarked upon political damage control. In March 1975 it held a weekend conference. In an interview with reporter for the *Pirate Press*, Jaime Casillas, the brother of Graciela and Arnulfo, stated that the purpose of the event was to recruit new members and to address false ideas about MEChA, since the remarks of Razo and Hernández confirmed in the eyes of many their view of the organization as exclusive, aggressively militant, and resolute in the *reconquista* of the Southwest. For the most part, however, the goals and objectives of the organization were moderate, inclusive of all people, regardless of ethnicity and race. Most of all the organization was reformist in character, in terms of its pursuit of progressive change within extant institutions.[63]

But the braggadocio of two of its members made MEChA politically vulnerable. Ventura College's Alpha Gama Sigma (AGS) ran a slate of candidates of its own in the spring 1975 election for the executive posts of the AS board. In previous elections incumbents often ran unopposed. But this cycle was different; AGS ran against Mechistas to diminish, if not demolish, the organization's power. As the campaign commenced, both AGS and MEChA candidates denied that their election would result in their favoritism of one group of students over others.[64] Michael C. Dill, AGS candidate for the Office of Finance, who ran against Mechista Tony Valenzuela, wrote a letter to the editor right before the election. He commended MEChA for the organization's engagement in campus affairs and how its activism inspired him to run for the AS board to break its political domination. The goal was not to eliminate completely MEChA's presence on the AS board, but he desired more balanced representation.⁶⁵ In the end, however, the Mechistas lost all seats on the board of student government.⁶⁶

A Contretemps of Identities

In addition to collective actions of self-determination on campuses and in their communities, Chicana-Chicano youth asserted their new identity in a more individualistic fashion in print distinctive from their elder counterparts with Mexican American or Mexicanist identities. Combined, local movements and the propaganda of the larger movimiento influenced the ways in which young men and women viewed themselves as a people. The term "propaganda" in U.S. culture connotes a certain stigma of bias and rhetoric; in the tradition of Mexican culture, however, propaganda involves public relations in the dissemination of values. In this regard Chicana-Chicano youth challenged those who questioned the identity they espoused. This debate, often heated, emerged in the letters to the editor within campus and community newspapers.

An extended conversation commenced on the label "Chicano" when the *Oxnard Press-Courier* reported in January 1970 California State College Hayward's implementation of a Chicano studies program. This raised the ire of city of Ventura resident R. De Leon, who emphasized the pejorative provenance of the moniker. De Leon argued that people who identified themselves as Chicano desired attention and held a "chip on their shoulders." Although De Leon respected the right of individuals to identify themselves as they wished, he challenged the newspaper's use of the label to describe the Mexican American community, since individuals like himself rejected it. The next month Jerry R. Rosalez, like De Leon, opposed the daily's identification of ethnic Mexicans as Chicano; this, in his opinion, referenced a group of impostors.⁶⁷ In the same edition of the newspaper that printed Rosalez's letter, however, Faye Villa, a resident of Ventura County's city of Camarillo, challenged De Leon's perspective. She asked rhetorically if he had taken a poll to determine that most ethnic Mexicans disliked the label "Chicano." Villa went on to contend that the Anglo use of the label "Spanish" was a euphemism and rebutted the notion that ethnic Mexicans were not different than "anyone else." In fact, Villa held, ethnic Mexicans suffered racism in the United States due to their appearance; she concluded her letter by stating that he should "accept it [being of a distinct ethnicity] and live with it—happily."[68]

Daniel E. Contreras did exactly this. The next day the *Oxnard Press-Courier* published a letter that defined his sense of the "Chicano" soubriquet. Contreras referenced the infamous opinion of Judge Gerald S. Chargin, who espoused a racist characterization of a Chicano youth convicted of raping his sister. Contreras mentioned three ways in which the Chicano, as a community, was "exercising his shoulders." One was by an unnamed Chicano lawyer working to have Chargin removed from the bench. The second entailed the recruitment of Chicanos to go onto college. Third, Contreras concluded, "in essence, to be a Chicano is to believe and live as one. One is born a Mexican but one becomes a Chicano by choice.... I don't relish encounters with people with chips on their shoulders, but it's just as bad, if not worse, dealing with people with no shoulders at all."[69]

Under the pseudonym "Nomas Milando" (roughly translated to "just observing"), a writer in the Voice of the People section, published on February 7, responded to the contribution of Rosalez. He contextualized the label in relation to the need for ethnic Mexicans to be prideful of their heritage within an "Anglo society" that denigrated every aspect of their being. Furthermore, to compel self-erasure, society forced ethnic Mexicans to identify with the moniker of "Spanish American." But what was important was that people determine their own identity. In fact, Nomas Milando contended, an internalized white supremacy grounded Rosalez's objection to the word "Chicano." This entailed the portrayal of ethnic Mexicans as criminally inclined, if not in fact criminal, and lazy. He also referenced a statement made by deceased senator Dennis Chávez of New Mexico that when Mexican Americans won a congressional medal of honor for valor, they were labeled "Latin American"; when they won political office they were "Spanish American"; and, when unemployed, society tagged them as "Mexican." Nomas Milando concluded, "So with this in mind, Mr. Rosalez, please do not lose sight of the 'real' problem. Direct your energies to stamp out the existing cancer [i.e., racism] of our society and do not waste your time bickering over an idiomatic term."[70]

As part of the ongoing contretemps, the *Oxnard Press-Courier* published an essay by Contreras in late February titled "Chicano Power Defined." Contreras referenced the song "Chicano Power" by the East Los Angeles band Thee Midniters to argue that the epithet encompassed all ethnic Mexicans with a U.S. life experience—at least with persons who identified as Mexican in the first place. "Chicano Power" signified the centrality of an education for the well-being and advancement of the ethnic Mexican community; a relevant curriculum would instill a positive self-concept and, in the process, challenge negative stereotypes perpetuated by a white, ethnocentric media. Contreras credited the Brown Berets for their promotion of cultural pride, like the Black Panthers. For him the Brown Berets were "tough-minded individuals" who struggled by way of direct action for positive social change.[71]

The initial letter of R. De Leon that protested the *Oxnard Press-Courier*'s use of the "Chicano" appellation predated by two weeks an op-ed by former *Los Angeles Times* reporter Ruben Salazar titled "Who Is a Chicano? And What Is It the Chicanos Want?" on February 6, 1970. In this piece Salazar discussed the nuances of the label as expressing a social consciousness of resistance. Conversely, the label "Mexican American" held an inverse connotation less critical of the subordination of ethnic Mexicans. In the words of Salazar, "Chicanos, then, are merely fighting to become 'Americans.' Yes, but with a Chicano outlook."[72]

Takeaway

An enthusiasm for actualizing positive change and achieving greater representation in society's institutions with élan inspired the young and old. Since Chicana-Chicano youth existed at all levels of education, campuses served as the grounds for dreaming (to borrow the concept from historian Lori Flores's work) an enriched condition for ethnic Mexican students in terms of the curricular inclusion of their experiences, support services, and greater representation in faculty and staff. These students, with the guidance of mentors from the Mexican American generation, learned, gained confidence, and worked collaboratively with others to achieve positive changes. Chicana-Chicano students of Ventura County, therefore, fought similar struggles as their counterparts in different parts of the nation, but with a rurban chic all their own.

Conclusion

This book sought to demonstrate the intergenerational character of El Movimiento in Ventura County, California. The question at the end of this project is how ethnic Mexican communities in Ventura County have continued to assert their sovereignty since 1975. After going off to college at California State University, Fresno, and then living in Orange County for nine years to start my career as an educator at Cypress College in 1992, I returned to Ventura County in 2001 to teach at California State University Channel Islands (CSUCI), the newest in the system and the first and only public four-year institution here. As part of an early cohort of tenure-track faculty, I toured the cities of Camarillo, Oxnard, Port Hueneme, Santa Paula, and Ventura with colleagues to flack the new campus. In the process I connected with long-time residents, many of them participants of El Movimiento. A significant number went on to be K–14 educators, health care providers, peace officers, entrepreneurs, social workers, and directors of nonprofit agencies.

In meeting these civically engaged residents and becoming familiar with their stories, the savoir faire with which they carried themselves captivated me as I learned how they deftly negotiated public and private institutions that for the most part lacked demographic diversity. In the expression of their concerns, these *veteranas* and *veteranos* (veterans) of El Movimiento invariably made sure that the underserved and underrepresented were not neglected, as had been the case during their coming of age. Therefore, in them, the Chicana-Chicano movement lives on.

As I got to know these community leaders over time, I discovered that most of them were, too, first-generation college students who successfully graduated against steep odds—with the guidance of mentors such as Tony Del Buono, Bert Hammond, Ernestine Webb, and Rodolfo F. Acuña. As the progeny of farmworkers, many carried forward a legacy of resistance in the face of racist labor exploitation and state violence. Hence, their activism was about equity in all forms to self-determine, as much as possible, services for the common good.

As I resettled in my hometown of Oxnard, I discovered in the heart of the city a site auspiciously named the Dr. Rodolfo F. Acuña Art Gallery & Cultural Center, devoted to the advancement of Chicana-Chicano culture as a way to encourage the development of wayward youth. Located on A Street at the city's heart, it was also monikered the Café on A, for short. It was here that Avie Guerra, an alum of the Chicano Studies Program at San Fernando Valley State College, now deceased, convened the Consortium for Higher Education to hold the new campus of CSU Channel Islands accountable to the interests of the ethnic Mexican community. Acuña and Jorge García (a city of Simi Valley resident), as CSU doyens, spoke at the café to educate the community on the stakes of the new university's advancement. Admissions, financial aid, inclusive hiring practices, access, curricular programs, and student support services were among the topics discussed. In the end Chicanas-Chicanos, many of them alumni of Valley State; the University of California, Los Angeles; and the University of California, Santa Barbara, steadfastly lobbied CSUCI for a bachelor's degree in Chicano studies and won.

This is to state unequivocally that the legacy of the El Movimiento Chicano in Ventura County not only continues, but also is defined by people of different generations. This was highlighted even further when the Oxnard Police Department and the Ventura County District Attorney's Office announced with calculated histrionics in the spring of 2004 their court filing for a constitutionally flawed civil injunction against the Colonia Chiques street gang. Although the majority of residents in Ventura County supported or were indifferent to the implementation of this racist tool of law enforcement that infringed upon the due process rights of largely penurious ethnic Mexican males, a cell of opposition arose that questioned the decision's overall constitutionality. In fact, in an op-ed in the *Ventura County Star* on March 30, 2004, Francisco "Chavo" Romero—with the brio of the leaders of the Community Service Organization and Brown Berets of the 1960s and early 1970s—castigated public officials for the adoption of this blunt device. As I watched with fascination Romero's weekly addresses to the city council on the public access channel, I witnessed a poised citizen of Generation X speak to power. The activism of the organization he represented, El Comité de Raza Rights, utilized the Café on A, owned and operated by Deborah De Vries and Armando Vázquez, as a space to mobilize community opposition. Moreover, it was at the café that I came to befriend William Terry, a past member of Harambee Uhuru and the city of Oxnard Community Action Commission, mentioned earlier in this book. During our weekly or biweekly community meetings, I associated with others who opposed the injunction under an organization labeled Chiques Organizing for Rights, Employment, Equity, and Education (CORE for short).[1] Through my association with Romero, I learned that he, too, was a native son of Oxnard, a middle-school educator, an alum of CSUN, and himself a victim of police violence. He was also a devotee of Chicano studies.

Vázquez, originally from the city of Pacoima, too, was a Valley State graduate with a degree in Chicano studies who got his professional start as an Operation Chicano Teacher educator in the city of Fillmore. Vázquez regularly challenged, directly and by example, patrons of the café to fearlessly speak truth to power and document their own stories, because their experiences, and that of their communities, comprised a power all their own. Otherwise our perspectives would disappear into the ether or be written for us by folks from the outside, perhaps to our dissatisfaction. Together the trio (De Vries, Romero, and Vázquez) served as the germinal collective that others, like me, would join to question the civil injunction's overall legitimacy. To this end, on May 11, 2004, the three headed a sparsely attended press conference in front of city hall just prior to the council's weekly meeting to publicly challenge the gang injunction. This spark ignited broader attention. As in the case of the CSO and the Ventura County National Association for the Advancement of Colored People (NAACP) in the 1960s, the county chapters of the League of United Latin American Citizens and, later, the NAACP, expressed their distinct reservations with the injunction, if not their opposition to it.[2]

The Café on A, since its establishment in 1998 and closing in 2017, provided restorative programing for youth and those under state supervision. Utilizing the arts as a remedy, the café tapped into the cultural capital of ethnic Mexicans—via paintings and sculptures, literature, and music—to instill an amour propre in traumatized youth so that they could, over time, learn to trust and love others. Once this was achieved, they would potentially become community leaders.

Therefore, in a new generation of youth, the central tenets of Chicana-Chicano cultural nationalism of El Movimiento continues. Its manifestation exists in a milieu unique yet akin to that of the 1960s and 1970s. For one, an ever-growing number of students in the county's grade schools and colleges are of greater indigenous lineage (as First American Mixteco, Zapotec, and Purépecha peoples, to name a few) and Central American origins. They or their families have migrated from southern Mexico, El Salvador, Guatemala, Honduras, and Nicaragua as economic and political refugees to escape ruthless right-wing dictatorships, somewhat surreptitiously supported if not put in place by the U.S. government during the presidency of Ronald Reagan. This demographic shift has changed the character of student bodies. At my campus alone, Hispanics make up over 50 percent (3,500 out of 7,000 plus) of students.[3] This allows CSUCI to be recognized as a Hispanic Serving Institution, which has qualified it to rake in millions in federal government funds for the enhancement of the institution's overall educational capacity. But, like the Oxnard Elementary School District in the 1970s, the faculty and administration of CSUCI, like other academic institutions throughout the nation, does not satisfactorily reflect the student body it serves. Nearly 60 percent of the faculty is white when an approximate percentage is made up of a plurality of racial-minority students, those labeled "Hispanic" being the largest. As a result a disjuncture exists in the cultural relevancy of the curriculum and services delivered.[4]

But incremental progress is being achieved with the growth of Chicano studies at CSUCI in terms of a group of Chicanx (the label is in transition) administrators, faculty, staff, and allies of various backgrounds committed to the ideals of El Plan de Santa Barbara. Consequently, Chicano studies tenure-track candidates are questioned about the principles of El Plan during the recruitment process. The Chicana/o Studies Department, in partnership with the administration, has also instituted an innovative interdisciplinary learning community in the name of Ventura County's literary lodestar, Michele Serros, author of the groundbreaking works *Chicana Falsa: And Other Stories of Death, Identity, and Oxnard* (1993) and *How to Be a Chicana Role Model* (2000), among others. Although Michele has left us, her authorial flamboyance continues to inspire students to be bold in the pursuit of their dreams and not to settle for unadventurous lives. Through characters such as La Letty and Bad Donna Rodriguez, Michele also messaged readers to confront the powers that be, wherever they be, with moxie, not with bowed heads and hats in hand. In her writings and presentations, Chicana Michele role-modeled for us how to express ourselves with confidence and wit in telling "our stories." But, whether recounted in print or audio, Serros gifted us rich narratives, with a sassiness all her own, that spoke to our nuanced regional reality as Chicanas-Chicanos since the 1970s.

I mention this incremental progress to argue that even though the school walkouts, farmworker protests, and rhetoric of El Movimiento has largely—but not completely—dissipated, the challenges, systemic racism, ideals, and the critical consciousness of that era *continua* (continues). In fact, Chicanas-Chicanos of El Movimiento currently serve as mavens and mentors to millennial professionals and youth just as leaders of the Mexican American generation had done, and continue to do, for them. Hence, the narratives that have yet to be written need to address in what ways El Movimiento in Ventura County has continued since 1975. The cultural fodder for this potential project exists in archives, personal papers, artistic collections, oral interviews, and reports, many yet to be discovered. And, as historian Gustavo Licón presciently points out, the legacy of resistance of El Movimiento reasserts itself when white supremacist anxiety surfaces in relation to immigration, public university admissions, and bilingual education.

In fact, not so long ago, in the 1990s, ballot initiatives backed by animus arose in the state of California, respectively, in Propositions 187, 209, and 227. In the present the racist impulses of these initiatives have gone viral throughout the United States with the unabashed and multifaceted hate of President Donald J. Trump.[5] This has been further evidenced by the police killings of African Americans such as George Floyd, Eric Garner, Meagan Hockaday, and Breonna Taylor. Therefore, a fundamental historical question needs be asked for the present and posterity: What have Chicanas-Chicanos of Ventura County done since the mid-1970s?

Although local newspapers such as the *Oxnard Press-Courier* and *Ventura County Star-Free Press*, with its crackerjack reporters, have significantly diminished since the early 1990s, with the advent of electronic media, historians can investigate the archives and interview the membership of organizations in Ventura County such as the Bell Arts Factory, the Cabrillo Economic Development Corporation, the Café on A, Clínicas del Camino Real, El Concilio Family Services, Future Leaders of America, Inlakech Cultural Arts Center, Latino Town Hall, and many others. Most, if not all, of these organizations are a direct or indirect manifestation of the work of agents of El Movimiento covered in this book with rich yet-to-be written histories all their own.

Lastly, to sample how *el espíritu* (the spirit) of El Movimiento has carried on since 1975, I end this book with a quote from Romero's March 30, 2004, appeal to the Ventura County community—again, reminiscent of the moxie of the CSO and Brown Berets—when officials of the city of Oxnard and Ventura County agreed amongst themselves to implement a civil gang injunction that targeted poor, marginalized, errant young Chicanos. Within this j'accuse, Romero captured the intergenerational essence of change and continuity in an emotive rhetoric of resistance determined to combat oppression in all its manifestations:

> The latest attempt to dehumanize, degrade, segregate and criminalize Raza youth by the Oxnard Police Department and District Attorney Greg Totten by petitioning for a civil injunction against Raza youth in Oxnard is the latest pre-emptive strike on the Mexican community in which there will be a lot of collateral damage....

The Committee on Raza Rights, an independent community-based organization, clearly and firmly stands in protest against the continued militarization of the community by the Oxnard Police Department. The CRR calls on the community to denounce and organize against this injunction by writing letters to the established political leaders, by holding rallies and forums exposing this attack on our community....

The solution is for Mexicano-indigenous people to commit ourselves to a positive, educational, cultural and political movement to uplift our community, our youth in particular, to a revolutionary level of consciousness.

By revolutionary, the CRR means that a serious change in the manner in which we address and listen to our misguided youth, how we construct and maintain our economic development, how and what we present as relevant education, and to how we create and establish our political future must be rooted in an independent, community-initiated, proactive and solution-based effort....

The systematic racism found within the economic and political system that feeds itself off the backs of the Mexican worker is the same system that petitions and calls for injunctions in the poorest sectors of our barrios, the incarceration and criminalization of our youth and the efforts against the righteous struggle for self-determination and community empowerment....

The answer is simple. We can choose to stand by with our hands in our pockets and watch our youth being attacked. Or, we can organize, educate and empower our community to realize our righteous struggle against blatantly racist laws....

Commit to a community-based movement to improve our own conditions. Commit to be part of the solution and not part of the problem. Commit to talk to our youth about our history, our humble roots and rightful duty to organize for self-determination and liberation. The solution lies within ourselves.[6]

Coda

After sixteen years contesting the constitutionality of civil gang junctions, the collective resistance of social justice activists, spearheaded by Romero and Vazquez, ultimately proved victorious. In July 2020 the Oxnard Police Department announced its abandonment of this blunt tool of law enforcement.[7]

NOTES

Epigraph

Brooks, "Chinua Achebe."

Introduction

1. Govea to Ortiz, February 2, 1971, UFWBCR, box 1; "In Support of Cesar Chavez," *Ventura County Star-Free Press*, January 30, 1971.
2. Approximately $6, adjusted for inflation in 2020.
3. Frank Del Olmo, "Eight Arrested in Fourth Day of Strike by Strawberry Pickers," *Los Angeles Times*, May 30, 1974; Leopoldo Urias, "Berry Pickers Strike Reaches Oxnard Fields," *Pirate Press*, May 31, 1974; "Flynn, Jewett to Confer with Strikers, Sheriff," *Ventura County Star-Free Press*, June 5, 1974; clippings, Walter Reuther Library, UFWIRDP, box 29; Roberto Flores, phone conversation with Frank P. Barajas, April 24, 2019; Bardacke, *Trampling Out the Vintage*, 342–43; Pawel, *Crusades of Cesar Chavez*, 342–43.
4. "Berry Harvesting Halted by Violence," *Ventura County Star-Free Press*, May 25, 1974; "Cesar Chavez to Aid Oxnard Berry Strike," *Ventura County Star-Free Press*, May 28, 1974; "Cesar Chavez to Aid Oxnard Berry Strike," *Ventura County Star-Free Press*, May 29, 1974; Fred Johnston, "Picketers, Deputies Clash in Berry Strike," *Ventura County Star-Free Press*, May 29, 1974; Del Olmo, "Eight Arrested"; "Flynn, Jewett."

5. Clippings, 1974, Walter Reuther Library, UFWIRDP, box 29; for a magisterial study of the history of ethnic Mexicans homicidally oppressed by the Texas Rangers, see Muñoz Martínez's *Injustice Never Leaves You*.
6. Mexicans have migrated to and from what is now the United States for centuries, if not millennia. Therefore, people from Mexico were not immigrants of the European variety that crossed the Atlantic. Therefore, I utilize the more suitable label of "migrant" to identify transnational workers on both sides of the U.S.-Mexico border; Roberto Hernández Chicana/o Studies Summit of Ventura County, April 27, 2019; Hernández, *Coloniality of the U.S./Mexico Border*, 32.
7. I utilize this label to include people of Mexican origin who were U.S. citizens (born and naturalized) as well as migrants with authorized or unauthorized residency.
8. I settled on the centrality of the spirit of El Movimiento shaping the identity of ethnic Mexicans from a conversation with CSU Channel Islands colleagues Nicholas Centino and Jennie Luna, April 22, 2019; I also adopted as well as adapted Ana Rosas's definition of emotive causes, or an emotional intelligence, that compels both individual and collective acts of resistance. Abigail Rosas also uses this definition in a manner closer to mine. Moreover, in social media, blogs, and podcasts, Rodolfo Acuña, Myriam Gurba, and Viet Thanh Nguyen have written on the significance of anger in the formulation of resistance; see Rosas, "Undocumented Emotional Intelligence"; Rudy Acuña, Facebook post, April 29, 2004; Myriam Gurba, "I Called Out American Dirt's Racism. I Won't Be Silenced," Vox, March 12, 2020, https://www.vox.com/first-person/2020/3/12/21168012/racism-american-dirt-myriam-gurba-jeanine-cummins; Viet Thanh Nguyen, "On the Uses of Rage and Anger," July 19, 2012, https://vietnguyen.info/2012/on-the-uses-of-rage-and-anger; Abigail Rosas, *South Central Is Home*.
9. Flores, *Grounds for Dreaming*, 10.
10. Rosales, "Mississippi West"; Louis Menand argues that activist, artist, and public intellectuals born before 1946 exercised a greater influence on the movements of the 1960s as much older adults than persons of the baby boom generation. In fact, Menand considers baby boomers as peripheral participants of the social movements of the time; see Menand, "Misconception about Baby Boomers," 1–5.
11. Jiménez, *Replenished Ethnicity*, 104–10.
12. George J. Sánchez identified Chicanos as U.S.-born but did not label migrant ethnic Mexicans as Chicanas-Chicanos despite the crux of his book arguing that the identities of people transformed with the adaptations made to the sociocultural environment in which they lived; see Sánchez, *Becoming Mexican American*.
13. Ruíz, *From Out of the Shadows*, xvi.

14. Alvarez, "*Los Re-Mexicanizado*," 15–23; Mario García, *Mexican Americans*; Monroy, *Rebirth*; Ruíz, *Cannery Women, Cannery Lives*; Sánchez, *Becoming Mexican American*; Zamora, *World of the Mexican Worker*; Weber, *From South Texas to the Nation*.
15. Arredondo, *Mexican Chicago*; Gutiérrez, *Walls and Mirrors*; Jiménez, *Replenished Ethnicity*; Patiño, *Raza Sí, Migra No*; Rodriguez, *Tejano Diaspora*; Valdes, *Mexicans in Minnesota*; Weber, *From South Texas to the Nation*.
16. Mario García's more recent books in this regard are *Blowout!* and *Chicano Generation*.
17. Acosta, *Revolt of the Cockroach People*, chapter 13; Thompson, "Strange Rumblings in Aztlan," 221–22.
18. Barajas, *Curious Unions*, 230.
19. The union was officially renamed the United Farm Workers after it received an AFL-CIO independent charter in 1972. For the sake of clarity, I use for the most part the UFW moniker; see García, *From the Jaws of Victory*, 299n1.

1. What's Their Provenance?

1. Barajas, *Curious Unions*, chapters 4–5.
2. Ross, *Conquering Goliath*, 4–5; CSO reporter, n.d., Community Service Organization, EGP, box 13.
3. Quoted in Flores, *Grounds for Dreaming*, 40; Barajas, *Curious Unions*, chapter 6.
4. Chávez to Ross, May 7, 1959, FRSC, box 3; Levy, *Cesar Chavez*, 143.
5. Ygnacio Coronado, "Voice of the People: Brown and Farm Labor," *Oxnard Press-Courier*, January 24, 1961.
6. "County Bracero Program Backed," *Oxnard Press-Courier*, April 13, 1961.
7. J. D. Rivera, "Voice of the People: Brown and Farm Labor," *Oxnard Press-Courier*, April 19, 1961.
8. Letters, EGP, box 13; Tjerandsen, *Education for Citizenship*, 105.
9. Allen to Becker, January 18, 1961; and Becker to Allen, February 21, 1961, MMC, box 8.
10. Apodaca, "Home Fires"; Burt, *Search for a Civic Voice*, 177–79, 199–201; Pitti, *Devil in Silicon Valley*, 163–64; "Oxnard Man Sees Brown Sign Bill," *Oxnard Press-Courier*, July 11, 1961.
11. Chávez, letters to Ross, FRSC, box 3; Levy, *Cesar Chavez*, 146–47.
12. Bardacke, *Trampling Out the Vintage*, 107–11; Pawel, *Crusades of Cesar Chavez*, 10, 12; Chávez, letters to Ross, FRSC, box 3; Ruben Salazar, "Prominent Ranch

Woman Works in Fields to Expose Pay Violations," *Los Angeles Times*, February 22, 1965, MMC, box 8.
13. Quarterly Report, Ventura County CSO Chapter to National Executive Board, March 1, 1962–June 1, 1962, CSO, FRSP, folder 3, box 11.
14. "City Declines to Seek Halt in Braceros," *Oxnard Press-Courier*, February 20, 1963. To supplement the controversial flow of braceros from Mexico, California growers successfully lobbied the federal government to create in 1956 a similar agreement with the government of Japan officially titled the Japanese Agricultural Workers Program; see Loza, "Japanese Agricultural Workers' Program," 661–90.
15. McWilliams, *Southern California*, 12–13.
16. Yvonne De Los Santos and Roberto Flores, interview by Frank P. Barajas, February 1, 2013.
17. "The Obvious Should Be Made Official," *Los Angeles Times*, June 9, 1963.
18. Ray Hebert, "Survey of Regional Traffic Tackles Host of Questions," *Los Angeles Times*, August 5, 1962; Avila, *Folklore of the Freeway*.
19. Over $250,000,000, adjusted for inflation; Al Johns, "Ventura County Comes to Life in New Population Explosion," *Los Angeles Times*, May 29, 1960; "L.A. Area to Get Most New Residents in '60s," *Los Angeles Times*, May 10, 1961.
20. Abrams to Griffin in San Francisco, April 16, 1946, NAACPR, carton 86; Lily Watkins, interview by Frank P. Barajas, June 4, 2003; Domingo Martínez, "Comparative Study"; Howard Kennedy, "Bias in Housing near Military Bases Noted," *Los Angeles Times*, September 23, 1967.
21. Richard Abrams to Noel Griffin in San Francisco, April 16, 1946, NAACPR, carton 86; "Prejudice in Oxnard Grows; Trouble Brews," *Neighborhood News*, March 21, 1946, 1, NAACP Papers, carton 86, folder 11; "Four Ejected from Oxnard Theatre as Friction Grows," *Eagle*, April 4, 1945, NAACP Papers, carton 86, folder 11.
22. Notes, NAACPR, carton 86; November 24, 1945, Emory McMurray, president, to Regional Office, November 24, 1945, NAACPR, carton 99, folder 8.
23. December 2, 1967, NAACP Papers, carton 59.
24. Abrams to Griffin, in San Francisco, April 16, 1946, NAACPR, carton 86, folder 11; "Prejudice in Oxnard Grows," *Neighborhood News*, 1; "Four Ejected from Oxnard Theatre," *Eagle*.
25. Notes, NAACPR, carton 86, folder 11; Emory Murray to Regional Office, November 24, 1945, NAACPR, carton 99, folder 8.
26. "Four Ejected from Oxnard Theatre," *Eagle*.
27. "Local Race Issue Hit by Trustee," *Oxnard Press-Courier*, June 14, 1963.

28. Anne Hetfield, "Oxnarders Speak Out on Race Turmoil," *Oxnard Press-Courier*, July 17, 1963.
29. Notes, NAACPR, carton 86, folder 11; NAACP Annual Report of 1967, NAACPR, carton 86, folder 13.
30. David García, Yosso, and Barajas, "Few of the Brightest"; David García and Yosso, "Capacity of Servant," 64–89; García, *Strategies of Segregation*; "Special Meeting Called to Discuss 'Segregation,'" *Oxnard Press-Courier*, April 29, 1963.
31. Watkins interview, 2003. (Disclosure: Lily Watkins was my first-grade teacher at Driffill Elementary.)
32. Notes on issues in NAACP Oxnard, December 2, 1967, NAACPR, carton 59, folder 38.
33. José Antonio Villareal, "Mexican-Americans and the Leadership Crisis," *Los Angeles Times*, September 25, 1966.
34. Jiménez, *Replenished Ethnicity*.
35. Villareal, "Mexican-Americans and the Leadership Crisis."
36. Rachel Murguia Wong, interview by Frank P. Barajas and David G. García, May 30, 2010.
37. Owens, chief of police, February 26, 1975, COC, box 28; April 22, 1975, "Report on a Proposed Civilian Complaint Review Board for the City of Oxnard," April 22, 1975, COC, box 28.
38. "Education Needs of Minority Young People," 1965 and 1966, COC, box 28.
39. Summer Report of 1971, COC, box 28.
40. Roberto Flores, interview by Frank P. Barajas, April 14, 2006; Rosas, *Abrazando el Espíritu*, 62.
41. Francisca "Kika" Friend, interview by Frank P. Barajas, May 4, 2006; Flores interview, 2006; "850 Wetbacks Rounded Up in County," *Ventura County Star-Free Press*, July 29, 1967; "Letters to the Editor: Wondering about Wetbacks," *Ventura County Star-Free Press*, August 1, 1967; Hernández, *Migra!*, 166; Patiño, *Raza Sí, Migra No*.
42. Friend interview, 2006; Fermín Herrera, interview by Frank P. Barajas, August 14, 2019; Rosa Rodriguez, interview by Frank P. Barajas, November 9, 2012; Flores, *Grounds for Dreaming*, 178.
43. Rosas, *Abrazando el Espíritu*.
44. "Council Candidates to Air Views at Meet," *Oxnard Press-Courier*, January 14, 1974.
45. Moses Mora, interview by Frank P. Barajas, June 1, 2016.

46. De Los Santos and Flores interview, 2013; Mora interview, 2016; "Voice of the People: Ex-teen Speaks," by Dan E. Contreras, *Oxnard Press-Courier*, January 5, 1969; Johnson, *Spaces of Conflict*, 12, 94.
47. Murguia Wong interview, 2010; Flores interview, 2006; Juan Lagunas Soria, interview by Frank Bardacke, January 25, 1996; Barajas, *Curious Unions*, chapter 5.
48. De Los Santos and Flores interview, 2013; Peggy Larios, interview by Frank P. Barajas, September 3, 2019.
49. Laura Espinosa, interview by Frank P. Barajas, May 30, 2012; Mora interview, 2016; Soria interview, 1996; Manuel Avila De Los Santos, manuscript, n.d.; Ray Tejada and Teresa Preciado Tejada, interview by Frank P. Barajas, June 26, 2012; Morales, *Dionicio Morales*.
50. Ismael "Mayo" de la Rocha, interview by Frank P. Barajas, May 15 and 22, 2014; Armando López, interview by Frank P. Barajas and David G. García, June 21, 2010; García and Castro, *Blowout!*
51. Jess Gutiérrez, interview by Frank P. Barajas, June 28, 2010; Mora interview, 2016; Oropeza, *¡Raza Sí! ¡Guerra No!*, 67–68; Nancy Matsumoto, "A Streetwise Latino Beams His Message," *Los Angeles Times*, February 19, 1994.
52. Manuela Aparicio-Twitchell, interview by Frank P. Barajas, July 22, 2014; De Los Santos and Flores interview, 2013; Murguia Wong interview 2010; Avie Guerra, manuscript, 2007; Licón, "Feminist Mobilization in MEChA," 76–110.
53. Aparicio-Twitchell interview, 2014; Tom Richter, "Seven Vie for Four Positions on A.S. Board Tuesday," *Pirate Press*, January 10, 1975; Tom Richter, "MEChA Sweeps A.S. Elections," *Pirate Press*, January 17, 1975.
54. Diana Borrego Martínez, interview by Frank P. Barajas, July 9, 2012; Lee Dye and Harry Trimborn, "286 Seized at Valley State Rally," *Los Angeles Times*, January 10, 1969; Bea Hartmann, "Plea for Police Probe Granted," *Oxnard Press-Courier*, August 14, 1968; "Pickets Protest at Police," *Oxnard Press-Courier*, January 25, 1969.
55. Thompson, "Strange Rumblings in Aztlan," 222–41; Gutiérrez interview, 2010. For quotes, see Kurt Sanders, "'La Raza' Peace March Goes off without a Hitch," *Ventura County Star-Free Press*, September 20, 1970; and "Year of the Chicano," *Ventura County Star-Free Press*, September 20, 1970.
56. Borrego Martínez interview, 2012; De Los Santos and Flores interview, 2013; Mora interview, 2016; Blackwell, *¡Chicana Power!*, 135; Frank Del Olmo, "Community Awareness behind Bars: Chicano Prison Inmates Find New Purpose," *Los Angeles Times*, August 24, 1971.

2. Mexican American Role Models

1. Burt, "Power of a Mobilized Citizenry," 421; Vargas, *Labor Rights Are Civil Rights*, 275; Ruíz, *From Out of the Shadows*, 132.
2. Chávez to Ross, December 20, 1960, File Correspondence 1959–60, FRSC, box 3; "Oxnard Will Host CSO Convention," *Oxnard Press-Courier*, February 17, 1964; Forbes, *Aztecs del Norte*, 257.
3. David White, "Camarillo Nurseryman Spends Time as Counselor to Mexican-Americans," *Oxnard Press-Courier*, February 3, 1959; "CSO Plans Registration Campaign," *Oxnard Press-Courier*, January 9, 1960; "CSO Opens Drive for Registration," *Oxnard Press-Courier*, March 1, 1960.
4. Bill Bitters, "Four Barred from Voting," *Oxnard Press-Courier*, November 9, 1960; Forbes, *Aztecs del Norte*, 255–57.
5. "City Council Candidate John Soria Favors Oxnard-Hueneme Consolidation," *Oxnard Press-Courier*, March 25, 1960; "Ten Candidates in a Race for 3 Oxnard Council Seats," *Oxnard Press-Courier*, April 5, 1962; Juan Soria, interview by Frank Bardacke, January 25, 1996.
6. "Editorials: Tomorrow's Election in Oxnard," *Oxnard Press-Courier*, April 11, 1960.
7. "Council Candidates to Speak Tonight," *Oxnard Press-Courier*, March 10, 1960; "Eight Candidates for Council Speak," *Oxnard Press-Courier*, March 11, 1960; "'Meet Your Candidate' Talk Brings Small Crowd," *Oxnard Press-Courier*, May 31, 1960; "CSO Delegates Arriving for Convention," *Oxnard Press-Courier*, March 13, 1964; quote from "Labor, Housing, Key CSO Issues," *Oxnard Press-Courier*, March 14, 1964; "Supervisor, Judge Race Forum Due," *Oxnard Press-Courier*, May 26, 1964; "Supervisor, Judge Forum Set by CSO," *Oxnard Press-Courier*, May 28, 1968; Mike Bird, "Heated Exchange in Colonia Forum," *Oxnard Press-Courier*, May 29, 1963; Laura Flores Espinosa, interview by Frank P. Barajas, May 30, 2012. In 1993 the Oxnard Elementary School District renamed the Juanita campus Cesar E. Chavez Elementary; see Matthew Mosk, "Oxnard: Cesar Chavez School Dedication Planned," *Los Angeles Times*, September 25, 1993; and HoSang, *Racial Propositions*, 83.
8. Ross, *Conquering Goliath*.
9. Rose, "Gender and Civic Activism," 189–90; section 2, Seventh CSO Annual Convention minutes, Saturday session, March 19, and Sunday session, March 20, 1960, Fresno CA; Saturday session, March 19, 1960, "Memorabilia, 50s & 60s," HGP, box A-14.

10. Barajas, *Curious Unions*, chapter 6; section 2, Seventh CSO Annual Convention minutes, HGP, box A-14; Herman Gallegos, interview by Frank P. Barajas, May 21, 2012; Flores Espinosa interview, 2012.
11. Pitti, *Devil in Silicon Valley*, 160; "Union Pickets Demolition of Oxnard Hotel," *Oxnard Press-Courier*, March 22, 1960; "Legal Notice," *Oxnard Press-Courier*, June 1, 1960; "Legal Notice," *Oxnard Press-Courier*, October 13, 1962; Jim Wilson, "Project Head Start Opens amid Good and Bad Omens," *Oxnard Press-Courier*, June 28, 1965; CSO Reporter 1958 Special Edition, 26–29, UFW:OPC, box 26.
12. "CSO Presents First Debutantes," *Oxnard Press-Courier*, June 25, 1969; "Easter Egg Hunts Depend on Aid to the City," *Oxnard Press-Courier*, April 12, 1960; "Benefit Barbecue Planned by CSO," *Oxnard Press-Courier*, March 31, 1961; "700 Colonia-Area Youngsters See Santa, Receive Presents," *Oxnard Press-Courier*, December 20, 1970; section 2, Seventh CSO Annual Convention minutes, HGP, box A-14.
13. "CSO Plans Program to Aid Youth," *Oxnard Press-Courier*, March 9, 1961; "Police to Talk on Youth Crime at CSO Meeting," *Oxnard Press-Courier*, March 30, 1961; "Principals Fail to Sway CSO Opposition to School Bonds," *Oxnard Press-Courier*, January 18, 1963.
14. Pardo, *Mexican American Women Activists*, 31; "CSO Crowns Queen at Ball Tonight," *Oxnard Press-Courier*, September 11, 1959; untitled article, *Oxnard Press-Courier*, September 14, 1959; "CSO Planning 2nd Annual Queen Contest," *Oxnard Press-Courier*, June 20, 1960; "CSO Presents First Debutantes," *Oxnard Press-Courier*; Flores Espinosa interview, 2012.
15. Stockton CSO letter to Stockton City Council concerning urban redevelopment, November 10, 1958, FRSP, box 4; Hernandez, Stockton CSO president, statement to Stockton City Council, January 12, 1959, FRSP, box 4; "Indenture," Ventura County Cerk and Recorder, January 23, 1913, Book 134, 547; "Indenture," Ventura County Clerk and Recorder, February 24, 1913, Book 134, 550; "Reservations, Restrictions, and Protective Covenants Applicable to the Eugene H. Agee Subdivision lot 132 of Patterson Ranch Subdivision of Ventura County," Ventura County Clerk and Recorder, June 18, 1951, Book 1005, 36; I am grateful to David G. García and Tara J. Yosso for sharing with me these covenants within residential deeds in Oxnard. The first two have the exact following language: "And said premises shall not, at any time, be sold or conveyed to any person of Negro, Japanese or Chinese race, nor to any Mexican or Indian." The last deed has the following restriction, "No person of any race other than the White or Caucasian race, nor

any Mexican, Indian or East Indian, nor any person who is a lineal descendant of the first or second degree of a person born in the Republic of Mexico shall use or occupy any building, or any parcel, except that this covenant shall not prevent occupancy of by domestic servants of a different race domiciled with an owner or tenant"; Chávez to Ross, December 4, 1961, FRSC, box 3; "Colonia Rebuilding Fight Vowed," *Oxnard Press-Courier*, December 1, 1961.

16. Avila, *Popular Culture in the Age of White*, 62, 167–68; Gallegos interview, 2012.
17. "Colonia Rebuilding Fight Vowed," *Oxnard Press-Courier*; Levy, *Cesar Chavez*, 34–35; Chávez to Ross, December 22, 1961, FRSC, box 3.
18. "Colonia to Begin Cleanup," *Oxnard Press-Courier*, January 20, 1962; "CSO Blasts Small-Lot Colonia Tract," *Oxnard Press-Courier*, February 7, 1962; "CSO Warns of Colonia Speculators," *Oxnard Press-Courier*, March 14, 1962; Alvarez interview, 2013.
19. Report of Ventura County CSO Chapter to CSO National Executive Board, 1962, FRSP, box 11; "CSO Wary of U.S. Urban Study," *Oxnard Press-Courier*, February 20, 1963.
20. "50 Join Committee Backing School Bonds," *Oxnard Press-Courier*, January 9, 1963; "NAACP, CSO to Meet to Air Bond Issue Stand," *Oxnard Press-Courier*, January 16, 1963; quote from "Principals Fail to Sway CSO," *Oxnard Press-Courier*; "NAACP Joins Foes on Bonds," *Oxnard Press-Courier*, January 18, 1963.
21. "Principals Fail to Sway CSO," *Oxnard Press-Courier*; Charles Reach, "Voice of the People: Bonds Are a Must," *Oxnard Press-Courier*, January 18, 1963; "School Board Head Replies to Foes of Bond Issue," *Oxnard Press-Courier*, January 19, 1963. To accommodate the racial separatism of white parents, since the early twentieth century the Oxnard Elementary School District manipulated attendance boundaries and established schools to segregate children from their white peers; see David García, Yosso, and Barajas, "Few of the Brightest," 1–20.
22. "Principals Fail to Sway CSO," *Oxnard Press-Courier*; "$3.2 Million Issue in Peril Tomorrow," *Oxnard Press-Courier*, January 21, 1963; "Voting Brisk on Elementary School Bonds," *Oxnard Press-Courier*, January 22, 1963.
23. "NAACP Wants Hearing on School Issue," *Oxnard Press-Courier*, January 28, 1963.
24. Ralph Kaminsky, "Juggling Schools Urged to Mix Races: Anti-Segregation Plan to Face Study," *Oxnard Press-Courier*, March 6, 1963; "'Minority Races' in Majority among Oxnard District Elementary Students," *Oxnard Press-Courier*, March 13, 1963.
25. Kaminsky, "Juggling Schools Urged to Mix Races."
26. Kaminsky, "Juggling Schools Urged to Mix Races."

27. "Editorials: There Is No Deep South Bias Here," *Oxnard Press-Courier*, March 18, 1963.
28. García, *Strategies of Segregation*.
29. "D.A. Ruling Backs Plan for Colonia Area School," *Oxnard Press-Courier*, April 3, 1963.
30. Chuck Andrews, "Mass Meeting Told No New Junior High: New Grade School Eyed in La Colonia," *Oxnard Press-Courier*, June 25, 1963.
31. Barajas, *Curious Unions*, chapter 4.
32. "Gang Injures Oxnard Policemen," *Oxnard Press-Courier*, December 23, 1946; "Seven Are Arrested after Forming Gang," *Oxnard Press-Courier*, December 23, 1946; "Police Cleared of Brutality Charge: Mexican Consul General's Charge Leads to Inquiry by State Attorney General," *Oxnard Press-Courier*, January 22, 1947; "Asserted Mistreatment of Mexicans Protested," *Los Angeles Times*, January 22, 1947.
33. "Police Probe No Smear," *Oxnard Press-Courier*, July 1, 1947; "Shannon Backs Police Chief," *Oxnard Press-Courier*, July 2, 1947; "Grand Jury Indicts For," *Oxnard Press-Courier*, July 3, 1947.
34. "Shannon Backs Police Chief," *Oxnard Press-Courier*.
35. Morales, *Ando sangrando*, 20.
36. "Police Car Battered by Bottles, Rocks," *Oxnard Press-Courier*, May 26, 1958.
37. Morales, *Ando sangrando*, 139; John Douglas, "Jewell Promises Force to Quell Colonia Gang," *Oxnard Press-Courier*, March 2, 1967.
38. Barajas, *Curious Unions*, chapter 6.
39. Burt, "Tony Rios and Bloody Christmas," 159–92.
40. Elliott Sopkin, "Chief Backs Men, Blasts Accusers," *Oxnard Press-Courier*, April 4, 1962; "'Brutality' Probe Asked by Council," *Oxnard Press-Courier*, April 5, 1962.
41. Cloromiro Camacho, "Voice of the People—Pressure Groups," *Oxnard Press-Courier*, April 17, 1962.
42. Camacho, "Pressure Groups."
43. Richard Lyttle, "Council Gets Report on State Probe," *Oxnard Press-Courier*, April 25, 1962.
44. Morales, *Ando sangrando*, 11, 20.
45. Bea Hartmann, "Plea for Police Probe Granted," *Oxnard Press-Courier*, August 14, 1968.
46. "Mexican-American Group Forms Oxnard Chapter," *Oxnard Press-Courier*, February 16, 1966.

47. "Mexican-American Group Forms Oxnard Chapter"; "MAPA to Install Officers Monday," *Oxnard Press-Courier*, March 20, 1966.
48. Herzog, *Minority Group Politics*, 299–300.
49. Ron Hosie, "Council, Schools Blasted by MAPA," *Oxnard Press-Courier*, January 23, 1968.
50. Hosie, "Council, Schools Blasted by MAPA."
51. "Sanchez Rebuts MAPA Blast," *Oxnard Press-Courier*, January 24, 1968.
52. Salvatore Sánchez Jr., "Voice of the People: Objects to Overtures," *Oxnard Press-Courier*, September 5, 1969.
53. John Soria, "Voice of the People: Sánchez Thanked," *Oxnard Press-Courier*, May 19, 1970.
54. David García, *Strategies of Segregation*; Valencia, *Chicano Students and the Courts*, 67–70; Oxnard School District Board of Trustees v. Soria et al., Supreme Court of the United States 416. U.S. 951; 94 S. Ct. 1961; 40 L. Ed. 2d 301; 1974 U.S. LEXIS 652; Ruben N. Martínez, interview by Frank P. Barajas, December 18, 2020.

3. The Young and the Restive

1. Roberto Flores, interview by Frank P. Barajas, April 4, 2006.
2. "CSO to Elect New Officers," *Oxnard Press-Courier*, January 20, 1960; "Soria Elected CSO President," *Oxnard Press-Courier*, January 29, 1960; Bea Hartmann, "Who Are the Guys in the Brown Berets," *Oxnard Press-Courier*, August 21, 1968; Armando López, email to author, March 5, 2007; Barajas, *Curious Unions*, chapter 6.
3. Flores interview, 2006; Roberto Flores, interview by Frank P. Barajas, June 11, 2010; William Terry, interview by Frank P. Barajas and David García, May 8, 2010; Bea Hartmann, "Brown Berets Aggressive in Spirit, Energetic," *Oxnard Press-Courier*, August 29, 1968.
4. Hartmann, "Brown Berets Aggressive"; quote from Bea Hartmann, "Who Are the Guys in the Brown Berets," *Oxnard Press-Courier*, August 21, 1968.
5. Peggy Larios, interview by Frank P. Barajas, September 3, 2019.
6. Wally Smith, "Picket, Walk Out: Brown Berets Protest 'County Farm Kingdom,'" Ventura County *Star Free-Press*, October 20, 1968.
7. Berger, *Dollar Harvest*.
8. Flores interview, 2006; Flores interview, 2010; Hartmann, "Guys in the Brown Berets."
9. "Oxnard Police Cleared of Brutality Complaints," *Los Angeles Times*, February 26, 1969.

10. Assembly Select Committee on the Administration of Justice Hearing, April 28, 1972, Los Angeles CA: Relations between the Police and Mexican-Americans, L500 J85 1972 no. 1, v. 1 c. 3.
11. Brekke to administrative staff, Oxnard School District memo, October 14, 1968, Oxnard School District Archives (OSDA), tape 194.
12. Brekke to administrative staff, October 14, 1968, OSDA.
13. Brekke to administrative staff, October 14, 1968, OSDA.
14. Flores interview, 2010.
15. Flores interview, 2010; Flores interview, 2006.
16. Flores interview, 2010; Flores interview, 2006; Brekke to administrative staff, October 14, 1968, OSDA.
17. Flores interview, 2010.
18. "Brown Berets Plan Meeting in Oxnard," *Oxnard Press-Courier*, December 25, 1968, 9; Richards, "Land Is Rich"; Fermín Herrera, interview by Frank P. Barajas, August 14, 2019; Bebout, *Mythohistorical Imaginations*, 8.
19. "Brown Berets Plan Meeting in Oxnard," *Oxnard Press-Courier*; "Unity Group Planned for Oxnard," *Oxnard Press-Courier*, December 29, 1968.
20. Hartmann, "Brown Berets Aggressive"; Flores interview, 2006.
21. Flores interview, 2006; Flores interview, 2010.
22. Flores interview, 2006; Flores interview, 2010; "Editorial: Study Project Deserves a Chance," *Oxnard Press-Courier*, July 5, 1969.
23. Approximately $900, adjusted for inflation; see "Editorial: Study Project," *Oxnard Press-Courier*.
24. "Chicano Educators' Aid to Be Requested," *Oxnard Press-Courier*, November 17, 1970; Larios interview, 2019.
25. Acuña, *Occupied America*, 346; Oropeza, *Raza Sí! ¡Guerra No!*
26. Acuña, *Occupied America*, 347–48; Oropeza, *¡Raza Sí! ¡Guerra No!*, 172; Thompson, "Strange Rumblings in Aztlan," 235.
27. Thompson, "Strange Rumblings in Aztlan," 220–21.
28. Quoted in Arthur Gómez, "Letters: Siesta Is Over!," *Ventura County Star-Free Press*, September 3, 1970. Ramírez echoed the sentiments of Gómez; see Juan Ramírez, "Letters: A Long Time," *Ventura County Star-Free Press*, September 7, 1970.
29. Rick Nielsen, "Chicanos Urged to Unite," *Oxnard Press-Courier*, September 20, 1970; Larios interview, 2019.
30. Larios interview, 2019; quote from "Mexican-Americans Slate Peace March," *Oxnard Press-Courier*, September 10, 1970.

31. "Mexican-Americans Slate Peace March," *Oxnard Press-Courier*, September 10, 1970; "Peace March Leaders Issue Conduct Code for Paraders," *Oxnard Press-Courier*, September 17, 1970; "Conduct Code Commendable," *Oxnard Press-Courier*, September 18, 1970; "Chicanos Set Sept. 19 for Oxnard Peace March," *Ventura County Star-Free Press*, September 10, 1970; "Peace Expected During Oxnard March," *Ventura County Star-Free Press*, September 18, 1970.
32. Quote from "Peace March Leaders Issue Conduct Code for Paraders," *Oxnard Press-Courier*, September 17, 1970; "2,000 Expected for Peace March," *Oxnard Press-Courier*, September 19, 1970.
33. Quote from "Praise for All," *Oxnard Press-Courier*, September 22, 1970. The moratorium protest and the concern for it was also in the context of the student uprising at the Isle Vista community at the University of California at Santa Barbara. "Conduct Code Commendable," *Oxnard Press-Courier*, September 18, 1970; Nielsen, "Chicanos Urged to Unite"; "Peace Expected During Oxnard March," *Ventura County Star-Free Press*, September 18, 1970.
34. Jess Gutiérrez, interview by Frank P. Barajas, June 28, 2010; Nielsen, "Chicanos Urged to Unite"; "Year of the Chicano," *Ventura County Star-Free Press*, September 20, 1970.
35. Richard Becerra, "Voice of the People: Joy to Be with You," *Oxnard Press-Courier*, September 25, 1970.
36. M. García, "Voice of the People: Just Cause for All," *Oxnard Press-Courier*, October 2, 1970.
37. Ruben N. Martínez, "Voice of the People: Leadership Questioned," *Oxnard Press-Courier*, September 20, 1970; Ruben N. Martínez, "Voice of the People: Choice Applauded," *Oxnard Press-Courier*, February 2, 1969.
38. Ruben N. Martínez, "Voice of the People: Question of Identity," *Oxnard Press-Courier*, February 15, 1970, 4; Ruben N. Martínez, "Voice of the People: Backs Mrs. Banuelos," *Oxnard Press-Courier*, October 18, 1971.
39. Ruben N. Martínez, "Voice of the People: Permissiveness Hit," *Oxnard Press-Courier*, September 27, 1970; Ruben N. Martínez, "Voice of the People: Permissiveness Hit," *Oxnard Press-Courier*, October 2, 1971. As president of the United Latin American Citizens for Nixon, Martínez endorsed and supported the Nixon election campaign; see "Ad. Minoria Olvidada," *Oxnard Press-Courier*, September 29, 1968.
40. Armando Morales, *Ando sangrando*, 91.
41. Rick Nielsen, "Officers Quell Disturbance in Colonia Area," *Oxnard Press-Courier*, July 12, 1971; Paul Scripps and Robert Arras, "'Hoodlums' Damage Oxnard Bank, School," *Ventura County Star-Free Press*, July 12, 1971; Gutiérrez interview, 2010.

42. Rick Nielsen, "Mob Cuts Destructive Swath through Colonia," *Oxnard Press-Courier*, July 19, 1971; Rick Nielsen, "Colonia Disorders Explored," *Oxnard Press-Courier*, July 20, 1971; Paul Scripps and John Willson, "Drug Store, Bank Firebombed: New Violence Hits Colonia Area," *Ventura County Star-Free Press*, July 19, 1971; "Oxnard Starts Cleanup after Violent Disturbance by Youths," *Los Angeles Times*, July 20, 1971.

43. "Editorials: Disturbances Must Be Halted," *Oxnard Press-Courier*, July 20, 1971, 4; $670,000, adjusted for inflation.

44. Nielsen, "Colonia Disorders Explored"; Scripps and Willson, "Drug Store, Bank Firebombed."

45. "Editorials: Good Example from Bad Episode," *Oxnard Press-Courier*, July 15, 1971; Rick Nielsen, "Garcia Honored by Elks for Saving 'Old Glory,'" *Oxnard Press-Courier*, July 27, 1971.

46. Nielsen, "Garcia Honored by Elks."

47. Bea Hartmann, "CRC Asks Council for Police Probe," *Oxnard Press-Courier*, July 20, 1971; Art Campos, "Oxnard Police Conduct Probed," *Ventura County Star-Free Press*, July 20, 1971.

48. "Chief Asks U.S. Aid in Colonia Troubles," *Oxnard Press-Courier*, July 21, 1971; Art Kuhn, "Meeting Marred by Bomb Threat," *Oxnard Press-Courier*, July 21, 1971; "Police Chief: Uneasiness at Colonia," *Ventura County Star-Free Press*, July 25, 1971. Chief Owens expressed appreciation for the revision of his department's revaluation of the use of firearms policy several years before. Up to July 1971 his officer did not use their guns once in La Colonia, contrasted with five times in 1970 and eleven times in 1968; no figures were provided for the year 1969. See "Police Chief: Uneasiness at Colonia," *Ventura County Star-Free Press*; John Willson and Robert Arras, "Troubled Times in La Colonia: Days of Anguish, Nights of Violence . . . and Tomorrow?," *Ventura County Star-Free Press*, July 25, 1971; and Peter Martínez, interview by Frank P. Barajas, June 23, 2020.

49. "Supervisors Rewarded with Jello," *Oxnard Press-Courier*, May 17, 1972.

50. In Ventura County the U.S. Border Patrol transported approximately eighty-five to ninety-five Mexican immigrants without immigration documents from its Oxnard office to Mexico; see "14 Illegal Aliens Arrested; Bakery in Ventura Closes," *Oxnard Press-Courier*, September 2, 1972.

51. "Council, CRC to Meet in Late August on Police, Job Issues," *Oxnard Press-Courier*, July 29, 1971; William Terry, interview by Frank P. Barajas and David García, May 8, 2010; Kelly Lytle Hernández, *City of Inmates*, 42, 164; for a trenchant

examination of racial formation via mobility restrictions, see Carpio, *Collision at the Crossroads*.

52. "SP Policeman Hit by Rock in Downtown Disturbance," *Santa Paula Daily Chronicle*, April 10, 1972; "5 Youths Apprehended, 2 Hurt in Santa Paula Melee," *Oxnard Press-Courier*, April 10, 1972.

53. "Youths Picket in Santa Paula," *Oxnard Press-Courier*, April 16, 1972; "Santa Paul Youth Protest Held in Cars," *Oxnard Press-Courier*, April 17, 1972.

54. "100 Lawmen Put Down Disturbances," *Santa Paula Daily Chronicle*, April 24, 1972; "35 Arrested in 5-Hour Melee in Santa Paula," *Oxnard Press-Courier*, April 24, 1972; "Shots Fired at Police during Santa Paula Chicano Protest," *Los Angeles Times*, April 24, 1972; "Car Firebombed Man Shot during Santa Paula Melee," *Redlands Daily Facts*, April 24, 1972.

55. "The Editor's Corner: 'What Do They Want?,'" *Santa Paula Daily Chronicle*, April 25, 1972; "All-City Trouble-Solving Council Proposed for SP," *Santa Paula Daily Chronicle*, April 26, 1972.

56. "Brown Berets Conduct 'Respectful' Meeting; City Has Calm Weekend," *Santa Paula Daily Chronicle*, May 1, 1972.

57. "Dozens of Store Windows Broken, One Shot, 31 Arrested in Outburst of Violence Here," *Santa Paula Daily Chronicle*, June 12, 1972; "Santa Paula Melee Quelled; 31 Nabbed," *Oxnard Press-Courier*, June 12, 1972; "1 Shot, 31 Arrested in Santa Paula Violence," *Los Angeles Times*, June 13, 1972.

58. Barajas, *Curious Unions*, 133–34; "Police Quell Colonia Riot," *Oxnard Press-Courier*, April 23, 1955; "Riot Stabbing Victim Still in Bad Shape," *Oxnard Press-Courier*, April 25, 1955; "Colonia Riot Suspects Freed," *Oxnard Press-Courier*, October 27, 1956.

59. "All-City Trouble-Solving Council," *Santa Paula Daily Chronicle*; Robert Borrego, emails to author, April 26 and 29, 2020.

60. "Marcha de la Reconquista," *Ideal*, May 16, 1971. Related to the deportation raids, Muñoz stated that La Marcha also demanded the end of the immigration Green Card program at the border; see "Southland: Latins in Quiet Protest March," *Los Angeles Times*, May 6, 1971; and Jack Jones, "Chicanos' 3-Month March to Capital Reaches Salton Sea," *Los Angeles Times*, May 6, 1971.

61. Yvonne De Los Santos and Roberto Flores, interview by Frank P. Barajas, February 1, 2013; "Marcha de la Reconquista," *Ideal*, May 16, 1971; Jones, "Chicanos' 3-Month March"; "Reconquista March Passes through Chino," *El Chicano*, June 11, 1971.

62. Jones, "Chicanos' 3-Month March"; Frank Del Olmo, "Chicanos: Protesters Pass through L.A. in March," *Los Angeles Times*, June 16, 1971; "Marcha de la Reconquista," *Grito del Norte*, August 20, 1971.
63. De Los Santos and Flores interview, 2013; Acuña, *Making of Chicana/o Studies*, 109.
64. De Los Santos and Flores interview, 2013; Acuña, *Making of Chicana/o Studies*, 109; Gutiérrez interview, 2010; "Reconquista Rally," *El Popo* 3, no. 3 (June 19, 1971): n.p.
65. De Los Santos and Flores interview, 2013.
66. De Los Santos and Flores interview, 2013; "Chicano March Ends in Near-Skirmish," *Los Angeles Times*, August 8, 1971.

4. Racially Segregated Schools

1. Rachel Murguia Wong, interview by Frank P. Barajas and David G. García, May 30, 2010.
2. Murguia Wong interview, 2010; Armando López, interview by Frank P. Barajas and David G. García, June 21, 2010; Roberto Flores, interview by Frank P. Barajas, November 6, 2010; Peggy Larios, interview by Frank P. Barajas, September 3, 2019.
3. Murguia Wong interview, 2010; "Panel to Review Housing Guidelines," *Oxnard Press-Courier*, February 23, 1971; Rick Nielsen, "Rachel Wong: Woman of Many Hats," *Oxnard Press-Courier*, February 27, 1972; "'Beautiful Activist' Rachel Wong Receives Award," *Oxnard Press-Courier*, May 25, 1973.
4. Murguia Wong interview, 2010, and telephone conversation, August 6, 2013; Ned McKay, "Controversial Figure: School Retains Colonia Aide," *Oxnard Press-Courier*, June 3, 1970.
5. McKay, "Controversial Figure."
6. McKay, "Controversial Figure."
7. "Oxnard District Voters Pick Trustee Tuesday," *Oxnard Press-Courier*, January 3, 1971; "Rachel Wong Winner in School Race," *Oxnard Press-Courier*, January 6, 1971.
8. Murguia Wong interview, 2010.
9. David García, Yosso, and Barajas, "Few of the Brightest," 1–25; David García, *Strategies of Segregation*.
10. "To Aid Integration: Oxnard Probes Shuttle System for School Kids," *Los Angeles Sentinel*, March 28, 1963.
11. "Pupil Enrollment, Ethnic Distribution, the Current Framework of the Law and Policy Dealing with School Integration, and the Implications These Factors Have

for School Construction and Site Acquisition in the OSDA," n.d. (ca. August–September 1968), OSDA, microfilm tape 194, foreword and 13.
12. "Anglo Students Outnumbered in Schools' Ethnic Make-Up," *Oxnard Press-Courier*, September 18, 1968; "Improving Racial and Ethnic Balance and Intergroup Relations: An Advisory Report to the Board of Trustees Oxnard School District," California State Department of Education, Division of Compensatory Education, Bureau of Intergroup Relations, April 1969, OSDA, microfilm tape 194, 7–8.
13. "Improving Racial and Ethnic Balance," 1–2.
14. "Improving Racial and Ethnic Balance," 9.
15. "Improving Racial and Ethnic Balance," 10.
16. The report allowed districts to consider feasibility factors in the creation of alternative plans based upon boundary determinations and the school organization by grade level, student demographics of a district, and its individual schools, see "Improving Racial and Ethnic Balance," 10–11.
17. The report also called upon the district to make cultural accommodations to that of the culture of Black and Mexican-origin students; see "Improving Racial and Ethnic Balance," 18–21.
18. "Improving Racial and Ethnic Balance," 34–37.
19. Cloene I. Marson, "Voice of the People: Supports Integration," *Oxnard Press-Courier*, November 1, 1969.
20. Marson, "Supports Integration." The matter was not an "us against them" issue; people of various ethnicities and backgrounds opposed and supported the idea of busing to remedy school segregation. As candidates for the OESD board in the spring of 1969, Paula Reach and Jean Comer supported busing when their political opponents either opposed it outright, opposed "mass" busing, or skirted the issue by arguing for increased federal and state funding to ensure equal education in all the schools of the district. See "School Board Hopefuls: Segregation Issue Dominates Forum," *Oxnard Press-Courier*, April 9, 1969.
21. Kenneth L. Mytinger, "Voice of the People: Forced Busing Opposed," *Oxnard Press-Courier*, October 20, 1969.
22. Flores interview, 2010; William Terry, interview with Frank P. Barajas and David G. García, May 8, 2010; Murguia Wong interview, 2010.
23. Ralph Kaminksy, "School Candidates Hold Divergent Opinions on 'De Facto' Segregation," *Oxnard Press-Courier*, March 14, 1963.
24. Thomas Malley, interview with Frank P. Barajas, May 10, 2010; Gilbert Cuevas, interview with Frank P. Barajas and David G. García, May 5, 2010; Terry interview,

2010; Murguia Wong interview, 2010; "School Trustees to Study Segregation," *Oxnard Press-Courier*, October 8, 1969.
25. Sue Nava, "Voice of the People: Motivation' Answer?," *Oxnard Press-Courier*, June 20, 1971.
26. "Times Editorial Views," *Los Angeles Times*, November 2, 1969.
27. See "School Integration Milestone," *Christian Science Monitor*, October 31, 1969.
28. "Editorials: A Necessity to Act," *Oxnard Press-Courier*, May 4, 1969.
29. "Cost Probe Ordered: Oxnard Trustees OK More Study for Racial Balance Plan," *Oxnard Press-Courier*, November 5, 1969.
30. The newspaper report referenced a year-long study that demonstrated sixth-grade children living in La Colonia and attending schools on the west side earning improved grades from that of their counterparts that remained in the schools of La Colonia; see "Oxnard School Trustees Nearly 'Stab' State over Segregation Issue," *Ventura Star-Free Press*, November 5, 1969.
31. "Necessity to Act," *Oxnard Press-Courier*. The editorial referenced the board resolution in support of integration; the newspaper also cited the commitment of district administrators to address the issue. In "Voice of the People: Racist Society Must Change; School Segregation Is Start," *Oxnard Press-Courier*, May 4, 1969, William and Margaret Thrasher detailed the history of racism in the nation from the perspective of slavery. The two characterized the nation as a racist society that must be ended with the desegregation of the schools. The letter of the Thrashers was in response to an April 30 "Voice of the People" letter by H. J. Johnson.
32. "Editorials: Time for Attention to School Problem," *Oxnard Press-Courier*, September 19, 1969.
33. "School Trustees to Study Segregation."
34. "Editorials: A Start Toward Solving the Problem," *Oxnard Press-Courier*, October 23, 1969.
35. "Public Forum on Segregation in Schools to Be Held Sunday," *Oxnard Press-Courier*, November 12, 1969.
36. "NAACP Plans Protest March," *Oxnard Press-Courier*, November 27, 1969.
37. "NAACP Marches for Desegregation," *Oxnard Press-Courier*, December 3, 1969.
38. "Editorials: A Promising Plan of Attack," *Oxnard Press-Courier*, December 18, 1969; OESD Regular Board Meeting, January 20, 1970, OSDA, microfilm tape 393; "School Integrating Plan Runs into First Obstacle," *Oxnard Press-Courier*, January 21, 1970.

39. OESD Regular Board Meeting, January 20, 1970, OSDA, microfilm tape 393; "School Integrating Plan," *Oxnard Press-Courier*.
40. I thank Antonia Arguelles Di Liello for forwarding me this clipping; see Scott Steepleton, "Juan Soria, Key Figure in School Desegregation Battle, Dies at Age 65," *Ventura County Star*, June 15, 1997.
41. "Court Orders Pasadena to Integrate All Schools," *Oxnard Press-Courier*, January 21, 1970; Gene Blake, "Pasadena Schools Told to Integrate," *Los Angeles Times*, January 21, 1970.
42. United Press International (Washington DC), "U.S. Busing Orders Opposed President," *Oxnard Press-Courier*, February 18, 1970.
43. Associated Press, "Key Civil Rights Official Forced Out," *Oxnard Press-Courier*, February 18, 1970.
44. Associated Press, "Personal Attack Avoided: Commission on Civil Rights Scores Nixon on Integration," *Oxnard Press-Courier*, April 12, 1970.
45. United Press International (Bradenton FL), "Kirk Aides Bar U.S. Marshals in School Fuss," *Oxnard Press-Courier*, April 9, 1970.
46. "NAACP Marches for Desegregation."
47. "Petition Prays Parental Consent: Busing Plea Splits Legislators," *Oxnard Press-Courier*, October 21, 1969.
48. Debbie and Doreen Soria et al., Plaintiffs, v. Oxnard School District Board of Trustees et al., Defendants, 70-00396 Docket, NARA; the names listed in the suit were Leticia Barrios (6), Ramona School; John Soria's nieces Debbie (7) and Doreen Soria (8), Ramona School; David Scott Frazier (11), Rose Avenue School; Michael Silva (6), Juanita School; Vincent Silva (9), Juanita School; Victor Bernard (7), Rose Avenue School; April Weisman (5), Juanita School; Lilly Treviño (10) and Diane Treviño (6), Rose Avenue School. See John Willson, "Oxnard Parents File Bias Suit," *Star Free-Press*, March 2, 1970.
49. Malley interview, 2010; "Legal Services: Challenging the Power," *Los Angeles Sentinel*, May 27, 1971.
50. Malley interview, 2010; Roos interview, 2010; Kalish interview, 2013.
51. Malley interview, 2010; Roos interview, 2010; Kalish interview, 2013; Flores interview, 2010; Terry interview, 2010; "Colonia Votes against Busing," *Ventura County Star-Free Press*, June 16, 1970; "'Substandard' Education in Colonia Rapped," *Ventura County Star-Free Press*, June 16, 1970.
52. "Supreme Court Upholds Busing for Integration," *Oxnard Press-Courier*, April 20, 1971.

53. Helen Reynolds, "Integration Issue: School Suit Ruling Due," *Oxnard Press-Courier*, May 11, 1971.
54. Debbie and Doreen Soria et al., Plaintiffs, v. Oxnard School District Board of Trustees, Defendant, Civ. No. 70-396 U.S. District Court for the Central District of California 328 F. Supp. 155; 1971 U.S. Dist. LEXIS 13328, May 12, 1971; "Court Rules That District Must Provide Racially Balanced Schools," *El Chicano*, June 4, 1971.
55. *Soria v. Oxnard School District Board of Trustees*, Civ. No. 70-396 U.S. District Court for the Central District of California 328 F. Supp. 155; 1971 U.S. Dist. LEXIS 13328; Civil No. 70-396-HP Interlocutory Order, OSDA microfilm tape 194.
56. *Soria v. Oxnard School District Board of Trustees*, U.S. District Court, Central District Court of California, Civil No. 70-396-HP Memorandum and Order for Judgement, July 21, 1971, OSDA, microfilm tape 194.
57. Six other schools were paired that did not involve the schools primarily cited in the case; see "A Summary of the Court Orders Directed to the Oxnard School District, Taken from the Federal District Court Judgment," July 21, 1971, OSDA, microfilm tape 194.
58. "Summary of the Court Orders."
59. "Summary of the Court Orders."
60. "Summary of the Court Orders."

5. No Way, José!

1. In this memo Tregarthen included a copy of the court order; see Tregarthen to staff, May 13, 1971, NARA, Exhibit E, 40, folder 70-396 v. 1.
2. Debbie and Doreen Soria et al., Plaintiffs, v. Oxnard School District Board of Trustees, Defendant, Notice of Appeal, VIV. no. 70-396-HP; the report made no mention of trustee and board president J. Keith Mason's vote or attendance. Other issues mentioned in the report was the hiring of an African American administrator, and an Emergency School Assistance application for $100,000 to advance integration in the district; see Art Kuhn, "Seek Stay of Judge's Order: School Hire Attorney in Integration Hassle," *Oxnard Press-Courier*, August 4, 1971.
3. "Oxnard District Seeks Stay of Busing Order," *Oxnard Press-Courier*, August 30, 1971.
4. "Plaintiffs Oppose Oxnard Busing Stay," *Oxnard Press-Courier*, September 3, 1971.
5. Richard Rodgers, "Voice of the People: Constitution Cited," *Oxnard Press-Courier*, June 25, 1971.

6. Art Kuhn, "300 Turn Out to Oppose Forced Busing of Children," *Oxnard Press-Courier*, July 7, 1971; Joe D. Olmstead, "Voice of the People: Busing Opposed," *Oxnard Press-Courier*, July 12, 1971.
7. "Antibusing Feelings Lead Poll," *Oxnard Press-Courier*, June 16, 1971.
8. Helen Reynolds, "School Integration Rule Widened: Oxnard District Must Include Kindergarten in Desegregation Plan," *Oxnard Press-Courier*, June 18, 1971.
9. Russ M. Likce, "Voice of the People: Defends Mrs. Wong," *Oxnard Press-Courier*, August 20, 1971; Carla M. Bard, "Voice of the People: Prevent Recall," *Oxnard Press-Courier*, August 20, 1971; Gilbert G. Cuevas, "Voice of the People: Educators Speak Out," *Oxnard Press-Courier*, August 22, 1971; Violet Burton, "Voice of the People: Pull Together," *Oxnard Press-Courier*, August 28, 1971; Daniel Philip Goodwin, "Voice of the People: Feelings Justified," *Oxnard Press-Courier*, August 28, 1971; Edward L. Lascher, "Voice of the People: Recall Appalling," *Oxnard Press-Courier*, August 24, 1971.
10. Art Kuhn, "Trustee May Take Children Out of School," *Oxnard Press-Courier*, September 8, 1971.
11. In other business of the district, the board passed an Affirmative Action Promotion of Employment Practices Resolution that declared the district's commitment to achieve ethnic balance in the ranks of its teachers and administrators. Trustee Murguia Wong and community member and Brown Beret Armando López questioned the actual will of the district to diversify its faculty and administration; see Kuhn, "Trustee May Take Children."
12. "Oxnard District to Press Court for Busing Stay," *Oxnard Press-Courier*, September 22, 1971.
13. In the meeting Superintendent Tregarthen detailed that district enrollment was down by 242 students and explained that a number of factors could have contributed to this drop. At the same time, district officials admitted that parents withdrew students due to the busing order; see "Oxnard District to Press Court."
14. Oxnard School District, Compensatory Education Advisory Committee, December 10, 1969, OSDA, tape 194.
15. Oxnard School District, Compensatory Education Advisory Committee, December 10, 1969, OSDA, tape 194; Brekke, memo, October 14, 1968, OSDA, tape 194.
16. Neil V. Sullivan, "Common Fears Related to Integration," OSDA, tape 194.
17. Quote from Sullivan, "Common Fears Related to Integration"; Mike M. and Milstein and Dean E. Hoch, "A Landmark in School Racial Integration: Berekeley, California," *Phi Delta Kappan* 50, no. 9 (May 1969): 524–29.

18. Waymon Wells, chairman, Compensatory Education Advisory Committee, June 11, 1970, OSDA, tape 194.
19. "Speakers Bureau Established to Explain Minority Views," *Oxnard Press-Courier*, September 24, 1971.
20. "'Chicano' Film Receives OK," *Oxnard Press-Courier*, October 6, 1971; *Chicano from the Southwest*, 1970, Encyclopedia Britannica, https://archive.org/details/chicanofromthesouthwest (accessed January 6, 2021).
21. "Editorials: Many Eyes on Oxnard School District," *Oxnard Press-Courier*, September 12, 1971; "Anti-busing Marchers in Pontiac," CBS Evening News, September 6, 1971, http://www.criticalcommons.org/Members/mattdelmont/clips/anti-busing-marchers-in-pontiac-9-6-71.
22. Quote of Trustee Mason from "Kirk Tells of Plans for Fight on Busing," *Oxnard Press-Courier*, September 1, 1971. Kirk pointed to the Charlotte-Mecklenburg case, in which Justice Warren Burger wrote that a "strict racial ratio" was necessary in the achievement of integration; see Art Kuhn, "Kirk Hits Edict on Compulsory Oxnard Busing," *Oxnard Press-Courier*, September 3, 1971. As the busing question intensified in Oxnard, twenty thousand parents planned to boycott busing to achieve integration in San Francisco; see "20,000 S.F. Parents Plan Busing Boycott," *Oxnard Press-Courier*, September 3, 1971.
23. Art Kuhn, "Meeting Marred by Bomb Threat," *Oxnard Press-Courier*, July 21, 1971.
24. "Antibusing Group Seeks Wong Recall," *Oxnard Press-Courier*, August 10, 1971; "Saturday Parade to Protest Busing," *Oxnard Press-Courier*, August 26, 1971. Other busing-related information was listed by this report having to do with walking distances to warrant busing, community relations, and funding related issues, see "Board Appeals to Citizens in Busing Hassle," *Oxnard Press-Courier*, August 18, 1971.
25. "Board Appeals to Citizens in Busing Hassle."
26. "School Trustees to Study Desegregation," *Oxnard Press-Courier*, October 8, 1969; Ned MacKay, "Trustees Take 2 Views of School Integration," *Oxnard Press-Courier*, October 22, 1969; "School Integration: Why? How? and When?," November 1969, OSDA, tape 194.
27. *Soria v. Oxnard School District Board of Trustees*, nos. 71-2369, 71-2929 U.S. Court of Appeals for the Ninth Circuit 467 F. 2d 59; 1972 U.S. App. LEXIS 7844, 16 ALR. Fed. 944, 21 August 1972; "Integration Stay Denied," *Oxnard Press-Courier*, January 5, 1972.
28. "Integration Stay Denied"; "More Details Sought in Appeal on Busing," *Oxnard Press-Courier*, June 8, 1972; "Nixon Pledges Minimum Busing," *Oxnard Press-Courier*, August 4, 1971.

29. Judge Pregerson's order also included the district's recruitment of minority faculty and administrators to achieve parity with the pupil population of the district, special programs, and projects to involve parents in the education of their children. Interestingly, Wong stated her inclination to set aside the busing order as long as the other parts of Pregerson's order were preserved and carried out; see "Oxnard Busing Halt Certain: New Legislation Gives District the Right to End Controversial Order," *Oxnard Press-Courier*, June 11, 1972; "U.S. Asks Oxnard Busing Case Role," *Oxnard Press-Courier*, July 22, 1972; and "U.S. to Challenge Integration Order," *Oxnard Press-Courier*, August 7, 1972. Ken Mytinger resigned from the OESD board after removing his daughter from the Haydock Jr. High School. Mytinger purchased a home in Camarillo to have his daughter educated outside the district. The report on the challenge to the Broomfield Amendment also detailed tensions at the junior high schools of the district; see "Issue of Busing Propels Oxnard into Spotlight," *Oxnard Press-Courier*, August 9, 1972. The Justice Department also challenged the ruling of Judge Pregerson based on it being a summary judgment and not a trial; see "Hearing Scheduled on Oxnard Busing Issue," *Oxnard Press-Courier*, August 10, 1972; and "Oxnard Bus Decision Weighted by Judges," *Oxnard Press-Courier*, August 11, 1972.

30. "Supreme Court Denies Appeal to Halt Oxnard School Busing," *Los Angeles Times*, October 25, 1972; "Court Ruling May Resolve Busing Fight," *Oxnard Press-Courier*, June 22, 1973.

31. "Lawyer Confident of Busing Reversal," *Oxnard Press-Courier*, July 11, 1973.

32. Quote from U.S. App. LEXIS 6846, 488 F.2d 579, 27 November 1973; Walter Stegmir, "Oxnard Busing Trial Ordered: School Integration Plan to Be Continued Pending Legal Ruling," *Oxnard Press-Courier*, 28, November 1973; "Trial Ordered on Charge of Oxnard School Segregation," *Los Angeles Times*, November 29, 1973; Valencia, *Chicano Students and the Courts*.

33. "Court Sets Date for Hearing on Oxnard School Busing Plea," *Oxnard Press-Courier*, July 7, 1973; Stephen E. Kalish, interview by Frank P. Barajas, August 2, 2013.

34. Walt Stegmeir, "Imbalance in Schools 'Known,'" *Oxnard Press-Courier*, September 25, 1974.

35. Stegmeir, "Imbalance in Schools 'Known.'"

36. Declaration of Protective Covenants, Conditions, and Restrictions Applicable to Vineyard Avenue Estates Unit No. 1, in Ventura County, California, applicable to Vineyard Avenue Estates Unit No. 1, in Ventura, May 12, 1949, W. C. Stroube

and Bessie Watts Stroube, NARA, folder 70-397 v. 1; David G. García, *Strategies of Segregation*, 43.

37. Barajas, *Curious Unions*, 188–92; David García, Yosso, and Barajas, "Few of the Brightest"; David García and Yosso, "Strictly in the Capacity of Servant," 64–89; David García, *Strategies of Segregation*. In fact, a year after the *Soria v. Oxnard School District Board of Trustees* trial, Jack McCurdy surmised in January 1975 that "what unfolded during the meetings in the late 1930s was a well-planned scheme of forced segregation which experts rank as one of the most blatant such episodes in school annals outside the South." See McCurdy, "School Board Minutes Play Big Role in Oxnard Desegregation," *Los Angeles Times*, January 19, 1975.

38. Walt Stegmeir, "Integration Ignored, Witness Tells Court," *Oxnard Press-Courier*, September 26, 1974.

39. Stegmeir, "Integration Ignored."

40. Walt Stegmeir, "School District Opens Case in Busing Trial," *Oxnard Press-Courier*, September 27, 1974; J. Keith Mason, deposition of April 16, 1974, NARA.

41. Walt Stegmeir, "Final Arguments Due Nov. 11: Testimony Ended in Integration Trial," *Oxnard Press-Courier*, September 28, 1974.

42. Thomas Kane, deposition of April 16, 1974, NARA.

43. 1963 board minutes, NARA; "Alternative Plans for the Elimination of De Facto Segregation in the Oxnard School District," November 1969, OSDA, tape 194.

44. Stegmeir, "Final Arguments Due Nov. 11."

45. Robert Pfeiler, deposition of April 16, 1974, NARA.

46. *Soria v. Oxnard School District Board of Trustees*, F. Supp. 539; 1974 U.S. Dist. LEXIS 11661 December 10, 1974.

47. *Soria v. Oxnard School District Board of Trustees*, F. Supp. 539.

48. *Soria v. Oxnard School District Board of Trustees*, F. Supp. 539.

49. Tregarthen to administrative staff, August 6, 1971, OSDA, tape 194; Oxnard School District, "Ethnic Census: Actual Enrollment after Busing, 1966–1971," OSDA, tape 393; "Mexican American Teachers Hired Last 9 Years," July 16, 1970, OSDA, tape 194; "Black Teachers Hired Last 9 Years," August 17, 1970. OSDA, tape 194. For the academic year of 1970–71, of the total 9,458 students in the OESD, approximately a 58 percent plurality consisted of students of color: ethnic Mexican at 4,364 (46 percent), Asian 179 (1 percent), and Black 1,031 (11 percent). The number of white students in the district stood at 3,884 (41 percent). Conversely, for the same academic year, the OESD employed a total of 388 teachers; 332 were white (86 percent), 23 Black (6 percent), 21 Spanish-surnamed (5 percent), Asian

11 (3 percent) and [Native American] Indian (1.25 percent). From 1961 to 1970, the district hired 26 Spanish-surnamed teachers. In the same time period, the district hired 25 Black teachers. The district archives for this microfilm tape did not have comparable numbers for other ethnic/racial groups. For the academic year of 1974–75, when Judge Pregerson issued his December 10 trial judgment, the number of teachers in the district decreased to 363. White faculty consisted of 258 of the faculty (71 percent), Black 36 (10 percent), brown 56 (15 percent), Asian 12 (3 percent), and 1 (0.275 percent) Indian; see Ethnic Survey of Personnel Oxnard School District, OSDA, tape 207.

50. Tregarthen to administrative staff, August 6, 1971, OSDA, tape 194; Oxnard School District, "Ethnic Census: Actual Enrollment after Busing, 1966–1971," OSDA, tape 393; "Mexican American Teachers Hired Last 9 Years," July 16, 1970, OSDA, tape 194; "Black Teachers Hired Last 9 Years," August 17, 1970. OSDA, tape 194; Ethnic Survey of Personnel Oxnard School District, OSDA, tape 207; Services for OESD, tape 207. The Emergency School Assistance Program Community Advisory Committee was also to be demographically diverse in its membership; see Oxnard School District Board of Trustees, agenda item, December 18, 1973, OSDA, tape 207.

51. Resendez to Brekke, December 12, 1973, OSDA, tape 207.

52. "Ontiveros Clears Up Job Status," *Oxnard Press-Courier*, August 23, 1968; "Mexican-American UCSB Course Topic," *Oxnard Press-Courier*, August 18, 1969.

53. In 1970 the average salary for a new teacher was $8,391 ($56,000, adjusted for inflation); see Summary of Recruitment Program: 1970–71, OSDA, tape 194.

54. Murguia Wong interview, 2013.

55. Murguia Wong interview, 2013.

56. Acuña, *Making of Chicana/o Studies*, 117; adjusted for inflation, the grant translates today to $2 million. See Narda Trout, "Grant to Help Teaching Jobs: Ford Foundation Provides $346,270 for CSN Program," *Los Angeles Times*, January 24, 1973.

57. DeGuzmán, "And Make the San Fernando Valley My Home"; "Operation Chicano: Teacher Program Students Sought," *Oxnard Press-Courier*, June 25, 1975.

58. "28 Teaching Jobs, Internship Plan Set," *Oxnard Press-Courier*, February 16, 1972.

59. John Johnson, "Oxnard Busing Orderly: Fifth Year of Plan Contrast to Trouble in East," *Oxnard Press-Courier*, September 21, 1975.

60. "5 Schools in Oxnard Balanced," *Oxnard Press-Courier*, May 15, 1975.

61. OSD, tape 518; John Johnson, "Minority Students Increase," *Oxnard Press-Courier*, May 18, 1975.

6. Laying the Groundwork

1. Jiménez, *Replenished Ethnicity*; "910 KOXR 910," *Oxnard Press-Courier*, October 28, 1963.
2. Murray Norris, "Plan to Train Citrus Workers Explained," *Oxnard Press-Courier*, March 4, 1965; John McCormick, "Imported Trio Heads County's Farm Labor Efforts," *Oxnard Press-Courier*, May 13, 1966; Individual Projects, MMC, box 9.
3. Lauwerys associated the FWOP with the American Friends Service Committee, a Quaker organization established in 1945; see "Treatment to Farm Problem Symptoms Hit by 'Agitator,'" *Oxnard Press-Courier*, March 18, 1969; and Norris, "Plan to Train Citrus Workers."
4. Katherine Peake lived at 1399 Schoolhouse Road in Montecito. See Administration, MMC, box 9.
5. Motion of the Board of Directors and Steering Committee, January 7, 1966, MMC, box 8; adjusted for inflation, $95,431 translates to nearly $640,000. See "A Review of Some Aspects of Operation Buenaventura," March 17, 1966, MMC, box 9.
6. Motion of the Board of Directors and Steering Committee, January 7, 1966, MMC, box 8; minutes of meeting of the Steering Committee of the Emergency of the Committee to Aid Farm Workers, June 12, 1965, MMC, box 8; "Review of Some Aspects."
7. Minutes of meeting, June 12, 1965; Operation Buena-Hands to ECB of Directors from Dan Lund, 3, MMC, box 8; memo from Max Mont (NO 2-1148), MMC Max Mont Papers, box 8; "Statistics Relating to the Use of Mexican National Contract Workers (Braceros) in California, 1962," MMC, box 9.
8. John McCormick, "Rules Lax for School Program for Farm Labor," *Oxnard Press-Courier*, May 14, 1966.
9. John McCormick, "Farm Worker Programs—Success or Waste?," *Oxnard Press-Courier*, May 12, 1966; John McCormick, "Imported Trio Heads County Farm Labor Efforts," *Oxnard Press-Courier*, May 13, 1966; John McCormick, "Rules Lax in School for Farm Labor," May 14, 1966.
10. McCormick, "Farm Worker Programs."
11. John McCormick, "County Farmers Critical of Two Federal Projects," *Oxnard Press-Courier*, May 16, 1966.
12. McCormick, "County Farmers Critical."
13. Case Studies of 1965, MMC, box 9.
14. Case Studies of 1965, MMC, box 9; "Employer-Landlord Setup Assailed: Rancho Sespe Eviction Cited in OEO Talks," *Oxnard Press-Courier*, January 26, 1966.

15. Case Studies of 1965, MMC, box 9.
16. Case Studies of 1965, MMC, box 9.
17. Ultimately, Guzmán found himself fired from the company; see case studies of 1965, MMC, box 9.
18. Case Studies of 1965, MMC, box 9.
19. Case Studies of 1965, MMC, box 9.
20. Case Studies of 1965, MMC, box 9.
21. "False Arrest in Santa Paula: Grower-Police Conspiracy," *El Malcriado*, no. 37, June 2, 1966.
22. Case Studies of 1965, MMC, box 9.
23. Bob Denman, "Family Asked to Leave Rancho Sespe House: Farm Workers Group Raps Fillmore Eviction," *Oxnard Press-Courier*, January 14, 1966; Case Studies of 1965, MMC, box 9; two works that detail the diaspora of ethnic Mexicans from Texas are Rodriguez, *Tejano Diaspora*, and Weber, *From South Texas to the Nation*.
24. Denman, "Family Asked to Leave"; Case Studies of 1965, MMC, box 9; "Wirtz Steals Workers, Citrus Manager Charges," *Ventura County Star Free-Press*, January 15, 1966.
25. Bob Denman, "Rancho Sespe Stands Firm on Plan to Evict Family," *Oxnard Press-Courier*, January 15, 1966.
26. "Soto Family Quits Sespe Ranch Home," *Oxnard Press-Courier*, January 19, 1966; "Employer-Landlord Setup Assailed."
27. "Soto Family Quits"; "Employer-Landlord Setup Assailed."
28. "CAP Chief Invited to Washington," *Oxnard Press-Courier*, January 14, 1966; Josephine Marquez was mentioned in the piece as an aide to Operation Buenaventura. See Bob Benman, "Farm Worker Showing Influences OEO Talks," *Oxnard Press-Courier*, January 26, 1966. The Economic Opportunity Act of 1964 required that one-third of Community Action Commissions consist of the poor from target areas, one-third from organizations of the type of the NAACP and CAP, and one-third of representatives from public bodies such as city councils, boards of supervisors, and health and welfare agencies. In this report it was mentioned that Rojas blasted the board of supervisors; see "Supervisors Must Ease Grip on CAC," *Oxnard Press-Courier*, February 1, 1966.
29. Benman, "Farm Worker Showing."
30. "CAP Chief Invited to Washington."
31. Al Rojas, interview by Frank P. Barajas, December 2, 2013.
32. Rojas interview, 2013.

33. The FWOP paid selected persons $279 ($2,250, adjusted for inflation) to participate in its educational program; see Dean Fairchild, "Farm Labor Shortages in Dispute," *Oxnard Press-Courier*, February 13, 1966.
34. "World's Largest Egg Producer Asks County for Permission to Expand," *Oxnard Press-Courier*, March 3, 1964; Joe O'Hara, "Workers Strike at Egg City; It's Illegal, Owner Asserts," *Oxnard Press-Courier*, July 14, 1967; "No Progress in Egg City Strike; Pickets Continue," *Oxnard Press-Courier*, July 18, 1967; "Egg City Buys Site at Los Berros," *Oxnard Press-Courier*, July 27, 1968; "Egg City Strike Idles 100," *Ventura County Star-Free Press*, July 14, 1967.
35. Virginia DeArmon, "Farm Workers' Union Continues Picket Lines," *Oxnard Press-Courier*, July 17, 1969.
36. "No Progress in Egg City Strike," *Oxnard Press-Courier*.
37. Gutiérrez, *Walls and Mirrors*, 2, 144–45, 153–62.
38. "Egg City Charges Pay Hike Refused," *Oxnard Press-Courier*, July 22, 1967.
39. "No Progress in Egg City Strike"; "Five Day Strike at Egg City Still Scrambled," *Ventura County Star-Free Press*, July 17, 1967; "Egg City Charges," *Oxnard Press-Courier*; "Picket Lines Spread to Ventura, Oxnard in Strike at Egg City," *Ventura County Star-Free Press*, July 18, 1967.
40. "5 'Wetbacks' Arrested at Egg City," *Oxnard Press-Courier*, July 19, 1967; "Egg City: That's No Walkout, It's a Strike," *Ventura County Star-Free Press*, July 19, 1967.
41. O'Hara, "Workers Strike at Egg City."
42. "Court Enjoins Egg City Strikers," *Oxnard Press-Courier*, July 19, 1967.
43. "Egg City Charges."
44. "Agreement Ends Egg City Strike," *Oxnard Press-Courier*, July 27, 1967; "Egg City Strike Ends Without Union Help," *Ventura County Star-Free Press*, July 27, 1967.
45. "Agreement Ends Egg City Strike"; "Egg City Strike Ends"; "Strike Still on at Egg City, Union Claims," *Ventura County Star-Free Press*, 28 July 1967.
46. Jay Ellis Ransom, "Brown Hailed as Farm Labor Hero," *Oxnard Press-Courier*, November 7, 1966.
47. Adjusted for inflation, the funds raised at Cal equaled approximately $40,000; see Ransom, "Brown Hailed."
48. "No Republicans," *Oxnard Press-Courier*, April 3, 1968; quote from "Chavez on Politics, Labor," *Oxnard Press-Courier*, April 3, 1968.
49. Bob Denman, "Chavez Promises Return to Oxnard," *Oxnard Press-Courier*, April 3, 1968.

7. ¡Que vivan las huelgas!

1. Wally Smith, "Talk or Face Strike, Chavez Warns Growers: Citrus Walkout Continues," *Ventura County Star-Free Press*, July 18, 1970; Kitty Dill, "Citrus Walkout Grows in County," *Ventura County Star-Free Press*, July 19, 1970; "No Citrus Walkout Talks Set," *Oxnard Press-Courier*, July 18, 1970; "Citrus Packer Strike; Chavez Backs Move: Attempts to Reopen Talks Fail," *Oxnard Press-Courier*, July 19, 1970; Pablo Izquierdo, letter of June 5, 1970, UFWIRDP, Part 2, box 39.
2. "No Citrus Walkout Talks Set"; Wally Smith, "Bitter Citrus Strike Launched Chavez's Viva La Causa," *Ventura County Star-Free Press*, July 26, 1970.
3. "No Citrus Walkout Talks Set"; "Citrus Packer Strike"; Wally Smith, "Citrus Pickers Boycott Jobs as Talks Snag," *Ventura County Star-Free Press*, July 17, 1970.
4. "Growers Poll Pickers on Union Issue," *Oxnard Press-Courier*, September 17, 1970; "Citrus Pickers Strike"; Dill, "Citrus Walkout Grows in County"; Wally Smith, "Citrus Picking Dwindles as Walkout Spreads," *Ventura County Star-Free Press*, July 20, 1970.
5. "Citrus Picking Dwindles"; Wally Smith, "Chavez Takes Charge of County Citrus Strike," *Ventura County Star-Free Press*, July 22, 1970; "Chavez in Lead as Citrus Pickers March in Strike," *Los Angeles Times*, July 23, 1970.
6. Manuela Aparicio-Twitchell, interview by Frank P. Barajas, July 22, 2014; Day, *Forty Acres*, 155–57; "No Citrus Walkout Talks Set"; Wally Smith, "Talk or Face Strike"; letter of Santa Paula UFWOC Committee, July 2, 1970, UFWIRDP, Part 2, box 39.
7. Wally Smith, "Chavez Takes Charge."
8. Wally Smith, "Pickers Reject Growers' Offer, Call for Election," *Ventura County Star-Free Press*, July 23, 1970.
9. Wally Smith, "Union Vote Impossible—Growers," *Ventura County Star-Free Press*, July 24, 1970; Wally Smith, "County Citrus Strike Ends: Chavez Union Demand Dropped," *Ventura County Star-Free Press*, July 29, 1970; "Editorial: A Welcome End to Citrus Strike," *Ventura County Star-Free Press*, July 30, 1970; "Agreement Ends 13-Day Walkout of Citrus Pickers," *Los Angeles Times*, July 30, 1970; "Citrus Workers Get Vacations," *Ventura County Star-Free Press*, August 23, 1970.
10. "Growers Poll Pickers on Union Issue"; "Text of Statement by Citrus Growers," *Oxnard Press-Courier*, September 17, 1970.
11. "Text of Statement by Citrus Growers"; apparently the statement was published in the *Oxnard Press-Courier* at least a week after it was distributed by the Limoneira Company.

12. Gonzalo R. Casillas, "Letters: 'Viva la raza!,'" *Ventura County Star-Free Press*, September 7, 1970.
13. V. H. Graig Jr., "Letters: 'Misrepresented,'" *Ventura County Star-Free Press*, September 10, 1970.
14. "Antle Had Teamsters Pact in '61," *Oxnard Press-Courier*, January 4, 1971; "Major Oxnard Grower, Chavez Sign Contract," *Ventura County Star-Free Press*, April 24, 1971.
15. "Major Oxnard Grower"; "Big Oxnard Grower Signs with Chavez," *Oxnard Press-Courier*, April 24, 1971; John Kendall, "Chavez Signs Nation's Largest Independent Lettuce Producer," *Los Angeles Times*, April 24, 1971.
16. "Major Oxnard Grower"; Kendall, "Chavez Signs."
17. "UFWOC Sparks Field Work Halt," *Oxnard Press-Courier*, September 16, 1971; "Farm Workers Return to Jobs, after 'Holiday,'" *Oxnard Press-Courier*, September 17, 1971; "Farm Workers' 'Fiesta' Blocks Buses to Fields," *Ventura County Star-Free Press*, September 16, 1971; "Farm Workers Back on Jobs after 'Holiday,'" *Ventura County Star-Free Press*, September 17, 1971; John Willson, "Oxnard High Violence Forces Closure," *Ventura County Star-Free Press*, September 24, 1971; Report No. 1, October 9, 1971, Oxnard, California, UFW:OPC, Part 2, box 36.
18. "Produce Ranch Picket Arrested," *Oxnard Press-Courier*, April 16, 1972; "Finerman Seeking Accord with UFW," *Oxnard Press-Courier*, April 18, 1972; "12 Lettuce Workers Arrested; Sit-In Clog's Packer's Office," *Ventura County Star-Free Press*, April 18, 1972; Rick Nielson, "Talks Collapse; County Lettuce Crop Imperiled," *Oxnard Press-Courier*, April 22, 1972.
19. "Oxnard Firm, Chavez Set Lettuce Pact Talk," *Ventura County Star-Free Press*, April 19, 1972; "Chavez Talks Stalemated," *Ventura County Star-Free Press*, April 22, 1972; "Lettuce Talks Resume," *Oxnard Press-Courier*, April 25, 1972; "Crop Feud Ends," *Oxnard Press-Courier*, April 26, 1972; "Southland," *Los Angeles Times*, April 27, 1972; "Lettuce Packer Sees Hope of Settlement with Chavez," *Ventura County Star-Free Press*, April 24, 1972; "Oxnard Lettuce Dispute Settled," *Ventura County Star-Free Press*, April 26, 1972.
20. "More Talks on Lettuce Dispute Set," *Ventura County Star-Free Press*, April 25, 1972; "Agriculture—Our No. 1 Industry," *Ventura County Star-Free Press*, January 11, 1974.
21. "$381 Million in Sales All-Time Sunkist High," *Ventura County Star-Free Press*, January 16, 1974. There were other packinghouses in Ventura County that operated independent of the Sunkist exchange.
22. Bob Carey, "200 Citrus Pickers Stay off Jobs in Pay Dispute," *Ventura County Star-Free Press*, January 27, 1974.

23. Wally Smith, "Idled Pickers Told of Chavez Offer to Help," *Ventura County Star-Free Press*, January 30, 1974.
24. "Citrus Growers Agree to Set Picking Rates," *Ventura County Star-Free Press*, January 31, 1974.
25. Wally Smith, "Pickers Reject Pay Offer, Ask Grievance Panel," *Ventura County Star-Free Press*, February 1, 1974; Jeff Fairbanks, "S.P. Workers Vote for Chavez Help," *Ventura County Star-Free Press*, February 3, 1974.
26. Wally Smith, "Growers Won't Accept S.P. Pickers' Proposal," *Ventura County Star-Free Press*, February 7, 1974; Fairbanks, "S.P. Workers Vote"; "Citrus Pickers Reject New Growers' Offer," *Ventura County Star-Free Press*, February 4, 1974; Jeff Fairbanks, "Citrus Pickers Seek $3 an Hour Average," *Ventura County Star-Free Press*, February 7, 1974.
27. Smith, "Idled Pickers"; "Citrus Walkout Ends, Pickers Approve Pact," *Ventura County Star-Free Press*, February 8, 1974.
28. "Berry Harvesting Halted by Violence," *Ventura County Star-Free Press*, May 25, 1974; "Cesar Chavez to Aid Oxnard Berry Strike," *Ventura County Star-Free Press*, May 28, 1974; Johnston, "Picketers, Deputies Clash in Berry Strike"; Frank Del Olmo, "Eight Arrested in Fourth Day of Strike by Strawberry Pickers," *Los Angeles Times*, May 30, 1974; "Flynn, Jewett to Confer with Strikers, Sheriff," *Ventura County Star-Free Press*, June 5, 1974.
29. "Cesar Chavez to Aid"; Fred Johnston, "UFW Vows $500,000 to Win Strike," *Ventura County Star-Free Press*, May 31, 1974.
30. "30 More Arrested in Labor Dispute," *Ventura County Star-Free Press*, May 31, 1974; "Hill Responds to Allegations of ACLU Head," *Ventura County Star-Free Press*, June 6, 1974; "Chavez Returning for Rally Tonight," *Ventura County Star-Free Press*, June 1, 1974.
31. Ken Hoover, "Assails Sheriff Hill: Chavez Urges Mass Arrests in County," *Ventura County Star-Free Press*, June 2, 1974; "Strikers Seek Help of County Supervisors," *Ventura County Star-Free Press*, June 4, 1974; quote from "Strikers Protest Tactics of Oxnard's Police Force," *Ventura County Star-Free Press*, June 6, 1974; Ken Hoover, "Farm Union Harassment Denied by Oxnard Police," *Ventura County Star-Free Press*, June 7, 1974.
32. "Strikers Seek Help"; "UFW Picketing to Be Limited . . . but a Little Less Lonely," *Ventura County Star-Free Press*, June 16, 1974; Dave Duffy, "UFW Vows Bigger, Better Strawberry Strike in 1975," *Ventura County Star-Free Press*, June 20, 1974.
33. Duffy, "UFW Vows Bigger."

34. Roberto Flores, interview by Frank P. Barajas, April 14, 2006; Jenaro Valdez, interview by Frank P. Barajas, June 19, 2019; Illegal Aliens: Reports, Oxnard and Coachella, California, 1974, UFWIRDP, Part 1, box 38.
35. "Noise Harassing of UFW Enjoined," *Ventura County Star-Free Press*, June 28, 1974; "Oxnard Won't Touch UFW Court Issue," *Ventura County Star-Free Press*, July 3, 1974; "UFW Picket Acquitted," *Ventura County Star-Free Press*, July 5, 1974; "UFW Organizer Acquitted of Rock-Throwing Charge," *Ventura County Star-Free Press*, July 12, 1974.
36. "Farm Workers Picketing Only One County Field," *Ventura County Star-Free Press*, June 3, 1974; "Substantial Wage Boost Announced for Farm Hands," *Ventura County Star-Free Press*, July 22, 1974.
37. "Citrus Pickers Walk Off Jobs in Santa Paula," *Ventura County Star-Free Press*, August 21, 1974.
38. "Citrus Pickers Walk"; Wally Smith, "S.P. Growers, Citrus Pickers in Pay Impasse," *Ventura County Star-Free Press*, August 22, 1974; "S.P. Citrus Pickers Remain Idled by Strike," *Ventura County Star-Free Press*, August 23, 1974.
39. "Striking S.P. Pickers to Ask Student Help," *Ventura County Star-Free Press*, August 24, 1974; Wally Smith, "Pickers: Growers Violated February Pact in 5 Areas," *Ventura County Star-Free Press*, August 27, 1974.
40. Smith, "Growers Violated February Pact."
41. Wally Smith, "Citrus Strike Grows, Talks Again Break Off," *Ventura County Star-Free Press*, August 30, 1974.
42. Wally Smith, "Chávez Tells Striking Pickers to Hold the Line," *Ventura County Star-Free Press*, September 5, 1975.
43. "Farm Workers to Meet with New Manager," *Ventura County Star-Free Press*, September 8, 1974; "Accord Reached in Citrus Strike; Pickers to Vote," *Ventura County Star-Free Press*, September 11, 1974; "S.P. Strikers Plan Boycott in Sta. Barbara," *Ventura County Star-Free Press*, September 12, 1974; "New Manager Hired by Citrus Growers," *Oxnard Press-Courier*, September 12, 1974.
44. "Teamsters Make Bid for Area Farm Hands," *Ventura County Star-Free Press*, December 1, 1974.
45. "Teamsters Sign Pacts with 3 Oxnard Firms," *Oxnard Press-Courier*, March 29, 1975. Earl Sterling served as the organizer for the Western Conference of Teamsters out of Local 186; see "Workers Awarded Back Pay," *Oxnard Press-Courier*, June 4, 1975; adjusted for inflation, $38,000 translates to nearly $190,0000 in 2020.

46. Pawel, *Union of Their Dreams*, 160–61; "Strike Reported at Egg Ranch to Protest Firing," *Ventura County Star-Free Press*, April 10, 1975; "Egg City Picketed; Strike Is Confirmed," *Ventura County Star-Free Press*, April 11, 1975; "Egg Strike in Third Day," *Ventura County Star-Free Press*, April 12, 1975; "Court Demands End to Strike at Egg City," *Ventura County Star-Free Press*, April 15, 1975; "Strikers Scorn Court Order at Egg City," *Ventura County Star-Free Press*, April 16, 1975.
47. Jerry Dyer, "Sheriff Says Strikers Can Ignore Court Order," *Ventura County Star-Free Press*, April 22, 1975.
48. Pawel, *Union of Their Dreams*, 162; "Chavez Due in Oxnard," *Oxnard Press Courier*, July 13, 1975; "Strikers Issue Set of Demands at Egg City," *Ventura County Star-Free Press*, April 17, 1975.
49. "Hungry Egg City Strikers Promised Help by CAC," *Ventura County Star-Free Press*, April 18, 1975; "Supervisors Question CAC Role at Egg City," *Ventura County Star-Free Press*, April 23, 1975; John Weigle, "CAC Officials Defend Help at Egg City," *Ventura County Star-Free Press*, April 25, 1975; Bud Weisbart, "Letters: CAC Rebuttal," *Ventura County Star-Free Press*, April 28, 1975.
50. Edward Díaz, "Letters: The Other CIA . . . Certified Illegal Aliens," *Ventura County Star-Free Press*, April 21, 1975; Larry Pryor, "Ballot Box Stolen in Farm Union Election," *Los Angeles Times*, October 15, 1977; Wally Smith, "UFW Protests Egg City Hiring Refugees," *Ventura County Star-Free Press*, July 31, 1975; Harry Bernstein, "Angry Union Demonstrators Protest Use of Viet Refugees as Strikebreakers," *Los Angeles Times*, October 22, 1975; Robert Lindsey, "Egg City Refugees in Crossfire: Vietnamese Called 'Scabs,'" *Ventura County Star-Free Press*, August 10, 1975; quote from Fred Johnston, "Clergy Aiding UFWA Barred at Egg City," *Ventura County Star-Free Press*, August 1, 1975.
51. "37 Arrested in County Illegal Alien Crackdown," *Ventura County Star-Free Press*, April 22, 1975; "Strikers Say Aliens Working at Egg City," *Ventura County Star-Free Press*, April 23, 1975.
52. Fred Johnston, "Egg City Vote Asked by UFW to Decide Issue," *Ventura County Star-Free Press*, July 1, 1975; "Union Election Gets Conditional Egg City Okay," *Ventura County Star-Free Press*, July 3, 1975.
53. Fred Johnston, "Unions Trade Taunt at UFW Rally," *Ventura County Star-Free Press*, July 13, 1975; "Chavez Urges Colonia Crowd to Organize," *Ventura County Star-Free Press*, July 14, 1975; Fred Johnston, "Chavez Gives Views on Ventura County," *Ventura County Star-Free Press*, July 15, 1975.
54. "Teamster Pact OK'd at Egg City," *Ventura County Star-Free Press*, July 29, 1975.

55. Fred Johnston, "UFW Expected to Repeat Bid to See Workers," *Ventura County Star*, July 29, 1975; Jerry Dyer, "Trom Won't Prosecute Egg City UFW Pickets," *Ventura County Star-Free Press*, August 7, 1975; "Judge Threatens Arrests If UFWA Tries Mass Entry," *Ventura County Star-Free Press*, September 2, 1975; Bob Holt, "UFWA Wins Round in Battle for Egg City," *Ventura County Star-Free Press*, September 3, 1975; Wally Smith, "15 Union Leaders Move into Ranch amid Cheers," *Ventura County Star-Free Press*, September 3, 1975.

56. Wally Smith, "UFWA, Teamsters Vie: Egg City Vote Set for Thursday," *Ventura County Star-Free Press*, September 8, 1975; Wally Smith, "200 Challenged Ballots May Upset Egg City Vote," *Ventura County Star-Free Press*, September 12, 1975.

57. "3 UFW Victories in County Certified," *Ventura County Star-Free Press*, November 5, 1975; Wally Smith, "Lengthy Inquiry Forecast in Egg City Labor Dispute," *Ventura County Star-Free Press*, November 15, 1975; Walt Stegmeir, "UFW, Teamsters Split Oxnard Farm Votes," *Oxnard Press-Courier*, October 8, 1975.

58. Associated Press, "UFW Wins Fight to Tally Disputed Votes of Strikers," *Los Angeles Times*, October 8, 1977; Pryor, "Ballot Box Stolen."

59. "The Southland: 6% Olympic Ticket Tax Okd," *Los Angeles Times*, April 19, 1978; "All Objections in Egg City Labor Election Dismissed," *Los Angeles Times*, June 11, 1978. In 1980 the strikers won an ALRB decision that granted reinstated workers their seniority at the plant that affected their benefits and vacation benefits; see "Labor Ruling Favors Farmworkers in Dispute with Egg City in Moorpark," *Los Angeles Times*, December 21, 1980.

60. "Workers Awarded Back Pay"; "UFW Files for County Labor Votes," *Oxnard Press-Courier*, September 4, 1975; Pawel, *Union of Their Dreams*, 166, 320–21.

61. "UFW Wins Tanaka Farm Labor Voting," *Oxnard Press-Courier*, September 25, 1975.

8. Chicana-Chicano Agonists

1. Yvonne De Los Santos and Roberto Flores, interview by Frank P. Barajas, February 1, 2013.

2. Roberto Flores, interview by Frank P. Barajas, April 14, 2006; Helen Galindo Casillas, interview by Frank P. Barajas, June 9, 2006; Armando López, interview by Frank P. Barajas, June 21, 2010; Rachel Murguia Wong, interview by Frank P. Barajas, May 30, 2010.

3. De Los Santos and Flores interview, 2013; Roberto Flores, interview by Frank P. Barajas, April 14, 2006; Galindo Casillas interview, 2006; Frank H. Barajas, interview by Frank P. Barajas, May 16, 2020.

4. De Los Santos and Flores interview, 2013.
5. Juan Lagunas Soria, interview by Frank Bardacke, January 25, 1996; Flores interview, 2006.
6. De Los Santos and Flores interview, 2013; Laura Espinosa, interview by Frank P. Barajas, May 30, 2012; Galindo Casillas interview, 2006; Moses Mora, interview by Frank P. Barajas, June 1, 2016; Ray and Teresa Tejada, interview by Frank P. Barajas, June 26, 2012.
7. Eva Barbara Brown, "New High School Clubs Rising to Meet Challenge of Ethnic Awakening," *Ventura County Star-Free Press*, February 1, 1970.
8. Brown, "New High School Clubs Rising."
9. Roberto Hernández, *Coloniality of the U.S./Mexico Border*, 24–27.
10. "Protesting CI Students Face Suspensions, Principal Says," *Oxnard Press-Courier*, February 27, 1969.
11. "Chicano Educators' Aid to Be Requested," *Oxnard Press-Courier*, November 19, 1970; "NAACP Charges Elks Discriminate," *Oxnard Press-Courier*, February 23, 1971.
12. "Farm Workers Return to Jobs After 'Holiday,'" *Oxnard Press-Courier*, September 17, 1971; "Fighting Disrupts Oxnard School," *Los Angeles Times*, September 24, 1971; "Oxnard Grid Game Canceled; Beatings Cut School Attendance," *Oxnard Press-Courier*, September 24, 1971; John Willson, "Oxnard High Violence Forces Closure," *Ventura County Star-Free Press*, September 24, 1971; "Oxnard Football Opener Canceled," *Oxnard Press-Courier*, September 25, 1971; "Monday Reopening: Oxnard High Seeking Calm," *Ventura County Star-Free Press*, September 26, 1971; Peter Martínez, interview by Frank P. Barajas, June 23, 2020.
13. "Minority Committee to Meet," *Oxnard Press-Courier*, October 3, 1971; "Smith's Resignation Offer Favored by Oxnard Board," *Oxnard Press-Courier*, November 12, 1971.
14. Art Kuhn, "Black Offered Job: Smith's Resignation Offer Favored by Oxnard Board," *Oxnard Press-Courier*, November 12, 1971.
15. Rick Nielsen, "Oxnard High School Firebombed," *Oxnard Press-Courier*, October 31, 1971; "U.S. Enters Oxnard High Probe," *Oxnard Press-Courier*, November 1, 1971.
16. "Editorials: Firebombing Act of Desperation?," *Oxnard Press-Courier*, November 2, 1971.
17. "OHS to Get New Principal Shortly," *Oxnard Press-Courier*, December 9, 1971.
18. Cindy Garcia, "Channel Islands MEChA Conducts Clothes Drive for Tijuana Needy," *Oxnard Press-Courier*, December 2, 1973.

19. Karly Eichner, "Candy Sale Contest Starts at Rio Mesa," December 2, 1973; "MEChA Sponsored Event Draws 100 Parents," *Oxnard Press-Courier*, November 12, 1972.
20. Diana Borrego Martínez, interview by Frank P. Barajas, July 9, 2012; De Los Santos and Flores interview, 2013.
21. Jess Gutiérrez, interview by Frank P. Barajas, June 28, 2010.
22. Borrego Martínez interview, 2012; De Los Santos and Flores interview, 2013; Acuña, *Making of Chicana/o Studies*, 95, 96.
23. Jess Gutiérrez lecture, CSUCI, April 2014; Manuela Aparicio-Twitchell, interview by Frank P. Barajas, July 22, 2014; "MC Opens to 1200 Day Students," *Moorpark College Reporter* 1, no. 1, September 29, 1967; "Campus News: Oxnard Repeats Bus Service to College," *Pirate Press*, September 19, 1969; "Commuter Bus Routes Approved," *Oxnard Press-Courier*, July 14, 1971.
24. "Berets Present Sheinbaum Today," *Raiders Reporter* 2, no. 3, October 4, 1968.
25. "Moorpark Students Engage in Peaceful Protest at Poverty Conf.," *Raiders Reporter* 2, no. 5, October 23, 1968.
26. "Of Campus Organizations: Berets Build 'Community Pride,'" *Raiders Reporter* 2, no. 5, October 23, 1968.
27. "Berets Build 'Community Pride.'"
28. Bill Bader, "Of Personalities: 'I'm Here to Educate You'–Soria," *Raiders Reporter* 2, no. 8, November 13, 1968.
29. Bader, "I'm Here to Educate You"; López interview, 2010.
30. "Unity Group Planned for Oxnard," *Oxnard Press-Courier*, December 29, 1968; Flores interview, 2006; "Voice of the People: Berets Give Service," *Oxnard Press-Courier*, February 3, 1969.
31. FBI File, February 5, 1969, courtesy of Milo Alvarez.
32. Reynaldo Rivera, "Chicanos Suffer in This Country," *Pirate Press*, December 12, 1969; "MEChA Group Nominates Officers, Representatives," by Michel Wolf, *Pirate Press*, May 22, 1970.
33. Robert Flores, interview by Frank P. Barajas, June 10, 2010; De Los Santos and Flores interview, 2013; Borrego Martínez interview, 2012; Gutiérrez interview, 2010; Ismael "Mayo" de la Rocha, interview by Frank P. Barajas, May 15 and 22, 2014; Fermín Herrera, interview by Frank P. Barajas, August 14, 2019; "Editorials: Study Project Deserves a Chance," *Oxnard Press-Courier*, July 5, 1969; Acuña, *Making of Chicana/o Studies*, 52–54.
34. "Mexican-America UCSB Course Topic," *Oxnard Press-Courier*, August 18, 1969.

35. Over thirty-five students belonged to Moorpark College MEChA; see Steve Horton, "MEChA Proposes MC Chicano Study Program: Confrontation with Administration Has Harmonious Start," *Raiders Reporter* 2, no. 25, April 23, 1969.
36. "Mexican Flag Flies at MC in Independence Day Fete," *Raiders Reporter* 3 no. 1, September 17, 1969; Muñoz, *Youth, Identity, Power*, 189–90.
37. Professor Reynoso was the brother of Cruz Reynoso, who would be appointed to the California Supreme Court in 1981 by governor Jerry Brown; see "New, Yet Familiar: MAS Head Reynoso Finds MC 'Exciting,'" *Raiders Reporter* 3, no. 4, October 8, 1969.
38. "MAS Conference Planned at MC," *Raider Reporter* 3, no. 9, November 12, 1969.
39. "MAS Conference Planned at MC"; "Chicano Studies Conference Slated at Moorpark College," *Oxnard Pres-Courier*, November 17, 1969.
40. Bill Sanchez et al., "To the Editor: Open Letter," *La Voz del Pueblo*, November 21, 1969.
41. "Julian Nava," *Raiders Reporter* 3, no. 24, April 15, 1970, 4. After his tenure at Moorpark College, Collins went on to continue his support of Chicano studies as president of Bakersfield college; see Rosales, "Mississippi West," 172–73.
42. Raoul Contreras, "Raoul Reacts: Black Power," *Pirate Press*, November 15, 1968; Borrego Martínez interview, 2012; Mayo de la Rocha, interview by Frank P. Barajas, May 15 and 22, 2014; "Meet Features SB Walk-Out," *Pirate Press*, October 1, 1968; Raoul Contreras, "Black Students, Officials Confront Problem Areas," *Pirate Press*, December 6, 1968.
43. Duane Warren, "Larry Ellis, Black Activities Head, Expounds upon BSU's Eight Demands," *Pirate Press*, January 9, 1970.
44. "MC Library Fuss Penalties Pressed," *Oxnard Press-Courier*, October 6, 1971; "Moorpark BSU Slates Black Events," *Oxnard Press-Courier*, March 3, 1971.
45. Emilia Alaniz, "Two Counselors Hired to Aid Disadvantaged," *Pirate Press*, December 4, 1970; "Minority Centers Form New Programs, Goals," *Pirate Press*, February 26, 1971.
46. Blackwell, *¡Chicana Power!*, 135; Montejano, *Quixote's Soldiers*, 126–27.
47. Jill Patrick, "4-Day Cinco de Mayo Event Begins Tues," *Raiders Reporter* 4, no. 28, April 28, 1971.
48. "MC Commemorates Cinco De Mayo," *Raider Reporter* 5, no. 29, May 3, 1972.
49. De Los Santos and Flores interview, 2013; Gutiérrez interview, 2010.
50. Dick Cooper, "People's Choice," *Oxnard Press-Courier*, April 15, 1973.

51. Michael Kremer, "MEChA Outlines Seven Proposals: Dr. Glenn Announces Steps to Implement Minority Plans," *Pirate Press*, May 15, 1970; "Minority Students' Informational Center Opens for Business on VC Campus," *Pirate Press*, October 2, 1970; "Campus News: MEChA, BSU Organize Tutoring for Disadvantaged," *Pirate Press*, October 23, 1970.
52. "BSU, MEChA Present Show," *Pirate Press*, December 8, 1972; Dennis McCarthy, "Minority Center Plans Festivities," *Pirate Press*, May 7, 1971.
53. Louis Zitnik, "Letters to the Editor: Minorities," *Pirate Press*, March 30, 1973.
54. Arnulfo Casillas, "Writer Differs with Letter to Editor," *Pirate Press*, April 13, 1973.
55. "MEChA Mounts Mural," *Pirate Press*, May 4, 1973; "Chicano Celebration Continues," *Pirate Press*, May 4, 1973.
56. "Chicano Speaks: The Mexican Fiesta—a Chance to 'Discharge the Soul,'" *Raiders Reporter* 2, no. 21, March 19, 1969.
57. Raoul Contreras, "Mexican Students Propose Festive Christmas Season," *Pirate Press*, November 8, 1968; "Mexicans Prepare Holiday Festivities," *Pirate Press*, December 6, 1968.
58. Silvia Monica Robledo, "Letters to the Editor: Chicana Reader Explains, Defends Movimiento, Challenges Campos to Meaningful Participation," *Pirate Press*, May 24, 1974.
59. Arnulfo Casillas, "Cinco de Mayo Explained," *Pirate Press*, April 27, 1973. For the study of the usages of history to situate the power of collectives in the Chicana-Chicano community, see Bebout, *Mythohistorical Imaginations*.
60. Aparicio-Twitchell interview, 2014; "Jeanette Valasco MEChA and Luedora Wallace BSU for Homecoming Queen," *Raiders Reporter* 4, no. 9, November 12, 1970; "Aurelia Aparicio MC Homecoming Queen," *Raider Reporter*, November 22, 1972; "Betty Luna Reigns as Homecoming Queen," *Pirate Press*, November 7, 1969; "Pirates' Royalty for Homecoming Crowned Today," *Pirate Press*, November 20, 1970.
61. "Hernández Endorses Luevano for Top Post," *Raiders Reporter* 2, no. 27, May 7, 1969; Becky Merrell, "New Winds of Activism: MAS Program Expanding Understanding," *Raider Reporter* 3, no. 14, December 17, 1969; "Rueles Elected as New Speaker of Parliament," *Raider Reporter* 5, no. 21, March 1, 1972.
62. Jenaro Valdez, interview by Frank P. Barajas, June 19, 2019. Tom Richter, "Seven Vie for Four Positions on A.S. Board Tuesday," *Pirate Press*, January 10, 1975; Tom Richter, "3 Percent Vote: MEChA Sweeps A.S. Elections," *Pirate Press*, January 17, 1975.
63. "Mechistas Hear Platform, Purposes," *Pirate Press*, March 7, 1975; Manuel Razo, "Letters to the Editor: So What Is MEChA All About?," *Pirate Press*, October 4, 1974.

64. Jill Boardmand, "Alpha Gamma Challenges MEChA: AS Election Set for Next Week," *Pirate Press*, May 23, 1975; Jill Boardman and Tom Richter, "Fall AS Board Candidates Fight for Leadership Positions," *Pirate Press*, May 30, 1975.
65. Michael C. Dill, "Letters to the Editor: Grouch Runs for Treasurer," *Pirate Press*, May 30, 1975.
66. Leigh Ann Dewey, "AS Board: Election Controversy Erupts," *Pirate Press*, June 6, 1976; Tom Richter, "AGS Wins AS Election; Voting Number Doubles," *Pirate Press*, June 6, 1975.
67. R. De Leon, "Voice of the People: Objects to 'Chicano,'" *Oxnard Press-Courier*, January 21, 1970; Jerry R. Rosalez, "Voice of the People: 'Chicano' Opposed," *Oxnard Press-Courier*, February 2, 1970.
68. Faye Villa, "Voice of the People: 'Chicanos' Challenge," *Oxnard Press-Courier*, February 2, 1970.
69. Dan E. Contreras, "Voice of the People: Chicano Spokesman," *Oxnard Press-Courier*, February 3, 1970.
70. Nomas Milando, "Voice of the People: More on 'Chicano,'" *Oxnard Press-Courier*, February 7, 1970.
71. Daniel Eugenio Contreras, "Voice of the People: Chicano Power Defined," *Oxnard Press-Courier*, February 23, 1970.
72. Ruben Salazar, "Who Is a Chicano? What Is It the Chicanos Want?," *Los Angeles Times*, February 6, 1970.

Conclusion

1. "Chiques" is the barrio nickname of the City of Oxnard.
2. Barajas, "Invading Army," 403.
3. "Fall Enrollment Snapshot," Academic Affairs Data Analytics, California State University, last updated October 8, 2019, https://oneci.csuci.edu/t/IRPEGuest/views/FallEnrollmentpublic/EnrollmentDashboard?:iid=1&:isGuestRedirectFromVizportal=y&:embed=y.
4. Faculty Affairs Senate Presentation, April 18, 2017.
5. Licón, "Ideological Struggle for Chicana/o Unity and Power," 151–72; Licón, "Feminist Mobilization in MEChA," 76–110.
6. Francisco Romero, "Injunction an Attack on Residents' Basic Rights," *Ventura County Star*, March 30, 2004.
7. Megan Diskin, "Oxnard Police Will Abandon Gang Injunctions, Department Announces," *Ventura County Star*, July 21, 2020.

BIBLIOGRAPHY

Manuscripts/Archives

Assembly Select Committee on the Administration of Justice Hearing, April 28, 1972, Los Angeles CA: Relations between the Police and Mexican Americans, L500 J85 1972 no. 1 [v. 1] c. 3. California State Library. Sacramento CA.
COC. City of Oxnard Collection. John Spoor Broome Library. California State University Press. Channel Islands, Camarillo CA.
EGP. Ernesto Galarza Papers. Cecil H. Greene Library, Stanford University, Stanford CA.
FRSP. Fred Ross Sr. Papers. Cecil H. Greene Library, Stanford University, Stanford CA.
FRSC. Fred Ross Sr. Collection. Wayne State University, Detroit MI.
HGP. Herman Gallegos Papers. Cecil H. Greene Library, Stanford University, Stanford CA.
MMC. Max Mont Collection. Oviatt Library, California State University at Northridge, Northridge CA.
NAACPR. National Association for the Advancement of Colored People Records. Bancroft Library, University of California, Berkeley, Berkeley CA.
NARA. National Archives and Records Administration. Perris CA.
OSDA. Oxnard School District Archive. Oxnard School District, Oxnard CA.
UFWBCR. United Farm Workers Boycott Central Records. Walter Reuther Library, Wayne State University, Detroit MI.

UFWIRDP. United Farm Workers Information and Research Department Papers. Walther Reuther Library, Wayne State University, Detroit MI.

UFW: OPC. United Farm Workers: Office of the President Collection. Walther Reuther Library, Wayne State University, Detroit MI.

Published Works

Acosta, Oscar Zeta. *The Revolt of the Cockroach People*. New York: Vintage, 1989.

Acuña, Rodolfo. *The Making of Chicana/o Studies: In the Trenches of Academe*. New Brunswick NJ: Rutgers University Press, 2011.

———. *Occupied America: A History of Chicanos*. 3rd ed. New York: HarperCollins, 1988.

Alvarez, Robert. "Los Re-Mexicanizado: Mexicanidad, Changing Identity, and Long-term Affiliation on the U.S.-Mexico Border." *Journal of the West* 40, no. 2 (2001): 15–23.

Apodaca, Maria Linda. "They Kept the Home Fires Burning: Mexican American Women and Social Change." PhD diss., University of California, Irvine, 1994.

Arredondo, Gabriela F. *Mexican Chicago: Becoming Mexican in Early Twentieth-Century Chicago*. Urbana: University of Illinois Press, 2008.

Avila, Eric. *The Folklore of the Freeway: Race and Revolt in the Modernist City*. Minneapolis: University of Minnesota, 2014.

———. *Popular Culture in the Age of White: Flight Fear and Fantasy in Suburban Los Angeles*. Berkeley: University of California Press, 2004.

Barajas, Frank P. *Curious Unions: Mexican Workers and Resistance in Oxnard, California, 1898–1961*. Lincoln: University of Nebraska Press, 2012.

———. "An Invading Army: A Civil Gang Injunction in a Southern California Chicana/o Community." *Latino Studies* 5, no. 4 (2007): 393–417.

Bardacke, Frank. *Trampling Out the Vintage: Cesar Chavez and the Two Souls of the United Farm Workers*. New York: Verso, 2011.

Bebout, Lee. *Mythohistorical Imaginations: The Chicano Movement and Its Legacies*. Minneapolis: University of Minnesota Press, 2011.

Berger, Samuel R. *Dollar Harvest: The Story of the Farm Bureau*. Lexington KY: D. C. Heath, 1971.

Blackwell, Maylei. *¡Chicana Power! Contested Histories of Feminism in the Chicano Movement*. Austin: University of Texas Press, 2011.

Brooks, Jerome. "Chinua Achebe, the Art of Fiction No. 139." *Paris Review* 133 (Winter 1994): https://www.theparisreview.org/interviews/1720/the-art-of-fiction-no-139-chinua-achebe (accessed November 5, 2020).

Burt, Kenneth C. "The Power of a Mobilized Citizenry and Coalition Politics: The 1949 Election of Edward R. Roybal to the Los Angeles City Council." *Southern California Quarterly* 85, no. 4 (2003): 413–38.

———. *The Search for a Civic Voice: California Latino Politics*. Claremont CA: Regina, 2007.

———. "Tony Rios and Bloody Christmas: A Turning Point between the Los Angeles Police Department and the Latino Community." *Western Legal History* 14, no. 2 (2001): 159–92.

Calavita, Kitty. *Inside the State: The Bracero Program, Immigration, and the I.N.S.* New York: Routledge, 1992.

Carpio, Genevieve. *Collision at the Crossroads: How Place and Mobility Make Race*. Berkeley: University of California Press, 2019.

Day, Mark. *Forty Acres: Cesar Chavez and the Farm Workers*. New York: Praeger, 1971.

deGuzmán, Jean-Paul. "'And Make the San Fernando Valley My Home': Contested Spaces, Identities, and Activism on the Edge of Los Angeles." PhD diss., University of California, Los Angeles, 2014.

De Los Santos, Manuel Avila. Unpublished manuscript, n.d.

Flores, Lori A. *Grounds for Dreaming: Mexican Americans, Mexican Immigrants, and the California Farmworker Movement*. New Haven CT: Yale University Press, 2016.

Forbes, Jack D. *Aztecs del Norte: The Chicanos of Aztlan*. Greenwich CT: Fawcett, 1973.

García, David G. *Strategies of Segregation: Race, Residence, and the Struggle for Educational Equality*. Berkeley: University of California Press, 2018.

García, David G., and Tara J. Yosso. "'Strictly in the Capacity of Servant': The Interconnection Between Residential and School Segregation in Oxnard, California, 1934–1954." *History of Education Quarterly* 53, no. 1 (February 2013): 64–89.

García, David G., Tara J. Yosso, and Frank P. Barajas. "'A Few of the Brightest, Cleanest Mexican Children': School Segregation as a Form of Mundane Racism in Oxnard, California, 1900–1940." *Harvard Educational Review* 82, no. 1 (Spring 2012): 1–25.

García, Mario T. *The Chicano Generation: Testimonios of the Movement*. Berkeley: University of California Press, 2015.

———. *Memories of Chicano History: The Life and Narrative of Bert Corona*. Berkeley: University of California Press, 1994.

———. *Mexican Americans: Leadership, Ideology, and Identity, 1930–1960*. New Haven CT: Yale University Press, 1989.

García, Mario T., and Sal Castro, *Blowout! Sal Castro and the Chicano Struggle for Educational Justice*. Chapel Hill: University of North Carolina Press, 2011.

García, Matt. *From the Jaws of Victory: The Triumph and Tragedy of Cesar Chavez and the Farm Worker Movement*. Berkeley: University of California Press, 2012.

Gómez, Alan Eladio. *The Revolutionary Imaginations of Greater Mexico: Chicana/o Radicalism, Solidarity Politics, and Latin American Social Movements*. Austin: University of Texas Press, 2016.

Guerra, Avie. Unpublished manuscript, 2007.

Gutiérrez, David G. *Walls and Mirrors: Mexican Americans, Mexican Immigrants, and the Politics of Ethnicity*. Berkeley: University of California Press, 1995.

Hernández, Kelly Lytle. *City of Inmates: Conquest, Rebellion, and the Rise of Human Caging in Los Angeles, 1771–1965*. Chapel Hill: University of North Carolina Press, 2017.

———. *Migra! A History of the U.S. Border Patrol*. Berkeley: University of California Press, 2010.

Hernández, Roberto D. *Coloniality of the U.S./Mexico Border: Power, Violence, and the Decolonial Imperative*. Tucson: University of Arizona Press, 2018.

Herzog, Stephen J. *Minority Group Politics: A Reader*. New York: Holt, Rinehart & Winston, 1971.

HoSang, Daniel Martinez. *Racial Propositions: Ballot Initiatives and the Making of Postwar California*. Berkeley: University of California Press, 2010.

Iber, Jorge, Jose Alamillo, Arnoldo De León, and Samuel Regalado. *Latinos in U.S. Sport: A History of Isolation, Cultural Identity, and Acceptance*. Champaign IL: Human Kinetics, 2011.

"Improving Racial and Ethnic Balance and Intergroup Relations: An Advisory Report to the Board of Trustees Oxnard School District." California State Department of Education, Division of Compensatory Education, Bureau of Intergroup Relations. April 1969, 7–8.

"Indenture." Ventura County Clerk and Recorder, Book 134, 23 January 1913, 547.

"Indenture." Ventura County Clerk and Recorder, Book 134, 24 February 1913, 550.

Jiménez, Tomás R. *Replenished Ethnicity: Mexican Americans, Immigration, and Identity*. Berkeley: University of California, 2010.

Johnson, Gaye Theresa. *Spaces of Conflict, Sounds of Solidarity: Music, Race, and Spatial Entitlement in Los Angeles*. Berkeley: University of California Press, 2013.

Levy, Jacques E. *Cesar Chavez: Autobiography of La Causa*. New York: W. W. Norton, 1975.

Licón, Gustavo. "Feminist Mobilization in MEChA: A Southern California Case Study." *Kalfou* 5, no. 1 (2018): 76–110.

———. "The Ideological Struggle for Chicana/o Unity and Power: A Short History of California MEChA." In *The Chicano Movement: Perspectives from the Twentieth Century*, edited by Mario T. García, 151–72. New York: Routledge, 2014.

Loza, Mireya. "The Japanese Agricultural Workers' Program." *Pacific Historical Review* 86, no. 4 (2017): 661–90.

Martinez, Domingo. "A Comparative Study of the Academic Achievement of the Mexican-American Students in the Wilson Junior High School, Oxnard, California." Master's thesis, Claremont University, 1956.

Martinez, Monica Muñoz. *The Injustice Never Leaves You: Anti-Mexican Violence in Texas*. Cambridge MA: Harvard University Press, 2018.

McWilliams, Carey. *Southern California: An Island on the Land*. Layton UT: Peregrine Smith, [1946] 1995.

Menand, Louis. "The Misconception about Baby Boomers and the Sixties." *New Yorker*, August 18, 2019, 1–5.

Milstein, Mike M., and Dean E. Hoch. "A Landmark in School Racial Integration: Berkeley, California." *Phi Delta Kappan* 50, no. 9 (May 1969): 524–29.

Mitchell, Don. *The Lie of the Land: Migrant Workers and the California Landscape*. Minneapolis: University of Minnesota Press, 1996.

Monroy, Douglas. *Rebirth: Mexican Los Angeles from the Great Migration to the Great Depression*. Berkeley: University of California Press, 1999.

Montejano, David. *Quixote's Soldiers: A Local History of the Chicano Movement, 1966–1981*. Austin: University of Texas Press, 2010.

Morales, Armando. *Ando sangrando / I Am Bleeding: A Study of Mexican American—Police Conflict*. La Puente CA: Perspectiva, 1972.

Morales, Dionicio. *Dionicio Morales: A Life in Two Cultures*. Houston: Piñata/Arté Publico, 1997.

Muñoz, Carlos, Jr. *Youth, Identity, Power: The Chicano Movement*. Rev ed. New York: Verso, 2007.

Oropeza, Lorena. *¡Raza Si! ¡Guerra No! Chicano Protest and Patriotism during the Vietnam War Era*. Berkeley: University of California Press, 2005.

Pardo, Mary S. *Mexican American Women Activists: Identity and Resistance in Two Los Angeles Communities*. Philadelphia: Temple University Press, 1998.

Patiño, Jimmy. *Raza Sí, Migra No: Chicano Movement Struggles for Immigrant Rights in San Diego*. Chapel Hill: University of North Carolina Press, 2017.

Pawel, Miriam. *The Crusades of Cesar Chavez: A Biography.* New York: Bloomsbury, 2014.
———. *The Union of Their Dreams: Power, Hope, and Struggle in Cesar Chavez's Farm Worker Movement.* New York: Bloomsbury, 2009.
Pitti, Stephen J. *The Devil in Silicon Valley: Northern California, Race, and Mexican Americans.* Princeton NJ: Princeton University Press, 2003.
"Reservations, Restrictions, and Protective Covenants Applicable to the Eugene H. Agee Subdivision lot 132 of Patterson Ranch Subdivision of Ventura County." Ventura County Clerk and Recorder, Book 1005, 18 June 1951, 36.
Richards, Harvey. *The Land Is Rich.* Oakland CA: Estuary Press, [1966] 2005. https://archive.org/details/6384_Land_Is_Rich_The_01_29_33_24 (accessed November 5, 2020).
Rodriguez, Marc Simon. *The Tejano Diaspora: Mexican Americanism and Ethnic Politics in Texas and Wisconsin.* Chapel Hill: University of North Carolina Press, 2011.
Rosales, Oliver Arthur. "'Mississippi West': Race, Politics, and Civil Rights in California's Central Valley, 1947–1984." PhD diss., University of California, Santa Barbara, 2012.
Rosas, Abigail. *South Central Is Home: Race and the Power of Community Investment in Los Angeles.* Stanford CA: Stanford University Press, 2019.
Rosas, Ana Elizabeth. *Abrazando el Espíritu: Bracero Families Confront the U.S.-Mexico Border.* Berkeley: University of California Press, 2014.
———. "Undocumented Emotional Intelligence: Learning from the Intellectual Investments of California's Undergraduates." *Boom California* (December 7, 2017): https://boomcalifornia.com/2017/12/07/undocumented-emotional-intelligence/.
Rose, Margaret. "Gender and Civic Activism in Mexican American Barrios in California: The Community Service Organization, 1947–1962." In *Not June Cleaver: Women and Gender in Postwar America, 1945–1960*, edited by Joanne Meyerowitz, 177–200. Philadelphia: Temple University Press, 1994.
Ross, Fred. *Conquering Goliath: Cesar Chavez at the Beginning.* Keene CA: El Taller Grafico, 1989.
Ruíz, Vicki L. *Cannery Women, Cannery Lives: Mexican Women, Unionization, and the California Food Processing Industry, 1930–1950.* Albuquerque: University of New Mexico Press, 1987.
———. *From Out of the Shadows: Mexican Women in Twentieth-Century America.* New York: Oxford University Press, 1998.
Sánchez, George J. *Becoming Mexican American: Ethnicity, Culture, and Identity in Chicano Los Angeles, 1900–1945.* New York: Oxford University Press, 1993.

——. "Edward R. Roybal and the Politics of Multiracialism." *Southern California Quarterly* 92, no. 1 (Spring 2010): 51–73.

——. "What's Good for Boyle Heights Is Good for the Jews: Creating Multiracialism on the Eastside during the 1950s." *American Quarterly* 56, no. 3 (September 2004): 633–61.

Thompson, Hunter S. "Strange Rumblings in Aztlan." *Rolling Stone*, April 29, 1971, 217–62.

Tjerandsen, Carl. *Education for Citizenship: A Foundation's Experience*. Santa Cruz CA: Emil Schwarzhaupt Foundation, 1980.

U.S. Bureau of the Census. *Characteristics of the Population*. Part 6. California. Section 1. Washington DC: Bureau of the Census, 1970.

Valdes, Dionicio. *Mexicans in Minnesota*. St. Paul: Minnesota Historical Society, 2005.

Valencia, Richard R. *Chicano Students and the Courts: The Mexican American Legal Struggle for Educational Equality*. New York: New York University Press, 2008.

Vargas, Zaragosa. *Labor Rights Are Civil Rights: Mexican American Workers in Twentieth-Century America*. Princeton NJ: Princeton University Press, 2005.

Weber, John. *From South Texas to the Nation: The Exploitation of Mexican Labor in the Twentieth Century*. Chapel Hill: University of North Carolina Press, 2015.

Zamora, Emilio. *The World of the Mexican Worker in Texas*. College Station: Texas A&M University Press, 1993.

Zirin, Dave. *What's My Name, Fool? Sports and Resistance in the United States*. Chicago: Haymarket, 2005.

INDEX

Abrams, Richard, 24
Action Farm Labor, 128
Acuña, Rodolfo F., 117–18, 172, 186
Affirmative Action Promotion of Employment Practices Resolution, 213n11
African Americans: Black studies program, 166, 174; civil rights movement of, 35; housing discrimination against, 22–23, 107, 111–12, 200n15; police killings of, 190; student population of, 52, 86, 173–74; theater discrimination against, 23; white terrorism against, 24. *See also* Black Panther Party for Self-Defense; Black Student Union (BSU); NAACP (National Association for the Advancement of Colored People); racism; residential racism and segregation; school (de)segregation
Agricultural Labor Relation Board (ALRB), 155, 157–59, 226n59

Agricultural Labor Relations Act (ALRA), 156–57
agricultural workers. *See* farmworkers
Ahuamada, Ramiro, 151
Alabama, 24
alcohol abuse, 27, 34, 56
Alexander v. Board of Education, 91
Alianza Hispano Americana, 14, 32
Alianza Latino Mexicano, 163
Allen, Patrick, 83
Allen, Steve, 17, 123, 126
ALRA, 156–57
"Alternative Plans for the Elimination of De Facto Segregation in the Oxnard School District" report, 109
Alurista, 175, 176
Alvarez, Leo, 44
AMAE, 62–64, 102, 165
Ameramex Club, 45, 56
American Beet Sugar Company (ABSC), 13

241

American Civil Liberties Union (ACLU), 25
American Federation of Teachers, 147
Los Amigos (organization), 62
Ando sangrando / I Am Bleeding (Morales), 50, 176
anger, 3, 80, 194n8
antiwar protests, 9, 34–35, 54. *See also* labor protests; peace marches; school protests
Aparicio, Aurelia, 180
Aparicio, Ben, 141
Aparicio-Twitchell, Manuela, 34, 141, 175, 180
Arredondo, Joseph, 63
arson, 71, 75, 150, 152, 166
Assembly Bill 5 (California), 17–18
Associated Farmers (organization), 140
Associated Students (organization), 177, 180–81
Association of Bilingual Educators, 172
Association of Mexican American Educators (AMAE), 62–64, 102, 165
Avenue barrio, Ventura, 30, 177, 179
Aztlán, 70. *See also* Movimiento Estudiantil Chicano de Aztlán (MEChA)

baby boomers, 98, 194n10. *See also* Mexican American generation, as term and identity
Baez, José, 148
Baeza, Andre, 3
Bank of A. Levy, 71
Bard, Carla M., 102
Barker, Harold N., 77
Barnard, Keith, 148
Barrios, Juan, 148
Barry, Joe, 60
Basolo, De Wayne, 152, 153
Beason, Eddie, 129
Becerra, Ermina, 157

Becerra, Richard, 69–70
Becker, William, 17
Becoming Mexican American (Sánchez), 5
Beekman, Jim, 148
Berkeley Plan, 104
Berzman, William, 118
betabeleros, 14. *See also* sugar beet industry
bilingualism, 30, 38–39. *See also* language differences
blackface theater, 25
Black Panther Party for Self-Defense, 7, 33, 184. *See also* African Americans
Black students, 52, 86, 173–74. *See also* African Americans; school (de)segregation
Black Student Union (BSU), 7, 11, 161, 174, 176–77, 180. *See also* African Americans
Black studies programs, 166, 174. *See also* African Americans; educational curriculum
"Bloody Christmas" event (1951), 48
Blowouts (1968 East Los Angeles protests), 8, 33, 60, 99, 174, 176. *See also* Los Angeles CA; Los Angeles Unified School District
bomb threats, 73, 107
Bonpane, Blase, 35, 68
border patrol. *See* Immigration and Naturalization Services (*la migra*)
Borrego, Robert, 78
Borrego Martínez, Diana, 34, 167
boycotts. *See* labor protests
Bracero Program, 15–17, 123, 126–28, 156, 196n14
Brekke, Norman, 59, 92, 101, 118, 119
Briggs Lemon Growers Association, 127–28, 148, 152
Brokaw Nursery, 159

Broomfield Amendment, 109
Brown, Edmund G., 16, 18, 136
Brown, Isaiah, 174
Brown Berets of Los Angeles, 65, 70
Brown Berets of Oxnard: on busing, 95–96; collaborations of, 62, 67, 168–69; Contreras opinion of, 184; CSO support of, 50; establishment of, 33, 56, 117; leaders of, 2, 11; Murguia Wong and, 82; protest actions by, 34–35, 56–59; on school (de)segregation, 89–90, 104; tutorial program of, 59–62, 63, 113, 170
Brown Berets of Santa Paula, 76–77
Brown v. Board of Education (1954), 9, 46, 85, 86, 91, 97
Bud Antle Lettuce Company, 144
Bureau of Intergroup Relations (California), 86, 87, 91
Burger, Warren, 96, 214n22
Burpee Seed Company, 127
Burt, Kenneth C., 18
Burton, Philip, 18
busing, 21; COB against, 101–3, 106–8; Kane on, 113–14; Kirk on, 107; in North Carolina, 96; opposition to, 10, 82, 89–95, 102–4, 213n13, 214n24; Pregerson's integration order on, 10, 96–98, 100, 110, 120; proposal to OESD for, 84, 85–86; support for, 82, 209n20. *See also* Oxnard Elementary School District (OESD); school (de)segregation; *and names of specific schools*
Bustillo, Luisa, 38–39
Butler, James Lloyd, 126

Café on A, 186–87, 188
California Committee for Fair Practices, 17, 19
California Department of Justice, 50, 59
California Fair Employment Commission, 23
California Farm Placement Service (CFPS), 15–16
California Lutheran College, 22
California State Board of Education, 86, 87
California State University Channel Islands (CSUCI), 185, 186, 188–89
California State University Hayward (CSUH), 182
California State University Northridge (CSUN), 117–18. *See also* San Fernando Valley State College (SFVSC)
Camacho, Cloromiro, 44, 49
campesinos. *See* farmworkers
Cannery and Agricultural Workers Industrial Union, 14
Cannery Women and Cannery Lives (Ruiz), 5–6
Cano, Antonio, 128
Cano, Gilbert, 79
Carmona, Richard, 35
La Casa del Mexicano, Santa Paula, 135, 140, 147, 153
Casillas, Arnulfo, 177, 179
Casillas, Gonzalo, 144
Casillas, Graciela, 34, 180–81
Casillas, Jaime, 181
Castañeda, George, 148, 153
Castro, Daniel, 171
Castro, Ruben, 135
Castro, Sal, 12, 60, 176
Castro, Sallie, 78
La Causa (publication), 174
celery farms, 1, 132, 146, 154. *See also* farmworkers; labor protests

Chambers, James, 84
Chancey, Lee, 147, 148
Channel Islands High School, 164, 165, 166
Chargin, Gerald S., 183
charity projects, 166–67, 176
Chavarria, Art, 154
Chavarria, Jesus, 172
Chávez, Benjamin, 157
Chávez, César: as CSO national director, 15; CSO resignation of, 18; description of, 19–20; ethnic identity of, 3, 137, 159; Johnson's war on poverty and, 121; marches led by, 2; Rojas and, 132; on urban redevelopment, 43; Ventura County work and, 14–15, 135–36, 140–43, 149–51, 153, 156, 157. *See also* National Farm Workers Association (NFWA); United Farm Workers (UFW)
Chávez, Dennis, 183
Chávez, Manuel, 149
Chávez Ravine redevelopment, Los Angeles, 42
Chicana-Chicano, as term and identity, 2–7, 66, 182–84, 194n7. *See also* Mexican American generation, as term and identity
Chicana-Chicano youth: celebration style and cultural expression of, 178–80, 182; early life experiences of, 28–31; employment programs for, 27–28, 63, 171; La Colonia rioting by, 71–72; national conferences for, 34, 65, 175; OPD brutality against, 47–50; political consciousness development of, 31–34, 159–60, 162–63; in Santa Paula, 74–78; student activist groups, 163–66. *See also* antiwar protests; child labor; Movimiento Estudiantil Chicano de Aztlán (MEChA); peace marches
Chicana Falsa (Serros), 189
El Chicano (band), 3
El Chicano (publication), 35, 174
Chicano from the Southwest (film), 105–6
Chicano Moratorium Peace March (1970), 35, 65–70. *See also* peace marches
"Chicano Power" (song by Thee Midniters), 184
Chicano Student Movement of Aztlán. *See* Movimiento Estudiantil Chicano de Aztlán (MEChA)
Chicano studies programs: alumni of, 117, 176, 186, 187; at CSU schools, 117–18, 172, 182, 186, 188–89; funding for, 78; in K–12 schools, 166, 167; at Moorpark College, 172–73; at Ventura College, 105. *See also* educational curriculum
Chicano Youth Conference (1970), 34, 65, 175
Childers, John, 96
child labor, 122, 141. *See also* Chicana-Chicano youth
Chiques Organizing for Rights, Employment, Equity, and Education (CORE), 187
Chumash, 21
Cinco de Mayo celebrations, 78, 175, 177, 179
Círculo Social Mexicano, 62–63
Citizens Against Poverty (CAP), 131, 132–33
citizenship classes, 15, 38
Citizens Opposed to Busing (COB), 101–3, 106–8
citrus farms, 22, 82, 123, 127–28. *See also* farmworkers
citrus strikes: (1941), 27, 31, 39, 140; (1970), 140–44; (1974), 147–48, 152–53. *See also* farmworkers; labor protests

civil unrest. *See* antiwar protests; labor protests; rioting; school protests
Clowes, Richard, 112, 116
Coachella Valley CA, 8
Coastal Growers Association, 153
Coleman, James S., 104
collective consciousness, 33–35. *See also* Chicana-Chicano, as term and identity; Mexican American generation, as term and identity
collective resistance. *See* antiwar protests; labor protests; school protests; unionization; *and names of specific organizations and events*
college recruitment and work-study program, 27–28, 63–64, 171. *See also* education
Collins, John, 172–73, 229n41
Colonades of La Colonia (drill team), 31
Colonia. *See* La Colonia CA
Colonia Chiques (gang), 186–87, 188, 190–91
Comer, Jean, 209n20
Comité de Campesinos de SP Growers Association, 148
Comité de Raza Rights, 187, 190–91
Committee on Farm Labor Problems (California), 17, 19
Committee on Raza Rights, 187, 190–91
"Common Fears Related to Integration" (Sullivan), 104, 105
Community Service Organization (CSO): on busing, 95–96; as organization, 4, 14–18, 37–39, 57; against police brutality, 48–49; against school (de)segregation, 44–46, 53, 81, 114; in support of Brown Berets, 50; against urban redevelopment projects, 42–44;

women leaders in, 40–41, 42. *See also* Oxnard Civic Improvement Association (OCIA)
Compensatory Education Advisory Committee (CEAC), 84, 103, 104, 105
Con Safos (publication), 35, 174
Contreras, Daniel E., 183, 184
Cooney, Maureen, 180
Corona, Bert, 26, 27, 35, 68, 136, 176
Coronado, Ygnacio, 16
el cortito, 29
Cristo Rey Catholic Church, La Colonia, 41, 48, 57
Cuevas, Gilbert G., 102, 105
Culbert site of OESD (proposed), 44–46, 112, 114. *See also* Oxnard Elementary School District (OESD)
Curious Unions (Barajas), 7
curriculum. *See* educational curriculum

Dark Corner (band), 175
Dave Walsh Company, 1–2, 154
Davis, Mary, 44, 46, 100
declaration of independence (work) contract, 143–44
Deem, Woodruff, 46
Delano CA, 18, 19
Del Buono, Tony: as community organizer, 38, 39; influence of, 57, 186; on school (de)segregation, 45; on women leaders, 40–41
DeLeon, Francisco, 170
De Leon, R., 182, 184
DeLeon, Ralph, 153
De Los Santos, Yvonne: as community organizer, 175; early life of, 20–21, 32, 162–63; La Marcha and, 79–80; MEChA and, 167

Democratic Party, 53, 136
Denman, Bob, 130
Denver Youth Conferences, 34, 65, 175
deportation raids, 150–51, 207n60
De Pue, Harold R., 112, 116
De Vries, Deborah, 187
Día de los Muertos celebrations, 179
Diez y Seis de Septiembre. *See* Mexican Independence Day celebrations
Dill, Michael C., 181–82
Dodgers Stadium, 42–43
Dr. Rodolfo F. Acuña Art Gallery & Cultural Center, 186, 187, 188
drug abuse, 27, 34, 56

Economic Opportunity Act (1964), 219n28. *See also* Office of Economic Opportunity (OEO)
Edelman, Joel, 110
education: college recruitment and work-study program, 27–28, 63–64, 171; IQ testing, 61; language differences and, 20–21, 29–30, 32–33, 60, 162; tutorial programs, 9, 59–62, 63, 113, 167. *See also* school (de)segregation; teaching faculty; *and names of specific schools and districts*
educational curriculum, 31–32, 42, 83, 98, 170. *See also* Black studies programs; Chicano studies program
Educational Opportunity Programs (EOP), 9, 171
Egg City, 133–35, 154–58, 226n59
electoral politics. *See* voter registration drives; voting campaigns
Ellis, Larry, 174, 177
El Rio Elementary School, 167
Emergency Committee to Aid Farm Workers (ECAFW), 19, 122–23

employment programs for youth, 27–28, 63–64, 171
environmental pollution, 56. *See also* pesticide exposure
"Equality in Educational Opportunity Report" (Coleman), 104
Escobar, Javier, 171
ethnic identity, 2–7, 66, 70, 139, 182–84, 194nn7–8, 194n12
ethnic studies curriculum, 42. *See also* Black studies programs; Chicano studies programs; educational curriculum

F and P Growers Association, 140, 141
Farm Home Administration (FHA), 131
Farm Labor Service Center (FLSC), 18–19, 122
Farm Worker Opportunity Project (FWOP), 11, 122–26, 220n33
farmworkers: Bracero Program and, 15–17, 123, 126–28, 156, 196n14; documentary film on, 61–62; employment grants for, 123; housing of, 127, 128, 129–30, 142; from Japan, 14, 122, 196n14; labor conditions of, 17, 29, 62, 121–22, 126–29, 156; Operation Buenaventura for, 11, 122, 124–26; Operation Harvest Hand for, 123; pensions for, 17–19, 62, 126; pesticide exposure of, 29, 144–45; from Philippines, 122; safety of, 144, 148; in sugar beet industry, 13–14; television show on, 17, 62; from Vietnam, 154, 155–56. *See also* labor protests; wages of farmworkers; *and names of specific organizations*
Farm Workers Committee of Santa Paula Growers Association, 148
Federal Housing Administration, 5, 107. *See also* residential racism and segregation

feminist movement, 35
Filipino farmworkers, 122
Fillmore CA, 140–44
Fillmore Citrus Association, 141, 142
Flores, Edward, 41
Flores, Lori, 3, 15
Flores, Peter, 43
Flores, Roberto: arrest of, 2, 149; Brown Berets and, 56–62, 117; as cultural teacher, 170; family and early life of, 55–56; OPD charges by, 55; as protest leader, 149, 150, 151; on school integration, 96; as student organizer, 175; work-study program by, 63–64
Flores Espinosa, Laura, 41
Flores Magón, Ricardo, 32
Flynn, John, 134
Forbes, Jack D., 24
Ford, John Anson, 123
Free Marketing Council, 145
Friel, Ed, 126
Friend, Kika, 29
Friends of the Farm Workers, 140, 141, 147, 151, 154, 155, 156
From Out of the Shadows (Ruiz), 6

Galarza, Ernesto, 17, 134
El Gallo (publication), 174
gang injunction, 186–87, 188, 190–91. *See also* Oxnard Police Department (OPD); racism
García, A. M., 70
García, David G., 46, 54, 111
García, Francisco, 79
García, Joe, 72
García, Jorge, 117, 186
García, Mario T., 5, 6
García, Roberto, 149

gender divisions in collective action, 34, 79–80, 82. *See also* women leaders
get-out-the-vote drives. *See* voting campaigns
Giant (Ferber), 106
Godina, Vincent, 134
Goldman, Julius, 133, 135, 155
Gómez, Arthur, 66, 140, 141
Gonzales, Connie, 78
Gonzales, Juan, 148
Gonzales, Oscar, 133–35
Gonzales, Rodolfo, 62, 175
Gonzales, Vera, 40
Gordon, Leon, 148
Govan, Ron, 84
Govea, Jessica, 1, 4, 20
Graig, V. H., Jr., 144
grapefruit industry, 22. *See also* citrus farms; citrus strikes; farmworkers
grape strike (1965), 11, 19, 137, 139, 140, 143, 173. *See also* labor protests
El Grito (publication), 174
Grossman, Marc, 158
Grounds for Dreaming (Flores), 3
G & T Berry Farms, 154
Guardianes de la Colonia, 14, 163
Guatemalan migrants, 188
Guerra, Avie, 186
Guilen, Tony, 150
Gutiérrez, David G., 6
Gutiérrez, Jess, 35, 69, 167–68, 175, 176
Gutiérrez, Nellie, 40
Guyer, Leland, 52
Guzmán, Frank, 127–28
Guzmán, Ralph, 33, 65

Hammond, Bert, 186
Hansberry, Lorraine, 112

Harambee Uhuru (organization), 57, 90, 174, 187
Hardison, Russel, 142
Hartmann, Bea, 56, 57
Hartmire, Wayne, 155
Harvest of Shame (television show), 17, 62
Harvey, Steve, 148
Heaton, Richard C., 154
Helstein, Ralph, 14
Hernández, Jesus, 181
Hernandez, Richard, 180
Hernández, Roberto D., 164
Herrera, Andrés, 56–57, 62, 65, 117, 170
Herrera, Fermín, 56–57, 65, 117, 170, 172
Herrera, Tomás, 57, 65
Higher Education Act (1972), 109
High Potential–High Risk program (UCLA), 60
high school protests. *See* school protests; *and names of specific schools*
Hiji Brothers Farm, 159
Hironymous, Jack, 47
Hod Carriers Building and Common Laborers Union, 41
Holverson, Dallas, 107
Honduran migrants, 188
La Hora del Chicano (Larios), 179
housing discrimination. *See* residential racism and segregation
How to Be a Chicana Role Model (Serros), 189
Huerta, Dolores, 17, 20, 175. *See also* National Farm Workers Association (NFWA)
Human Relations Council, 25

"I AM Joaquin" (Gonzales), 62
Immigration and Naturalization Services (*la migra*), 28–29, 55–56, 151, 206n50
indigenous groups, 21, 62, 188, 191
Ingersoll, James, 44
integration of schools. *See* school (de)segregation
IQ testing, 61. *See also* education
Izquierdo, Pablo, 129, 140

Jackson v. Pasadena City School District, 87
Jalaty, Al, 154–55
Japanese Agricultural Workers Program, 196n14
Japanese farmworkers, 3, 14, 122
Japanese Mexican Labor Association (JMLA), 14
Japanese-Mexican Sugar Beet Strike (1903), 3
Jewell, Al, 47–48, 49
Jewett, Frank, 73
Jim Crow traditions, 23–25. *See also* racism
Jiménez, Tomás R., 5, 26, 122
Johnson, Lyndon, 7, 41, 121
Jones, Fred, 49–50
Juanita Elementary School: burning of, 71; community events at, 40, 42, 61, 136, 149; personnel of, 25, 44, 83; proposed improvements to, 96; student body of, 52, 86; tutorial program at, 170. *See also* Oxnard Elementary School District (OESD)

KACY radio, 179
Kalish, Stephen, 95, 97, 110, 116
Kane, Thomas, 84, 91, 93, 113
Kennedy, Robert, 136
Keyes v. School District No. 1, Denver, Colorado, 110
Kirk, Claude, 94–95, 106–7, 214n22
K. K. Ito Farms, 159

Klu Klux Klan (KKK), 24, 25, 106
Knowles, Clive, 123
KOXR radio, 30

labor conditions, 17, 29, 62, 121–22, 126–29, 156. *See also* farmworkers; wages of farmworkers
labor protests, 8; citrus strikes, 27, 31, 39, 140–44, 147–48, 152–53; in Egg City, 133–35, 154–58, 226n59; grape strike, 11, 19, 137, 139, 140, 143, 173; lettuce strike, 144–47; police violence against, 2, 7, 47, 149–50; by Rojas, 132; strawberry strikes, 1–2, 148–51; sugar beet strike, 3, 14. *See also* farmworkers; peace marches; wages of farmworkers
La Colonia CA: descriptions of inequality in, 30–31, 72–74; OPD violence in, 47–50, 55–56, 73, 206n48; peace march in, 9, 67–69; redevelopment plan of, 42–43; rioting in, 71–72; study on education in, 210n30. *See also* farmworkers; labor protests; Oxnard CA; Oxnard Elementary School District (OESD); Oxnard Police Department (OPD); school (de)segregation
La Colonia Youth Services program, 27–28
Lagomarsino, Robert, 95
Lake, Ellen, 149–50
The Land Is Rich (film), 61–62
language differences: farmworkers and, 129, 141, 142, 152; school and, 20–21, 29–30, 32–33, 60, 162; voter discrimination due to, 38–39. *See also* bilingualism
Larios, Bernardo, 179
Larios, Peggy, 57–58, 67
Lascher, Edward, 100, 102, 107, 109
Latin American Veterans Club, 32, 41

Lattrell, Bill, 108
Lauwerys, Peter, 123, 125, 130, 131, 132
League of United Latin American Citizens, 188
Legal Aid Association, 148
lemon farms, 22, 152. *See also* citrus farms; citrus strikes; farmworkers
Leon Pharmacy, 71
lettuce farms, 144–45, 146. *See also* farmworkers
lettuce strikes (1971), 144–47. *See also* farmworkers; labor protests
Lewis, Bill, 49
Licke, Russ M., 102
Licón, Gustavo, 189
Limoneira Company, 144
Little League baseball, 31
Loehr, Ray E., 173, 174, 177
Lombard, T. A., 133
London, Eddie, 92–93, 96
López, Armando: on 1971 riots, 73; Brown Berets and, 11, 51, 56–57, 117, 168; Gutiérrez and, 167–68; on school (de)segregation, 104; in student organizations, 45; tutoring by, 170; as veteran, 33
Lopez, Jayne, 180
López Tijerina, Reies, 60, 175
López Tijerina, Reies, Jr., 175
Los Angeles Brown Berets, 65, 70
Los Angeles CA, 42–43, 48, 65–66. *See also* Blowouts (1968 East Los Angeles protests); Los Angeles Unified School District
Los Angeles Sentinel (publication), 86
Los Angeles Times (publication), 8, 65, 75, 91, 184
Los Angeles Unified School District, 33, 113. *See also* Blowouts (1968 East Los Angeles protests)

Lucero, Val, 18
Luevano, Angel, 180
Luna, Betty, 180
Lund, Daniel, 123, 125

Magdalena, Ramon, 127
Maggipinto, Francis X., 179
El Malcriado (publication), 35, 129, 174
Malley, Thomas, 95, 96, 100, 110
Manatee County School District, 94
Manking, William, 145
MAPA. *See* Mexican American Political Association (MAPA)
Marcha de la Reconquista (1971), 9, 54, 78–80, *81*, 175, 207n60. *See also* peace marches
marches. *See* peace marches
Mariachi Uclatlan, 175
Marina West School, 98, 116. *See also* Oxnard Elementary School District (OESD)
Marquez, Josephine, 131
Marshall, John, 84
Marson, Cloene I., 89
Martínez, Ann L., 128
Martínez, Cecil, 148
Martínez, Diana Borrego, 167
Martínez, Domingo, 44
Martínez, Peter, 165
Martínez, Ruben, 70, 205n39
Martínez Berry Company, 148–49
Mason, J. Keith, 93, 101, 107, 112–13
Massie, Bob, 47
Matilija Growers Association, 142
Maynez, Raul, 63
McCormick, John, 125
McCurdy, Jack, 216n37
McDaniel, Ivan, 140
McDonald, J. K., 95

McDonnell, Duncan, 148
McFarland, Don, 47
McGrath, Nancy, 102, 107
McWilliams, Carey, 8
MEChA. *See* Movimiento Estudiantil Chicano de Aztlán (MEChA)
Mechistas. *See* Movimiento Estudiantil Chicano de Aztlán (MEChA)
Medina, Eliseo, 154, 155, 157, 158–59
Mel Finerman Company, 144–45, 146
Menand, Louis, 194n10
Menashe, Abe, 135
Menchaca, Blas, 177–78
Mendez v. Westminster School District, 87
Mendoza, Joe, 64, 105
Mercurio, Richard J., 59
Mexican American generation, as term and identity, 2–3, 4, 66, 70, 184. *See also* Chicana-Chicano, as term and identity
Mexican American Opportunity Foundation, 32
Mexican-American: Past, Present, and Future (course), 171–72
Mexican American Political Association (MAPA): on busing, 95–96; on Collins, 173; mission of, 62; as organization, 26, 27, 36, 56, 122; against police violence, 59; rise of, 50–53; voting campaigns by, 51, 122, 136
Mexican Americans (García), 5
Mexican American studies programs. *See* Chicano studies programs
Mexican American Youth Organization (MAYO), 164
Mexican Independence Day celebrations, 145–46, 165, 175, 179
la migra. *See* Immigration and Naturalization Services (*la migra*)
migrant, as term, 194n6, 194n12

Minority Affairs Committee (MAC), 166
Mississippi, 24, 91, 94
Mitchell, James P., 17
Mitchell, John N., 109
Monroy, Douglas, 6
Mont, Max, 19, 123
Montenegro, Raquel, 172
Moorpark College: Chicano Studies program at, 172–73; establishment of, 168; student newspaper of, 8, 169, 173, 178; student organizations of, 4, 34, 67, 147, 168–70, 180–81
Mora, Moses, 30, 32
Morales, Armando, 47, 50, 71, 176
Movimiento Estudiantil Chicano de Aztlán (MEChA): *la causa* of farmworkers and, 121–22, 147; educational programs by, 113, 167; ethnic identity and, 2–3, 194n8; at high schools, 166–68; leadership of, 34; legacy and influence of, 11, 185–90; Martínez's opinion of, 70; of Moorpark College, 34, 67, 147, 168–70, 172–73, 180–81; of Ventura College, 147, 174, 179, 181–82
moxie, as term, 3, 7, 189
Muñoz, Rosalio, 34, 35, 59, 65, 67
Mupu Citrus Association, 152
mural, 177–78
Murguia family, 27, 82
Murguia Wong, Rachel: civic engagement by, 82–83; family and early life of, 27, 82; OCT program by, 10, 117–18; OESD positions of, 83–85; on school board responsibilities, 105; on school integration, 96
Murrow, Edward R., 17
music, 30–31, 175, 178–79
Mytinger, Kenneth L., 89, 95, 100, 215n29

NAACP (National Association for the Advancement of Colored People), 9–10; on busing, 95–96; against gang injunction, 188; against police brutality, 49; against residential racism, 23, 25; on school (de)segregation, 44, 45–46, 53, 81, 85–86, 92, 114. *See also* African Americans
National Association for the Advancement of Colored People. *See* NAACP (National Association for the Advancement of Colored People)
National Chicano Moratorium Committee (NCMC), 65, 78. *See also* peace marches
National Farm Workers Association (NFWA), 10; protests by, 20, 78, 137, 139; publication by, 35, 129. *See also* United Farm Workers (UFW)
National Labor Relation Act, 142
Native American civil rights movement, 35
Nava, Sue, 90–91
Navarro, Carlos, 117
Neff, Ted, 111
Neighborhood Youth Corps (NYC), 28
Newman, John V., 133
Nicaraguan migrants, 188
Nixon, Richard, 70, 94, 109
North Carolina, 96
North from Mexico (McWilliams), 83
North Oxnard Methodist Church, 92
Northrup Institute of Technology, 22
Nowlin, Herb, 110
Nuestra Raza (publication), 167

Oaxaca, Virginia, 105
Ochoa, Nicholas, 105
Office of Economic Opportunity (OEO), 124–25, 131

Old Age Security Adjustment, 17–18
Olivares, Robert, 59, 92
Ontiveros, Jose, 68
Operation Buenaventura, 11, 122, 124–26
Operation Chicano Teacher (OCT), 10, 118, 187
Operation Harvest Hand, 123
Operation Wetback, 29
orange farms, 22, 129, 141, 142, 152. *See also* citrus farms; citrus strikes; farmworkers; labor protests
Ortiz, Barbara, 146
Ortiz, Gale Ray, 146
Ortiz, Ray, 1
Owens, Robert, 67–73, 78, 206n48
Oxnard Brown Berets. *See* Brown Berets of Oxnard
Oxnard CA, 13–14; barrio nickname of, 231n1; urban redevelopment in, 42–44. *See also* Chicana-Chicano youth; La Colonia CA; Oxnard Elementary School District (OESD); Oxnard Union High School District (OUHSD); *and names of specific agencies and organizations*
Oxnard Civic Improvement Association (OCIA), 9, 14, 38, 57. *See also* Community Service Organization (CSO)
Oxnard Community Relations Commission (OCRC), 64, 73
Oxnard Elementary School District (OESD): 1971 court-mandated integration order, 10, 96–100, 110, 117, 119–20; 1974 trial on school (de)segregation, 110–17; board's legal appeal against desegregation, 100–103, 109–11; bomb threats in board meetings of, 73, 107; Brown Berets work with, 9, 59–62, 63, 113; Bureau of Intergroup Relations study on, 87–88, 91; Culbert site conflict, 44–46, 112, 114; lawsuit against, 10, 53, 84, 90–91, 93, 95–98, 216n37; MAPA on, 51–52; Murguia Wong and, 83–85; school (de)segregation in, overview, 9–10, 51–52, 84, 85–91, 201n21; student population statistics of, 83, 86, 119, 216n49; teaching faculty of, 10, 117–18, 213n11, 215n29, 216n49; tutorial program of, 9, 113. *See also* busing; Chicana-Chicano youth; Juanita Elementary School; La Colonia CA; Ramona Elementary School
Oxnard Farm Labor Service Center (FLSC), 18–19
Oxnard High School, 165–66
Oxnard Legal Aid Association, 131
Oxnard Police Department (OPD), 2, 47–50, 58–59, 77, 149–50, 186, 191. *See also* police violence
Oxnard Press-Courier (publication), 8; on AB 5, 18; on Bracero Program, 16; on Brown Berets, 56; on Chicano as term and identity, 182–84; on Chicano film presentation, 106; on farmworkers' housing, 127, 130, 131; on labor protests, 39, 134; on La Colonia rioting, 71, 72; on OCT program, 118; on OESD trial, 111; on Operation Buenaventura, 124–26; on peace march, 67; on police brutality, 49; on race relations, 24; on school (de)segregation issue, 46, 89, 92, 101; on work-study program, 64
Oxnard Union High School District (OUHSD), 64, 165. *See also* Chicana-Chicano youth

Oxnard Wakefield Initiative, 89
Oxnard Youth Employment Services (OYES) program, 27–28

Packard Bell Electronics, 22
Padilla, Gilbert, 141
Panetta, Leon, 94
Papageorge, Harry, 49
Pasadena School District (PSD), 85, 87, 93, 95, 98, 106
Paz, Suni, 175
peace marches, 11; 1970 Chicano Moratorium Peace March, 35, 65–70; 1971 Marcha de la Reconquista, 9, 54, 78–80, *81*, 175, 207n60; of farmworkers, 135, 145–46, 149, 153; against school segregation, 92. *See also* antiwar protests; labor protests; school protests
Peake, Katherine, 19, 123, 124, 125, 131, 218n4
pension benefits for farmworkers, 17–19, 62, 126. *See also* farmworkers
Pérez, Eddie, 39
Pérez, Joe, 18
Perez, Ralph, 159
pesticide exposure, 29, 144–45. *See also* environmental pollution; farmworkers; labor conditions
Peto, Howard, 126
Peyton, Deborah, 158
Pfeiler, Robert, 90, 91, 92, 93, 101, 112, 114
picketing. *See* antiwar protests; labor protests; school protests
piece rate. *See* wages of farmworkers
Pirate Press (publication), 8, 181. *See also* Ventura College
El Plan de Santa Barbara (1969), 163, 170, 176, 189. *See also* Santa Barbara Conference of El Plan

Plessy v. Ferguson, 87
Pocho (Villareal), 26
police violence: against African Americans, 190; CSO's agenda against, 18, 37, 49; against labor protests, 2, 7, 47, 149–50; in Los Angeles, 48, 65–66; military violence and, 67; Morales's book on, 176; by Oxnard PD, 47–50, 206n48; peace march and, 35, 67–70, 78; rioting in protest of, 71–74, 75; in Santa Paula, 74–78. *See also* Oxnard Police Department (OPD); racism; Santa Paula Police Department; Texas Rangers
El Popo (publication), 35
Poss, J. N., 24
poverty alleviation. *See* war-on-poverty projects
Powell, Clifford, 165
Pregerson, Harry: 1971 school integration mandate by, 10, 96–100, 110, 117, 119–20, 215n29; 1974 trial decision by, 114–17. *See also* Oxnard Elementary School District (OESD); school (de)segregation
propaganda, 182
protest marches. *See* antiwar protests; labor protests; peace marches; school protests
Public Law 78 (California), 15
El Pueblo Opina (radio show), 30, 83
Pulido, Alex, 105

Quaker Religious Society of Friends, 57, 132
Quevedo, Eduardo, 26
quinceañeras, 41, 42
Quiroz, Isecelia, 2

INDEX 253

racism: Forbes on, 24–25; gang injunction, 186–87, 188, 190–91; Jewett on, 74; long-term effects of, 105; op-eds on, 182–84; Poss on, 24–25; student organizations against, 166; Thrashers on, 210n31; white flight, 8, 119; white supremacy, 24–25, 74. *See also* police violence; residential racism and segregation; school (de)segregation; terrorism
radio broadcasts, 30, 83, 179
rage. *See* anger
Raider Reporter (publication), 8, 169, 173, 178. *See also* Moorpark College
A Raisin in the Sun (play), 112
Ramona Elementary School: poor quality of, 96, 116; proposed closure of, 91; student body of, 52, 86; tutorial program at, 170. *See also* Oxnard Elementary School District (OESD)
Rancho de los Campanos CA, 141
Rancho Sespe CA, 127, 130–31, 141
La Raza (publication), 35, 174
La Raza Moratorium Peace March, 35, 65–70. *See also* peace marches
Razo, Lupe, 181
Razo, Manuel, 181
Reach, Paula, 209n20
Reagan, Ronald, 78, 188
Real, Manuel L., 93, 95
Rebirth (Monroy), 6
redevelopment. *See* urban redevelopment
redlining, 107. *See also* racism; residential racism and segregation
Republican Party, 53
residential racism and segregation, 4–5, 25, 111–12, 200n15; against African Americans, 22–23, 200n15; as cause of school (de)segregation, 85–87; against farmworkers, 127, 128, 129–30, 142; MAPA on, 51; redlining, 107; in Vineyard Estates, 111. *See also* Federal Housing Administration; racism; school (de)segregation; white flight; white supremacy
Reta, Joe, 18
revolutionary icons, 32
Reyes, Ray, 174, 177, 178, 180
Reynolds, Blanche T., 111
Reynoso, Amado, 172, 178
Richards, Harvey, 62
right-to-work contract, 143–44
Riles, Wilson C., 90
Rio Mesa High School, 164, 167, 170
Rios, Anthony P., 48
rioting: 1971 La Colonia, 71–74; 1972 Santa Paula, 74–78
Rivera, José, 15–16, 18
Roberts, Jack B., 109
Rodríguez, José, 152, 153
Rogers, Richard, 101
Rojas, Al, 11, 131–33
Romero, Francisco, 187, 190–91
Roos, Peter, 95, 110
Rosalez, Jerry R., 182
Rosas, Ana, 29
Rose, Margaret, 40
Rose Avenue School, 93, 98, 116. *See also* Oxnard Elementary School District (OESD)
Roussey, R. H., 74
Roybal, Edward R., 37, 43
Ruelas, Zeke, 180
Ruiz, Vicki, 5–6
rurban, as term, 8

Sabo, Ron, 110
safety of farmworkers, 29, 144–45, 148. *See also* farmworkers; labor conditions

Salazar, Frank A., 179
Salazar, Rubén, 65–66, 80, 184
Salinas Valley CA, 1–2, 8, 15, 143
Salvadoran migrants, 188
Sánchez, David, 60, 61
Sánchez, George J., 5
Sánchez, Salvatore, 52–53, 166
San Fernando Valley State College (SFVSC), 4, 9, 10, 34, 167. *See also* California State University Northridge (CSUN)
sanitation, 116, 141–42. *See also* labor conditions
San Joaquin Valley CA, 3, 8, 11, 18–19, 20, 139, 143
Santa Barbara Committee to Aid Farm Workers, 134
Santa Barbara Conference of El Plan, 175. *See also* El Plan de Santa Barbara (1969)
Santa Clara River Valley CA, 147
Santana, Javier, 30, 83
Santa Paula Brown Berets, 76–77
Santa Paula CA, 74–78, 141–42
Santa Paula Citrus Association (SPCA), 152
Santa Paula Daily Chronicle (publication), 75, 76, 77
Santa Paula Daily Courier (publication), 76
Santa Paula Farm Workers Committee (SPFWC), 141
Santa Paula Lemon and Orange Growers Association, 128, 129, 153
Santa Paula Police Department, 75–76. *See also* police violence
Saticoy CA, 19, 20, 75, 79, 135, 146, 159, 162, 177
Schary, Dore, 123
Schlichter, Walter, 43
school (de)segregation: in Berkeley, 104; Brown Berets on, 60; Coleman on, 104; in Denver, 110; MAPA on, 51; NAACP on, 44, 45–46, 53, 81, 85–86, 92, 114; in Pasadena, 85, 87, 93, 95, 98, 106; report on, 86, 87, 91, 209nn16–17; Sullivan on, 104, 105; Thrashers on, 210n31. *See also* busing; education; Oxnard Elementary School District (OESD); residential racism and segregation; *and names of specific court cases*
school and language differences, 20–21, 29–30, 32–33, 60, 162. *See also* education
school busing. *See* busing
school protests: in East Los Angeles, 8, 33, 60, 99, 174, 176; at OUHSD, 64, 165; in UCSB–Isle Vista, 68–69, 205n33. *See also* antiwar protests; labor protests; peace marches
Scott, Hugh, 94
Scott Amendment, 94
Serling, Rod, 123
Serros, Michele, 189
Serros, Robert, 73
SFVSC. *See* San Fernando Valley State College (SFVSC)
Sharp, James, 148
Shaw, Robert L., 157
Sheinbaum, Stanley, 134, 169
Shelton, Debbie, 180
Sierra Linda Elementary School, 98, 102, 106, 116. *See also* Oxnard Elementary School District (OESD)
Simi High School, 165
Simmons, Althea, 45, 46, 85–86, 88, 114. *See also* NAACP (National Association for the Advancement of Colored People)
Sociedad Internacional de Beneficios Mutuos, 41

Soria, John: FLSC work by, 18–19, 122; lawsuit against OESD, 10, 53, 84, 90–91, 93, 95–98, 216n37; MAPA work by, 52, 136; on school (de)segregation, 93, 95, 96; on voting discrimination, 39; work on peace march, 67
Soria, Roberto, 84, 95, 168–69
Soria v. Oxnard School District Board of Trustees, 10, 53, 84, 90–91, 93, 95–98, 216n37
Sosa, Juan, 47
Soto, Mario, 130–31
Soto, Raquel, 45
Soto, Roberto, 127
SP Growers Association, 147, 148, 153
sports, 31, 163
State Department of Employment Development, 150
Stennis, John D., 94
Stewart, Seawright H., 93, 119
Storke, Charles, 136
Strategies of Segregation (García), 111
strawberry farms, 128–29, 149, 154. *See also* farmworkers
strawberry strikes (1974), 1–2, 148–51. *See also* farmworkers; labor protests
Stroube, Bessie and W. C., 111
student protests. *See* school protests
Students for a Democratic Society (SDS), 7, 11, 33, 161
suburbanization. *See* urban redevelopment
sugar beet industry, 13–14. *See also* farmworkers
sugar beet strike (1903), 3, 14. *See also* farmworkers; labor protests
Sullivan, Neil V., 104, 105
Sunkist, 146
Swancutt, Dale, 134–35

Swann v. Charlotte-Mecklenburg, 96
systemic racism. *See* racism

Taft-Hartley Act (1947), 133
Tanaka Brothers Company, 154, 159
Taylor, Wallace, 165
teaching faculty: of CSUCI, 188; of OESD, 10, 117–18, 213n11, 215n29, 216n49; of PSD, 93; salary for, 216n53. *See also* education
Teague, Charles, 72, 134
Teamsters Union, 143–45, 151, 154–59
Teatro Aztlán, 176
Teatro Campesino of Santa Barbara, 62, 155
Teatro Quetzalcoatl, 176
Technology Instrument Corporation, 22
Teen Toppers, 45, 56
terrorism, 2, 24, 25, 106. *See also* police violence; racism
Terry, William, 73, 96, 103, 165, 174, 187
Texas Rangers, 2, 7, 149, 194n5. *See also* police violence
theaters, discrimination in, 23, 25
Thee Midniters (band), 175, 184
Thompson, Hunter S., 66
Thrasher, Margaret and William, 210n31
Tinklepaugh, Kenneth N., 91, 93, 100
Tolbert, William, 16
Tolmach, Jane, 39
Tolston, Fred, 23
toxic waste, 56. *See also* pesticide exposure
tradition of resistance by Mexican and Mexican American communities, 28, 31–32, 36, 62, 121. *See also* antiwar protests; labor protests; school protests; *and names of specific organizations*
Tregarthen, Doran W., 98, 99, 101, 107, 119–20, 213n13

Trom, C. Stanley, 155
Trump, Donald J., 190
Tull, Ray, 75, 76, 77
Turner, Irene, 23
tutorial programs, 9, 59–62, 63, 113, 167. *See also* education

UCLA, 4, 9, 60, 168
UCSB, 4, 9, 147–48, 168, 205n33
UFW. *See* United Farm Workers (UFW)
UFWOC, 140, 142–59, 165
Uhuru (organization), 57, 90, 174, 187
Ulloa, Alfred, 48
unionization, 31–32. *See also* farmworkers; labor protests; National Farm Workers Association (NFWA); Teamsters Union; United Farm Workers (UFW)
Unión Patriótica Benéfica Mexicana Independiente (UPBMI), 14, 32, 163
United Celery Growers, 154
United Church Women, 25
United Farm Workers (UFW): organizational name of, 10, 195n19; in Ventura County, 122, 140–59, 165. *See also* Chávez, César; farmworkers; labor protests; National Farm Workers Association (NFWA)
United Farm Workers Organizing Committee (UFWOC), 140, 142–59, 165
United Latin American Citizens for Nixon, 205n39
United Latin Americans, Inc., 53
United Mexican Americans Students (UMAS), 34, 163, 164
United Packinghouse Workers of America (UPWA), 14, 15, 39, 123, 135
University of California, Los Angeles (UCLA), 4, 9, 60, 168

University of California, Santa Barbara (UCSB), 4, 9, 147–48, 168, 205n33
University Study Center (USC), 171
UPWA, 14, 15, 39, 123, 135
urban redevelopment, 42–44, 200n15. *See also* racism; residential racism and segregation; white flight
Urias, Al, 78
Urias, Leopoldo, 154, 156
U.S. Border Patrol. *See* Immigration and Naturalization Services (*la migra*)
U.S. Commission on Civil Rights, 48, 94
U.S. Department of Labor, 16
U.S. Manpower Development and Training Agency (MDTA), 123
U.S. Naval Construction (SEA BEE) Base Center, 144

Valdez, Luis, 62
Valenzuela, Tony, 181
Vanoni, Ives, 153
Vargas, Santiago, 84
Vásquez, Tim, 171
Vázquez, Armando, 187
Velasco, Jeanette, 180
Ventura, Donato, 105
Ventura College: Minority Student Center, 176–78; student newspaper of, 8, 181; student organizations at, 4, 147, 173–74, 179, 181–82
Ventura County Agricultural Association (VCAA), 150, 151
Ventura County CA, overview, 21–22. *See also* Chicana-Chicano youth; farmworkers; labor protests; La Colonia CA; Oxnard CA; *and names of specific agencies and organizations*
Ventura County Citrus Growers Association (VCCGA), 16, 133, 140, 147

Ventura County Community Action Commission (CAC), 131–32, 155, 187
Ventura County CSO. *See* Community Service Organization (CSO)
Ventura County Fruit Growers Exchange, 140
Ventura County Jewish Council, 25
Ventura County Star-Free Press (publication), 1, 8, 66, 71, 140, 144, 146, 150, 187
Ventura Organizations Council for Agricultural Labor, 134
Veterans Administration, 5
Vietnamese farmworkers, 154, 155–56
Vietnam War, 7; Chávez's opposition to, 137; Chicano servicemen in, 33, 65, 69
Vietnam War protests. *See* antiwar protests
Villa, Faye, 182
Villa, Pancho, 32
Villanueva, Ernie, 39
Villareal, José Antonio, 26
voter registration drives, 15, 38–40, 136–37
voting campaigns: by Chávez, 15, 135, 136; by CSO, 38–40; by MAPA, 51, 122, 136

wages of farmworkers: Bracero Program and, 15, 126–29; fixed system of, 29, 62, 78, 125, 127; labor protests on, 14, 134–35, 147, 149, 152–53; minimum wage legislation, 16, 18; piece rates, 28, 128–29, 144, 147, 148, 154; theft of, 28, 141. *See also* farmworkers; labor protests
Wakefield, Floyd L., 89, 95
Walls and Mirrors (Gutiérrez), 6
war-on-poverty projects, 7, 58, 121–26
Washington, H. H., 49
Watanabe Ranch, 159
Waters, Tony, 110, 112
Waters, William A., 97
Watkins, Lily, 22–23, 25
Watts riots (1965), 8

Webb, Ernestine, 42, 45, 186
Wegis, Warren F., 140, 143
Weinstock, Richard, 148
Wells, Waymon, 84
West Foods, 159
wetback, as term, 26, 29, 133–34
white flight, 8, 119. *See also* racism; residential racism and segregation; urban redevelopment
white supremacy, 24–25, 74. *See also* police violence; racism; residential racism and segregation
white terrorism. *See* terrorism
"Who Is a Chicano?" (Salazar), 184
Williams, Rose, 50, 53
Willoughby, Patricia, 107
Wilson, Thomas, 65
women leaders: of civic organizations, 79–80; of CSO, 40–41, 42; of student organizations, 34; of union organizations, 17, 20. *See also* gender divisions in collective action
work-study programs, 27–28, 63–64, 171. *See also* education
The World of the Mexican Worker in Texas (Zamora), 5
Woven, Paul, 52

Yang-Na, 21
Yokut, 21
You Can't Take It with You (theatrical production), 25
Youth Employment Services (YES) program, 28
Yslas, Carmen, 40, 41

Zamora, Emilio, 5
Zamora, Hector, 150
Zapata, Emiliano, 32
Zitnik, Louis, 177

CPSIA information can be obtained
at www.ICGtesting.com
Printed in the USA
LVHW041316140723
752402LV00004B/78